Beyond the HEDGES

FROM TAILGATING TO TEA PARTIES

JUNIOR LEAGUE OF ATHENS
Athens, Georgia

Beyond the HEDGES

FROM TAILGATING TO TEA PARTIES

634 Prince Ave.
Athens, Georgia 30601
Phone: 706-549-8688
www.juniorleagueofathens.org

To order additional copies see order form in back of book.

First Printing   November 2007   5,000 copies
Second Printing   September 2010   5,000 copies

©2007 Junior League of Athens
ISBN: 978-09796590-0-3

Manufactured by
Favorite Recipes® Press
An imprint of

FRP.INC

P.O. Box 305142
Nashville, Tennessee 37230
800-358-0560

Printed in China

Foreword

The year 2010 marks our 75th year of service to the Athens community, and to celebrate, we are proud to present the second printing of *Beyond the Hedges: From Tailgating to Tea Parties!*

When people think of Athens, certainly the University of Georgia and spectacular gridiron match-ups come to mind. Our Bulldogs' winning history "between the hedges" of Sanford Stadium along with the beloved rites of each game day are Athens traditions and must be experienced to understand so much of what "The Classic City" is all about. There is perhaps no more quintessential form of entertaining here than tailgating, which has become for us something dearer and far more lovingly executed than a mere sandwich and a cold drink leaning against the back of the car. However, readers of this cookbook will indeed travel "Beyond the Hedges" and into the kitchens of our League members and local residents to enjoy culinary delights as storied and savory as Saturdays in autumn, with enduring flavors that continue to delight and nourish throughout the year.

The South offers some of the best food anywhere and, surprisingly, not all of it is deep-fried. The recipes on these pages mirror the diversity of a town with both international ties and an ever-modernizing League, and at the same time reflect how rapidly our "down home" ways of cooking are changing as we transition from fatback to olive oil. Athens' affinity for music and its thriving cultural arts scene is characterized by variety on all levels, just as our cookbook offers a wide array of dishes to suit any particular taste, occasion, or day of the week.

This book has been a joyous undertaking and a true labor of love as our membership collected and quadruple-tested recipes from our own members, our families, friends, and neighbors. We could not be more pleased with the result of our hard work as we bring you the second printing of this book. We hope that you will turn to this cookbook over and over again and that it will become as cherished a "classic" in your own home as Athens is itself.

We want to commend the entire membership of the Junior League of Athens, actives as well as sustainers, for such a successful first printing. We thank the Greater Athens community and beyond for supporting our first cookbook in forty years. As you read through this cookbook and prepare the meals within for your friends and family, remember that proceeds from the sale of this book go toward our Food 2 Kids program. The Food 2 Kids program is a cooperative effort between the Junior League of Athens and the Food Bank of Northeast Georgia to ensure that children in our local school district—children who would otherwise go without food—have enough to eat over the weekend. To read more about this project, to buy this cookbook, and to learn about other projects the Junior League of Athens supports, log on to www.juniorleagueofathens.org.

Congratulations to the 2009–2010 Cookbook Committee for their hard work and dedication to the success, sale, and reprint of this cookbook. So enjoy a great read and awesome recipes and help a worthwhile cause—all at the same time. Who could ask for anything more?

Rebecca McClure Farmer, *Cookbook Committee Chair, 2006–2007*
League President, 2008–2009

Shona Foster, *Cookbook Committee Chair, 2007–2008*
League President, 2009–2010

Natalie Glenn, *League President, 2010–2011*

The Junior League of Athens extends its heartfelt thanks and appreciation to the committee members and their families. Without their hard work and generosity, the accomplishment of this book would not have been possible.

Chairwomen

Rebecca Farmer,* Chair 2006-2007

Shona Foster, Chair 2007-2008

Beth Rivenbark,* Co-Chair 2007-2008

Beth Segars,* Co-Chair 2007-2008

Heather Kaplan, Chair 2008-2009

Beth Ricketson, Co-Chair 2008-2009

Pattie Strickland, Chair 2009-2010

Sumner Markwalter, Co-Chair 2009-2010

Susan Dodson,* *Editor*

Original Cookbook Committee 2006–2007

Susan Brodrick*

Katie Campbell

Ashley Carter*

Allison Cass*

Laura Childers

Rebecca Chisolm

Jodi Conner*

Sheila Parker Dunham

Ginna Ezernack*

Meghan Garrard*

Megan Henning

Heather Kaplan*

Valerie Langley*

Amy Lannae

Amy Lazenby

Kacy Lehn

Kate Lindsey*

Krista Mitchell*

Colleen Pruitt

Whitney Swann*

Lee Thornton

Jennifer Worley*

**denotes a minimum of two years service*

Acknowledgements

The committee would like to extend a special thank you to our local restaurants who shared their fabulous recipes and to other notable residents for being generous enough to share their "tried and true" Athens favorites. Many of these recipes are legendary, some have won food contests, and some were well-kept secrets—until now.

A special thank you goes to past members Mrs. Joy Wingfield, Mrs. Gwen Griffin, Mrs. Jane Eldridge and all of their friends. They were essential in helping to choose the "Classic" recipes that were taken from the Athens Junior Assembly's first cookbook, *A Cook's Tour of Athens*.

The Junior League of Athens

Mission
The Junior League of Athens is an organization of women committed to promoting voluntarism, developing the potential of women and improving communities through the effective action and leadership of trained volunteers. Its purpose is exclusively educational and charitable.

Vision
The Junior League of Athens is dedicated to reducing poverty in our community and to empowering and guiding women and children into a productive life using the diverse talents of passionate, trained volunteers.

Reaching Out to All Women
The Junior League of Athens represents a wide range of talents and diverse backgrounds. Our organization reaches out to women of all races, religions and national origins who demonstrate an interest in and commitment to voluntarism.

Our History
The Junior League of Athens (JLA) has been serving the citizens of the Athens community for 75 years. In 1935, 25 caring women chartered the Junior Assembly of Athens. Through their dedicated work, the Junior Assembly was the primary charitable resource for maternity and baby care for the Athens area. Enlisting the cooperation of local doctors and nurses, the Assembly was able to envision, oversee, and maintain numerous health and wellness clinics for children of all ages in Athens and surrounding areas well into the mid-1970s.

In 1968 the Assembly established its permanent location, in the boyhood home of Henry W. Grady, on Prince Avenue. In September of 1978, the Junior Assembly of Athens submitted a formal application for membership to the Association of Junior Leagues International and on October 28, 1980, the Junior Assembly of Athens became the 243rd Junior League in the Association of Junior Leagues, and incorporated as the Junior League of Athens, Georgia, Inc. Along with this affiliation came national recognition, but the Junior League of Athens was then and is to this day, dedicated to keeping its charity and volunteer commitments at the local level. Nearly three decades later, the Junior League of Athens continues to call the Taylor-Grady House home.

Following the national Junior League affiliation, the local membership elected to carry on their commitments to children by making the children of the Athens area the focus of the league's works. In the early 1980s, they established their Child Advocacy Substance Abuse Prevention Committee and focused much of their work in an effort to keep children away from the dangers of drugs and alcohol. In the 1990s the Junior League of Athens expanded their focus on children by spearheading the local "Don't Wait to Vaccinate" effort, and setting up After School programs with some of the neighborhood schools. In the year 2000 the Junior League, aided by the Athens Housing Authority, the Department of Family and Child Services, and $60,000 from the state budget, set up the Granny House, a community outreach center for at-risk children. Over the past 75 years the Athens Junior League has stood the test of time and continues to be a successful service-driven organization of hard-working women who truly want to create positive opportunities for their community, and the families that reside there.

Cookbooks Now and Then

Beyond the Hedges: From Tailgating to Tea Parties is not the first cookbook printed by the Junior League of Athens. **A Cook's Tour of Athens** was first published in 1963. If you look closely, you may recognize some recipes borrowed from the original book. The October 1965 edition of **American Home Magazine** recognized **A Cook's Tour of Athens** for its exceptional recipes for southern cooking. It had seven reprints, and over 13,000 copies were sold over the next 20 years.

We hope that we have given you dozens of useful and tasty recipes that will make your **"Tea Party"** special and your **"Tailgate"** famous. Enclosed you will find recipes from your favorite University of Georgia coaches, local musicians and celebrities, and Athens area restaurants.

The History Behind Athens and Clarke County

When Abraham Baldwin and the Georgia General Assembly charted the first state supported university in the nation, the University of Georgia, on January 27, 1785, the city of Athens was little more than a stop on a trail along the banks of the Oconee River. The university was only a concept until John Milledge, a future Georgia governor, bought 633 acres of land and donated it for the cause of building the college. Milledge held high hopes for his endowment to become a leading city for culture and learning. He named it Athens, in honor of the ancient Greek city of enlightenment.

As with many southern towns during the same time period, much of Athens' early economy was driven by cotton farming and production. Athens was a leader in cotton production technology, and in the mid 1800s, a group of local businessmen worked to build a railroad that would eventually connect Athens with larger cities for its distribution, Augusta and Atlanta.

During Sherman's march through Georgia, he largely ignored Athens, thus many beautiful antebellum homes remain standing, shading the sidewalks of the town. Though the architecture was left largely untouched, the Civil War remade the Athens community during the fighting and long afterwards. Men and boys departed for battle, while refugees from other parts of the state and traveling soldiers made wartime homes in Athens, and the University was closed from September of 1863 until January of 1866. When Federal troops occupied Athens in May of 1865, the slaves who had made up half of the town's population were emancipated.

Athens' major contribution to the war effort—one of the world's first double-barreled cannons—is a tribute to its history of innovative technology. The success of the invention has been debated, and over the years, some of the history of the cannon has morphed into legend. Today, it serves as a popular tourist curiosity, crouching behind City Hall and facing defiantly north, protecting the proud city from invasion, just in case....

Following the war, the University gained recognition as an educational hub, and as it grew so did Athens and its reputation for commerce. The turn of the century found Athens with an emerging downtown business district, and the beginning of its suburbs and subdivisions. The first commuters in Athens rode streetcars pulled by mules, up and down what is now Prince Avenue and the historic Boulevard neighborhoods. Cotton still drove much of the economy in Athens into the mid 1900s as the University grew into a major research center, and the Athens college scene began to emerge.

Today, Athens is nationally famous mostly for its "scene." For many, Athens means music, and for others it is the Georgia Bulldogs, but what makes Athens unique is that it is an eclectic blend of the historical and the modern, the Classic City that holds true to the vision of John Milledge so many years ago, a true epicenter of culture and education.

Sources:
* *A Portrait of Historic Athens and Clarke County* by Frances Taliaferro Thomas
* Courthouse informational marker
* *Athens, Georgia: Celebrating 200 Years at the Millennium* by Conoly & Al Hester

Contents

The teapot symbol placed alongside certain recipes in the book indicates that this is a Classic Recipe selected and shared from *A Cook's Tour of Athens*, the cookbook initially published by the League in 1963.

About the Artist

Hazel Caldwell was born and raised in Macon, Georgia. She studied at the College of Charleston in South Carolina, where she received her Bachelor of Arts degree in Studio Art, with a minor in Psychology. During this course of study she spent much time studying art abroad in Italy, where she gained an appreciation for architecture, portraits, and landscape. From there she went to Eastern Virginia Medical School and received her Master of Science in Art Therapy. She has been commissioned to do murals in Charleston, SC, and historical homes and churches in Macon, Valdosta, Charleston, Mississippi, and Athens. She has worked as an art therapist in both private practice and for the State for Georgia. She has worked with cancer patients at the Children's Hospital of the King's Daughters in Virginia as well as a psychiatric hospital at the veteran's hospital, and a juvenile detention facility. All of her work as a therapist has been to help treat mentally ill patients through the use of art. She is currently working full time as an artist and displaying her work in exhibits and galleries throughout the southeast. While her husband attended Veterinary School at the University of Georgia, she and her family lived in Athens, where Hazel became a member of the Junior League.

Hazel now resides in Forsyth, Georgia with her husband, Butler, and her two girls, Blain and Catharine.

The Tree That Owns Itself

(Pictured on the front and back liner and in the sidebars.)

According to local legend, Colonel William H. Jackson so loved sitting in the shade tree of a white oak located at the corner of Finley and Dearing Streets that, upon his death in 1832, he willed to itself the tree and the surrounding eight feet of land in which it grew.

The original oak fell in a windstorm on the evening of October 9, 1942. And in 1946, the Junior Ladies Garden Club planted a sapling which had been grown from one of the beloved tree's acorns.

This tree still stands today and receives many visitors every year. In 1975 it was listed in the National Register of Historic Places and was declared an Athens Historical Landmark in 1988.

Beverages

Beverages

Marti's at Midday Famous Mint Sweet Tea

1 gallon water

1 bunch fresh mint (about ½ cup)

10 to 12 large tea bags

2 cups sugar

Bring water and mint to a boil. Add tea bags. Let stand 10 minutes. Remove tea bags and mint. Add sugar to hot tea, stirring until sugar dissolves. Add 6 cups ice to cool.

Mama's Boy Strawberry Lemonade

Great served as a mixer with gin, rum, or vodka.

4 cups freshly squeezed lemon juice (about 20 lemons with pulp)

3 cups fresh strawberries, hulled and halved

4 to 5 cups sugar

1 gallon hot water

Pour lemon juice and strawberries into blender and purée. Dissolve sugar in hot water and allow to cool. Combine strawberry purée and sugar water. Mix well and chill.

The Ashford Manor Mint Julep

1 shot bourbon

¼ shot Campari

3 shots simple sugar (1 part water to 1 part sugar, boil until sugar dissolves, then chill)

Fresh mint sprigs

Confectioners' sugar

1 silver mint julep cup

1 rocking chair

1 front porch

In small pitcher, stir bourbon, Campari, simple syrup, and mint sprigs together. Pour over crushed ice in silver Mint Julep cup. Garnish with mint sprig and confectioners' sugar sprinkled on top. Add small cocktail straw and enjoy while sitting in a rocker on your favorite porch.

Serves 1

Marti's at Midday has become a supper club salvation, dishing up savory entrees, salads, and Southern-style staples for dine-in or take-away. Building on the success of Normaltown's eclectic mix of businesses, the restaurant's cheery dining area and sunroom offer a place where you can relax and enjoy your company as much as your food.

Leave it to these transplanted Yankees in Watkinsville to mess with a Southern icon. The "classic" version of this recipe calls for ¼ shot of bitters. They substituted Italian Campari. It enhances the color of the liquid as it mingles with the ice and mint. And Campari's complexity of bitter flavors provides this Southern staple with continental sophistication.

Shiraz's Shirley Temple-Tea Punch

4 cups red tea, cooled to room
    temperature

8 cups cold water

2 cups lemon juice

4 cups orange juice

6 cups cranberry juice

4 cups ginger ale

1 jar maraschino cherries,
    undrained

1 orange, sliced into thin rounds

Mix tea, water, and juices in punch bowl and stir well. Just before serving, stir in ginger ale and entire contents of jar of cherries. Add ice cubes and garnish with orange slices.

The recipe for syllabub hails from England and dates back to the 17th century. It was traditionally made by adding sweet wine directly to fresh milk and was then made bubbly by whipping with a whip or twig. The Butts family adopted the recipe, switched the wine to bourbon, and made the drink a Christmas tradition.

Wally Butts' Syllabub

1 pint whipping cream

1 pint whole milk

¾ cup sugar

½ to ¾ cup bourbon

Pour cream and milk into chilled 3-quart bowl. Add sugar, stirring until dissolved. Stir in bourbon. Whip with whisk or hand mixer. Skim off foam and eat with a spoon. Whip and skim again until all has been eaten.

Local resident Terry Wingfield has always been known for his kind nature and generosity. To him, we owe our gratitude for sharing this (until now) secret recipe for his Heavenly Tiddlies, which he invented and has been making for friends and family for over 30 years. This recipe has become a true classic among Athens residents.

Terry Wingfield's Famous Heavenly Tiddlies

2 (½-gallon) containers Blue Belle
    coffee-flavored ice cream,
    slightly thawed

2 cups brandy

1 cup white crème de cocoa

Transfer ice cream to large mixing bowl. Pour brandy and white crème de cocoa over ice cream. Using potato masher, mash ice cream and liquor to blend to slushy consistency. (A few lumps are alright.) Use a cup to dip and transfer mixture to glass container with lid, leaving enough room at top for any expansion, and freeze. Remove from freezer in time to slightly thaw before serving. Stir well and serve with a long spoon in mint julep cups.

Sweet Almond Punch

2½ cups sugar

1 cup water

1 tablespoon vanilla extract

1 tablespoon almond extract

¼ cup lemon juice

2 (2-liter) bottles ginger ale

To make concentrate, heat sugar and water in saucepan over medium-high heat, stirring continually until sugar dissolves. Remove from heat and stir in extracts and lemon juice. Makes 2 cups.

To make punch, pour 2 cups concentrate into punch bowl and add ginger ale, stirring until mixed. The concentrate for this punch can be made and refrigerated a few hours before serving.

This is a delicious year-round punch that is great for events like bridal and baby showers, Christmas parties, and luncheons.

Lucy's Mint Julep Punch

1 can frozen orange juice
   concentrate, diluted with
   3 cans water

1 can frozen lemonade
   concentrate, diluted with
   2 cans water

1 large can pineapple juice

1 cup confectioners' sugar

1 cup bourbon

12 mint sprigs for garnish

In large bowl, combine concentrates and pineapple juice with sugar and bourbon. Mix well. Pour into 12 serving glasses and garnish with mint.

Serves 12

This punch is festive and not very strong. Perfect to serve guests while watching the Kentucky Derby and excellent served with cheese straws.

Festive Ambrosia Punch

1 (15-ounce) can cream of
   coconut

1 large can pineapple juice

8 cups orange juice

1 (2-liter) bottle ginger ale

1 bottle champagne

Combine cream of coconut, juices, ginger ale, and champagne in punch bowl. Stir well to combine and enjoy. This recipe can be doubled or tripled to serve a crowd.

To make an ice ring, simply place slices of your favorite fruit into any size mold that will fit your punch bowl (try a Bundt pan). Arrange the fruit mold and add enough water or juice to fill the ring. Freeze until firm. When you are ready to serve the punch, dip the mold into warm water to loosen, and add to your punch bowl. For an extra special touch, try freezing mint leaves, slices of fruit, or edible flowers in an ice ring for a beautiful presentation!

Knock Your Socks Off Punch

½ gallon good quality vodka

Powdered pink lemonade mix

2 large cans pineapple juice

2 (2-liter) bottles lemon-lime flavored carbonated drink

In large punch bowl, combine vodka and 4 vodka bottle capfuls powdered pink lemonade mix, stirring until lemonade dissolves. Add juice and lemon-lime drink. Stir well and serve over ice.

Godfrey Punch

3 cups cranberry juice cocktail

2 cups pineapple juice

2 cups orange juice

1 liter ginger ale

½ orange, sliced

½ cup raspberries

In large pitcher, combine juices and chill up to 8 hours. Stir in ginger ale. Float orange slices and raspberries. Pour into individual glasses filled with ice and serve immediately.

Sanford Slush

Slush will melt as you mingle — great on a hot August afternoon!

1 (12-ounce) can frozen orange juice concentrate

1 (12-ounce) can frozen lemonade concentrate

½ bottle lemon juice concentrate

1 (2-liter) lemon-lime flavored carbonated drink

2 cups bourbon

In large bowl, combine concentrates, lemon-lime drink, and bourbon. Stir until frozen juices melt. Pour into freezable containers with large mouth. Freeze 8 hours or overnight. To serve, slightly thaw, and scoop frozen drink mixture into glasses with heavy spoon. Return unused drink mixture to freezer and keep frozen.

Serves 6-12

Golden Punch

Fresh strawberries may be used to add extra flavor and color.

2½ cups sugar

4 cups water

1½ cups lemon juice

1½ cups orange juice

½ cup pineapple juice

1 quart ginger ale

Boil sugar and 1 cup of the water for 5 minutes; remove from heat and cool. Combine the juices, sugar mixture, and the additional 3 cups water. Just before serving add ginger ale and crushed ice.

Serves 10

Tutti Fruitti Party Punch

1 (6-ounce) can frozen orange juice concentrate, partly thawed

1 (6-ounce) can frozen lemonade concentrate, partly thawed

3 cups pineapple juice, chilled

1½ quarts cranberry juice, chilled

2 quarts ginger ale or lemon-lime flavored carbonated drink, chilled

Vodka (optional)

Orange slices (optional)

In pitcher, combine concentrates and juices, stirring well. Add water according to fruit concentrate can directions. Add ginger ale or soda, vodka, and orange slices just before serving.

The juices in this punch may be mixed the day before and refrigerated. A frozen ring or mold may aid in keeping the punch cold during the party. Vodka may also be added for a delicious, "spiked" version.

Warm Spiced Punch

1 (6-ounce) can frozen lemonade concentrate, thawed

2 quarts cranberry juice cocktail

2½ cups apple juice

1½ cups orange juice

1 (46-ounce) can pineapple juice

4 cinnamon sticks

2 teaspoons ground ginger

Place concentrate and juices in 30-cup percolator. Place cinnamon and ginger in percolator basket according to percolator directions. Perk through one cycle and serve warm.

Makes 1 gallon

This punch is a delicious drink that warms the soul. Perfect for a holiday party!

Elegant Strawberry Champagne Punch

Not too sweet ... just right!

3 (12-ounce) cans frozen
   lemonade concentrate,
   thawed
10 cups water

2 pints fresh strawberries,
   capped and sliced
3 quarts ginger ale
3 bottles champagne, chilled

In large pitcher, combine concentrate, water, and strawberries; chill 4 hours. Just before serving, stir in ginger ale and champagne.

Makes 2 gallons

Strawberries and champagne are often indicative of a celebration. This punch is a perfect way to toast a bride-to-be!

Berry Good Eggnog

2 (12-ounce) cans frozen
   cranberry-raspberry juice
   concentrate, thawed

2 quarts dairy eggnog
1 quart lemon-lime flavored
   carbonated drink, chilled

In a pitcher, combine concentrate, eggnog, and lemon-lime drink. Gently stir and mix well.

Serves 20

Traditionally, eggnog is made in England with white wine. In America, we generally make it with bourbon, and in Germany they usually make eggnog with beer. This yummy version is alcohol-free and may be enjoyed by people of all ages!

Old-Fashioned Eggnog

30 eggs, separated
2 cups sugar
1 quart whipping cream

1 fifth whiskey
¼ teaspoon salt
Nutmeg

Beat egg yolks with sugar and add whiskey. Fold in egg whites, beaten stiff, and add salt. Whip cream and fold in. Nutmeg may be sprinkled on top.

Makes 40 servings

Georgia Peach Punch

2 cans frozen peach daiquiri mix, thawed

1 can frozen limeade concentrate, thawed

1 can frozen orange juice concentrate, thawed

1 quart club soda, chilled

1 (2-liter) bottle ginger ale, chilled

1 bottle white wine, chilled

1 to 2 fresh peaches, pitted and sliced for garnish

In large container, combine daiquiri and concentrates along with club soda and mix well. Pour over ice in pitcher or punch bowl; add ginger ale and wine. Garnish glasses with peach slices.

Serves 20

To make this punch a little drier, add more wine and less ginger ale. This drink is the perfect way to cool down after an afternoon in the hot Georgia sun!

Tennessee Tea

4 family-sized tea bags

2 cups sugar

2 quarts boiling water

2 quarts cold water

Mint leaves for garnish (optional)

Lemon or lime slices for garnish (optional)

1 can frozen lemonade concentrate, thawed

1 cup whiskey

2 (2-liter) bottles ginger ale

Brew tea by placing tea bags and sugar in gallon-sized glass or ceramic container; pour in boiling water, stirring until sugar dissolves. Add cold water and mix well.

If you want traditional Southern tea, you can stop here and serve over ice in glasses garnished with mint or a slice of lemon or lime.

To make Tennessee Tea, combine lemonade concentrate and whiskey in large plastic container. Add brewed tea, stirring until well combined. Freeze 4 to 6 hours or until slushy. Using an ice cream scoop, place 2 to 4 scoops in individual glasses and top with ginger ale. Serve immediately with mint leaf as garnish.

Serves 16 to 20

This is a modern twist to the traditional drink favored by the landed gentry in the horse country of Tennessee. It is so cool and refreshing! Just imagine rocking on the veranda among the magnolia blossoms and fields of clover!

Emerald Coast Margarita

1½ ounces (or 18 ounces) Sauza
    Commemorative Tequila

¼ ounce (or 3 ounces)
    Malibu Rum

¼ ounce (or 3 ounces)
    Blue Curaçao

⅛ ounce (or 1½ ounces) midori

¼ ounce (or 3 ounces)
    peach schnapps

1 ounce (or 12 ounces)
    sweet and sour mix

1 ounce (or 12 ounces)
    pineapple juice

2 ounces (or 24 ounces)
    orange juice

In glass (or large pitcher), combine tequila, rum, Curaçao, midori, schnapps, sweet and sour mix, and juices. Mix well and chill. Serve chilled.

Serves 1 (or makes ½ gallon)

Blue Caribbean Margaritas

1 ounce tequila

1 ounce Blue Curaçao

Splash of orange juice

Margarita mix

Fill margarita glass with ice. Add tequila, Blue Curaçao, and splash of orange juice. Top off with margarita mix. Stir well and serve.

Serves 1

Rose's Lime Juice can be found with the mixed drink ingredients in grocery or liquor stores. It is a sweetened, condensed lime juice that can also be used to make vodka and gin gimlets.

Mile High Margaritas

1 can frozen limeade concentrate

¾ to 1 can tequila

1 can water

½ bottle Rose's Lime Juice

1 bottle Mexican beer

In pitcher, combine concentrate, tequila, water, juice, and beer. Stir well and serve over ice.

Summer Sipper
Great summer drink!

1 (750-milliliter) bottle
    Chardonnay, chilled
    (or other white wine)

¼ cup Triple Sec

1 (12-ounce) can guanabana nectar

1 (12-ounce) can frozen limeade
    concentrate, thawed

1 (12-ounce) can frozen lemonade
    concentrate, thawed

1 (10-ounce) can frozen piña
    colada drink mix, thawed

1½ cups vodka

1 (2-liter) bottle lemon-lime
    flavored carbonated drink,
    chilled

2 to 3 lemons, sliced

2 to 3 limes, sliced

2 cups ice

In large pitcher, combine Chardonnay, Triple Sec, nectar, concentrates, piña colada mix, vodka, and lemon-lime drink. Mix well and add fruit slices. Add ice just before serving. Alcohol may be omitted and additional lemon-lime drink added for a children's version.

Makes 5 quarts

White Sangría
Wonderful summertime drink!

1 bottle dry white wine

½ cup Curaçao

¼ cup sugar

1 orange, thinly sliced

1 lemon, thinly sliced

1 lime, thinly sliced

4 to 5 large strawberries, sliced

1 (10-ounce) bottle club soda

In pitcher, combine wine, Curaçao, and sugar, stirring until sugar dissolves. Add sliced fruits, cover, and chill at least 1 hour. Just before serving, add soda and ice cubes. Stir gently to mix. Serve in wine glasses.

Serves 6

Guanabana nectar is a popular drink in Latin cultures. It can be found in the Mexican/International section of your local grocery store.

STOCK UP!

If you want to stock a full bar, most people's needs can be met by having the following items on hand:

* Vodka

* Rum

* Gin

* Scotch

* Bourbon

* Blended whiskey

* Tequila

Wine and Beer Basics

* Plan on stocking 5 bottles of wine for every 10 drinkers. You should get roughly 5 servings per bottle.

* Stock 5 six-packs for 10 people, based on a 12-ounce serving.

Sassy Sangría

¼ cup sugar

1 cup water

1 bottle red or white wine

6 ounces sparkling water

1 orange, thinly sliced

1 lime, thinly sliced

In small mixing bowl, combine sugar and water, stirring until sugar dissolves. In pitcher, combine sugar mixture, wine, and sparkling water. Add fruit and gently stir. Chill and allow flavors to blend. Pour into individual glasses filled with ice and garnished with additional fruit.

Serves 6

Berry Sparklers are a festive addition to any holiday party...they are great and easy to prepare for a crowd!

Berry Sparklers

2 cups cranberry juice cocktail, chilled

2 cups raspberry liqueur

1 (750-milliliter) bottle champagne, chilled

Fresh raspberries for garnish

In large pitcher, combine juice and liqueur. Stir in champagne. Pour into glasses and serve over ice, if desired. Garnish each glass with 3 raspberries.

Makes 8 cups

This drink makes a dramatic presentation with a fizzing sugar cube. It is perfect for a New Year's Eve party!

Pom Fizz

A festive holiday beverage!

2 tablespoons pomegranate juice

10 tablespoons cold champagne

1 sugar cube

Pour pomegranate juice into champagne flute. Just before serving, slowly pour in champagne and add sugar cube.

Serves 1

Vickie's Summer Cocktail

1½ ounces lemon vodka

½ ounce Grand Marnier™

Splash of Chambord

Juice of ½ lemon

In cocktail shaker filled with ice, combine vodka, Grand Marnier™, Chambord, and lemon juice. Shake well and strain into chilled martini glass.

Serves 1

24-Hour Cocktail

1 dozen lemons, rind and juice

1 cup sugar

2 cups boiling water

1 quart "corn-likker"

1 dozen oranges, juiced

1 (32-ounce) can pineapple juice

Small jar cherries

Squeeze lemons. Add juice to sugar, water, and "corn-likker." Put in a crock, adding the lemon rind. Keep in crock overnight. Strain and add pineapple juice, orange juice, and cherries. Serve in punch bowl over big chunks of ice.

If you are not connected with any bootleggers and cannot seem to find any dust-covered "corn-likker" in your grandmother's basement, just drive to your local package store and ask for a bottle of the strongest stuff they have!

This recipe originated when Athens was a dry county like most of the surrounding southern region at that time.

Old-Fashioned Bloody Mary Mix

1 (46-ounce) can tomato juice

¼ cup Worcestershire sauce

3 tablespoons horseradish

⅓ cup lime juice

⅓ cup lemon juice

Hot pepper sauce

Freshly ground black pepper

10 to 12 celery stalks

Vodka (optional)

In large saucepan over medium-high heat, combine tomato juice, Worcestershire, horseradish, juices, and hot pepper sauce; bring to a boil. Remove from heat, cool, and chill. Pour mixture into individual glasses filled with ice. Sprinkle with black pepper, add celery stalk, and serve immediately. (Add 1 ounce vodka to each ½ cup Bloody Mary mix.)

Serves 10-12

Bloody Mary's may be garnished with a celery stalk, a skewer of olives, a pickle, or even a shrimp. As with a margarita, this drink is delicious when served from a salt-rimmed glass.

Refined Scarlett O'Haras

1 (32-ounce) bottle cranberry
    juice cocktail, chilled
1½ cups chilled champagne

1 ounce Triple Sec
4 to 6 lime slices

Combine juice, champagne, and triple sec. Gently rub edge of champagne glasses with lime slice. Pour drink into glasses, place lime on glass edge for garnish, and serve immediately.

Serves 6

Go ahead and ask Rhett for a refill and enjoy because these Scarlett O'Hara's are so good you won't be worrying about anything until tomorrow!

Pimm's Cup

2 cups Pimm's #1 (found at
    large package stores)
4 cups ginger ale
6 cucumber spears

6 orange slices
    (sliced ¼-inch thick)
6 lemon slices
    (sliced ¼-inch thick)

Fill six (12-ounce) Collins glasses with ice. Pour ⅓ cup Pimm's #1 in each glass. Top each glass with ⅔ cup ginger ale. Garnish each serving with cucumber spear, orange slice, and lemon slice. Serve immediately.

Serves 6

A wonderfully refreshing gin-based drink served in England during the summertime.

Palomas

Pinch of kosher salt
1 ounce tequila
1 to 2 fresh limes, halved

Squirt® brand grapefruit flavored
    soft-drink (no substitute)

Fill straight-sided pint glasses or 16-ounce plastic cups three-fourths full with small ice cubes or cracked ice. Sprinkle salt directly onto ice. Pour tequila over ice. Place half of lime in lime press. Crush in press, flipping rind inside out. Pour juice in glass and garnish with rind. Fill glass with Squirt®. Stir gently with swizzle stick, dissolving remaining salt, while preserving the soda's effervescence. Serve immediately.

This is a light and refreshing, but potent margarita-like cocktail. It is perfect for a girl's night out!

The Lady Godiva Martini

Perfect for cocktails or dessert!

Chocolate syrup
½ ounce premium vodka
1 ounce Godiva liqueur

1 scoop vanilla-bean ice cream
½ ounce half-and-half
4 cubes ice

Two hours before serving, drizzle chocolate syrup into martini glass and freeze. In blender, combine vodka, liqueur, ice cream, half-and-half, and ice cubes, pulsing until smooth. Pour into frozen glass, and enjoy!

Serves 1

Southern Pecan Pie Martini

1 teaspoon butter pecan extract
1 teaspoon brown sugar
1 ounce brandy

3 ounces vodka
Whole pecan for garnish

In cocktail shaker, combine butter pecan extract, brown sugar, and brandy, stirring until sugar dissolves. Fill shaker half-full with cracked ice. Add vodka and shake 1 minute. Strain into chilled martini glass. Garnish with skewered pecan and serve immediately.

Serves 1

Pomegranate Martinis

1½ cups pomegranate juice
4 ounces citrus-infused vodka

1 ounce Cointreau or Citronage
Lime wedges

In cocktail shaker filled with ice, combine juice, vodka, and Cointreau or Citronage and shake well. Strain and pour into chilled martini glasses. Squeeze lime wedge into glass and use as garnish on glass edge.

Serves 4

Because of its numerous seeds and red color, pomegranates have been linked with fertility since ancient times. They are an excellent source of vitamin C and antioxidants.

Granny Smackers

2 (12-ounce) cans frozen limeade
  concentrate

2 cans beer
5 ounces vodka

In pitcher, combine concentrate, beer and vodka, mixing well. Chill until ready to serve.

Serves 6

Wide Awake Shirley Temple

½ can lemon-lime flavored soda
½ can Red Bull

1 to 2 tablespoons maraschino
  cherry juice
Maraschino cherries

Combine soda, Red Bull, and juice in glass and stir. Garnish with cherries.

Serves 1

You can substitute cola or diet cola to create a "Wide Awake Roy Roger." When using a diet drink, change the name to a "skinny!" This is the perfect pick-me-up on a sluggish afternoon.

Wassail Punch

2 quarts apple cider
2 cups orange juice
½ cup lemon juice
12 whole cloves

4 cinnamon sticks
1 pinch ground ginger
1 pinch ground nutmeg

In slow cooker or Dutch oven over low heat, combine cider and juices. Season with cloves, cinnamon, ginger, and nutmeg. Bring to a simmer. If using slow cooker, allow to simmer all day. Remove and discard cloves and cinnamon sticks before serving. Serve hot.

Serves 12

This delicious holiday favorite will warm you up after a chilly night of caroling!

Spiced Apple Cider

1 (64-ounce) bottle apple cider
1½ cups cranberry juice cocktail
6 cinnamon sticks
2 teaspoons whole all-spice
2 tablespoons honey

2 tablespoons lemon juice
1 teaspoon whole cloves
2 oranges, sliced
1 cup spiced rum (optional)

Combine cider, cranberry juice, cinnamon sticks, all-spice, honey, lemon juice, cloves, orange, and rum in crockpot. Simmer 2 hours (or more) on low. Serve warm.

Serves 10

Gluhwein

1 bottle red wine
4 cups apple juice
1 orange, sliced

1 lemon, sliced
8 to 10 whole cloves
½ cup sugar

In large saucepan, combine wine, juice, orange, lemon, cloves, and sugar, stirring gently until sugar dissolves. Bring to a boil; reduce heat and simmer until ready to serve.

Russian Tea

2 cups sugar
2 cups water, divided
4 tea bags
10 cups boiling water
1 (6-ounce) can frozen orange
    juice concentrate

1 (6-ounce) can frozen pineapple
    juice concentrate
1 (8-ounce) bottle lemon juice
1 tablespoon ground cloves

In medium saucepan over medium-high heat, combine sugar and 1 cup water, stirring until sugar dissolves. Remove from heat and set aside. Make weak tea by steeping tea bags in boiling water only a few minutes. Combine sugar-water, tea, concentrates, juice, and cloves, mixing well. Serve hot.

Serves 12

One-fourth cup heavy syrup from pickled peaches may be added for an extra spicy taste.

Instant Hot Spiced Tea

6 cups water   ¼ cup Tang
2 teaspoons instant tea   ½ cup lemon juice
¾ cup sugar   2 tablespoons whole cloves

Bring water to a boil, remove from heat and add tea and sugar, stirring until dissolved. Add Tang and lemon juice. Boil cloves in 2 cups water for 5 minutes. Remove from heat, brew for 5 to 10 minutes. Strain and add to tea. Cover container of tea and let stand for a few minutes.

Makes 2 quarts

Did you know that coffee is the second most traded commodity in the world economy after oil? One coffee tree yields less than one pound of coffee!

Creamy Mocha Punch
Perfect for a brunch shower!

1 quart boiling water   2 quarts cold water
8 tablespoons instant coffee   2 quarts milk
2 cups sugar   2 quarts vanilla ice cream
1 tablespoon vanilla   2 quarts coffee ice cream
1 (5½-ounce) can chocolate syrup

In large bowl, combine boiling water with instant coffee, sugar, vanilla, and chocolate syrup, stirring until sugar dissolves and chocolate melts. Stir in cold water and milk. Cover and chill overnight. Place ice cream in large punch bowl. Pour coffee mixture over ice cream 30 minutes before serving. Break up ice cream and stir occasionally.

Serves 40

Iced Coffee Punch

Leftover punch freezes beautifully.

1 gallon coffee (1½ strength)	1 cup sugar
¼ cup Jamaican rum	1 quart fudge-ripple ice cream
½ gallon coffee cream	

Make coffee in advance, add sugar and allow to cool in the refrigerator. Immediately prior to serving, add coffee cream and rum, and pour over ice cream.

Serves 40

Kahlúa Kozies

Give with a bottle of Kahlúa for a "kozy" holiday gift!

1 (30-ounce) box instant chocolate drink mix	2 cups flavored powdered coffee creamer
1 (16-ounce) box confectioners' sugar	1 (8-quart) box powdered milk
	Kahlúa, to taste

In large bowl, combine dry ingredients and mix well. To make cocoa, add 2 heaping tablespoons of mix to 1 cup hot water. Add Kahlúa to taste.

Serves 20

Gone are the days where many go to the trouble of "putting on the dog" by pulling out fine linen napkins, sterling silver and china. But the ladies of the Junior Assembly were a group of refined women with excellent taste who knew how to throw a tea party, luncheon or a simple girl's get-together. Never was a stone left unturned as the guests would always arrive at these gatherings donned in their finest gloves and hats.

Store powdered cocoa in plastic airtight container or give as a gift in a plastic zip top bag with mix instructions.

Appetizers

Sun-Dried Tomato Pâté

1 garlic clove

6 basil leaves

1 cup shredded Parmesan cheese

⅓ cup sun-dried tomatoes packed in oil

2 tablespoons tomato paste

2 ounces cream cheese, softened

⅛ cup sour cream

Salt and pepper to taste

Drizzle of olive oil

Place garlic and basil in food processor and pulse. Add Parmesan, tomatoes, tomato paste, cream cheese, sour cream, and salt and pepper to taste. Process until blended. Add olive oil while processing. Process until smooth. Serve with crackers, veggies, or toasted baguette.

This recipe is a favorite of Widespread Panic percussionist Sunny Ortiz.

Georgia Peach Salsa with Bulldog Ranch Crisps

Recipe created by Melanie Felton on behalf of the makers of Hidden Valley® Original Ranch® dressings.

GO BULLDOGS PEACH SALSA

4 peaches, halved, pitted, and cut into ½-inch dice

½ small red onion, cut into ¼-inch dice

4 green onions, including green tops, thinly sliced

2 medium tomatoes, cored, seeded, and cut into ½-inch dice

1 jalapeño chile, seeds and ribs removed, finely minced

½ cup chopped fresh cilantro leaves

Juice of 1 large lemon

Juice of 1 lime

2 tablespoons pure olive oil

1 (1.0-ounce) package Hidden Valley® Original Ranch® Salad Dressing & Seasoning Mix

In medium bowl, combine peaches, red onion, green onions, tomatoes, jalapeño, and cilantro. In measuring cup, stir together lemon juice, lime juice, oil, and package Hidden Valley® Original Ranch® Salad Dressing & Seasoning Mix. Stir until seasoning mix dissolves, then pour over peach mixture. Stir gently to combine. Transfer to serving bowl, cover, and set aside 1 hour to allow the flavors to meld.

Serves 12

Serve with tortilla chips, corn chips, pita chips, or Bulldog Ranch Crisps.

BULLDOG RANCH CRISPS

1 cup canola oil

1 tablespoon red pepper flakes

1 package (1.0 ounces) Hidden Valley® Original Ranch® Salad Dressing & seasoning Mix

1 box (1 pound) saltine crackers

In a bowl, combine the oil, red pepper flakes, and package of Hidden Valley® Original Ranch® Salad Dressing & Seasoning Mix. Stir to combine.

In an extra large bowl, place the crackers. Spoon the oil mixture over the crackers, gently tossing the crackers and distributing the dressing until the crackers are evenly coated. Arrange in a large serving bowl or basket. The crackers will keep for several days in a tightly covered container.

Rebecca Lang learned to cook from her mother and grandmother, both of whom are wonderful Southern cooks. Her formal training in culinary arts was at Johnson & Wales University, and she has apprenticed with Nathalie Dupree, has been an assistant food editor and recipe developer for Oxmoor House, is a food columnist for four newspapers and a private cooking instructor and professional speaker.

Roasted Pepper Crostini

Rebecca Lang

1 baguette, cut into ½-inch slices

¼ cup olive oil

4 ounces goat cheese

Freshly ground pepper

1½ cups roasted red bell pepper strips

2 tablespoons chopped oregano

Preheat oven to 400 degrees. Brush baguette slices with olive oil. Arrange slices on rimmed baking sheet. Bake 5 minutes, or until browned slightly. Turn over slices and bake additional 3 to 5 minutes. Transfer slices to platter. Spread goat cheese on each slice. Sprinkle pepper over goat cheese. Top each slice with 2 to 3 slices roasted pepper. Sprinkle with oregano.

Makes 30 pieces

Hot and Spicy Artichoke Spinach Dip

2 (9-ounce) bags frozen creamed spinach, thawed and drained

4 cups shredded mozzarella cheese, divided

1 cup shredded Parmesan cheese, divided

1 (14-ounce) jar artichoke hearts, drained and cut into ½-inch pieces

2 teaspoons hot pepper sauce

Preheat oven to 425 degrees. In mixing bowl, combine spinach, 3 cups mozzarella, ½ cup Parmesan, artichokes, and hot pepper sauce. Pour into 3-quart casserole dish and top with remaining cheeses. Bake 18 to 22 minutes. Serve with toasted pita wedges or cocktail pumpernickel and rye breads.

Serves 8-10

Warm Bacon Cheese Spread

1 (16-ounce) round loaf
    sourdough bread
1 (8-ounce) package cream
    cheese, softened
1 (12-ounce) container sour
    cream
2 cups shredded Cheddar cheese

1½ teaspoons Worcestershire
    sauce
¾ pound sliced bacon, cooked
    and crumbled
½ cup chopped green onions
Assorted crackers

Preheat oven to 325 degrees. Cut top quarter off of bread and set aside. Carefully hollow out bread, leaving a 1-inch shell. Cut removed bread and loaf top into cubes and set aside. In large mixing bowl, beat cream cheese with electric mixer. Add sour cream, Cheddar, and Worcestershire, mixing well until combined. Stir in bacon and onion. Spoon into bread shell. Wrap in heavy foil. Bake 1 hour, or until thoroughly heated. Serve with crackers and reserved bread cubes.

Crab and Artichoke Dip

1 (14-ounce) can artichoke hearts,
    drained and chopped
2¼ cups mayonnaise
2 cups shredded Parmesan cheese

2 (16-ounce) cans lump crabmeat,
    drained
⅓ cup seasoned bread crumbs
1½ teaspoons garlic salt
1 teaspoon lemon pepper

Preheat oven to 325 degrees. In mixing bowl, combine artichokes, mayonnaise, Parmesan, crabmeat, bread crumbs, garlic salt, and lemon pepper, blending well. Pour into prepared 3-quart baking dish. Bake 20 to 25 minutes, or until heated thoroughly. Serve warm or at room temperature with crackers.

APPETIZERS IN A BLINK

* Roasted Red Pepper Toasts
Top toasted baguette slices with diced roasted red peppers. Sauté garlic in olive oil, and lemon juice and drizzle over peppers. Garnish with chopped parsley.

* Chorizo Bites
Top 1-inch thick slices of chorizo sausage with thin slices of Manchego cheese and spear with a toothpick.

* Prosciutto Spirals
Roll one roasted red pepper in a slice of prosciutto ham. Serve on baguette toasts brushed with garlic-infused olive oil.

CREAMY CROISSANTS

1 cup butter (do not use
    margarine)
2 cups small curd cottage
    cheese
2 cups all-purpose flour
2 (3-ounce) packages of
    cream cheese with
    chives

Beat butter and cottage cheese together. Stir in flour. Divide into four balls and chill. Roll each ball out into a pie shape and cut into 16 wedges. Place a small amount of cream cheese on each wedge and roll up as crescents. Bake at 350 degrees 30 minutes or until brown. Serve warm.

Hot Crab Dip

1 can cream of celery soup
1 can cream of asparagus soup
1 stick butter or margarine

1 pound crabmeat
2 tablespoons sherry

Heat soups and butter in a heavy pan, stirring often to keep from burning. When mixture begins to boil, add carefully picked crabmeat and continue stirring, intermittently until it comes to a boil again. Add sherry and when thoroughly mixed, pour into heated chafing dish. Serve with crisp toast points or very thin small biscuits.

Serves 20-30

San Fran Annie Artichoke Dip

1 (14-ounce) can artichoke hearts,
    drained
1½ cups chopped onions
1 large clove garlic, minced
½ cup mayonnaise

1 (8-ounce) package cream
    cheese, softened
⅔ cup shredded Parmesan cheese
1 (6-ounce) package soft goat
    cheese

Preheat oven to 350 degrees. In food processor, combine artichoke, onion, garlic, mayonnaise, cream cheese, and cheeses in food processor. Pulse until blended. Transfer mixture to 8-inch casserole dish. Bake, uncovered, 30 minutes, or until lightly brown. Serve with corn chips or tortilla chips.

Serves 8-10

Mexicorn Dip

1 can Mexican style corn, drained

1 can sweet corn, drained

2 cups mayonnaise

2 cups sour cream

1 cup Mexican blend shredded
    cheese

3 green onions, chopped

Salt and pepper to taste

1 teaspoon chopped green onions,
    for garnish

Preheat oven to 350 degrees. In large mixing bowl, combine corns, mayonnaise, sour cream, cheese, and half of the green onion. Season with salt and pepper to taste. Garnish with remaining green onion. Pour mixture into loaf pan. Cover with foil and bake 20 to 30 minutes. Remove foil and bake until cheese lightly browns. Serve with tortilla chips.

Serves 10-20

Hot Bacon and Swiss Dip

½ cup mayonnaise

1 (8-ounce) package cream
    cheese, softened

1 (8-ounce) package Swiss cheese,
    cubed

1 (3-ounce) package real bacon
    bits

¼ cup onion, chopped

Dash hot sauce

Preheat oven to 350 degrees. In mixing bowl, combine mayonnaise and cream cheese. Fold in Swiss, bacon bits, and onion. Add hot sauce. Bake in an 11 x 7-inch pan for 15 minutes or until bubbly. Serve warm with crackers.

Serves 12

Serve something salty, something crunchy, something sweet, and fruit. For an early afternoon tea or shower, estimate 5 to 10 bites per person, and for early evening 12 to 15 bites per person. Place 5, 7, or 9 items on a cocktail buffet, less for an afternoon party (5), but for heavy hors d'oeuvres, serve 9 to 10 different items.

Buffalo Chicken Dip

Great appetizer for tailgates!

2 (8-ounce) packages cream
  cheese, softened

2 cans shredded white meat
  chicken, drained

1 cup ranch dressing

¾ cup Texas Pete wing sauce

1½ cups shredded Cheddar
  cheese

Celery

Scoop-style corn chips

Preheat oven to 350 degrees. In large mixing bowl, combine cream cheese, chicken, dressing, wing sauce, and cheese. Transfer mixture to an 11 x 7-inch baking dish. Bake 20 minutes, or until mixture is heated through. Stir well. Serve with celery and chips.

Serves 12

A nation's eternal thanks go to Teressa Bellissimo for creating and serving the original wing for which Buffalo, New York is famous (at the Anchor Bar in 1964). A marvelous adaptation of the original appetizer, this dip calls for ranch dressing instead of the typical bleu cheese.

Pepperoni Pizza Dip

1 (8-ounce) package cream
  cheese, softened

1 (14-ounce) jar pizza sauce

½ cup chopped green onions

¼ cup chopped green bell pepper

2 cups shredded mozzarella
  cheese

½ cup chopped black olives

1 (3-ounce) package sliced
  pepperoni, chopped

Tortilla chips

Preheat oven to 350 degrees. Press cream cheese into bottom of prepared 9-inch pie plate and spread with pizza sauce. Layer with green onions, bell pepper, mozzarella, olives, and pepperoni. Bake 20 minutes. Serve with tortilla chips.

Hot Tailgate Dip

1 (8-ounce) package cream
    cheese, softened

1½ cups sour cream

2 cups shredded sharp Cheddar
    cheese

1 jar chipped beef

1 (4-ounce) jar green chilies,
    drained

1 round loaf sourdough bread

Preheat oven to 325 degrees. In large mixing bowl, combine cream cheese and sour cream. Stir in Cheddar, chipped beef, and chilies. Cut top quarter off of bread and discard. Carefully hollow out bread, leaving a 1-inch shell. Spoon cheese mixture into bread shell. Wrap in foil and bake 2 hours. Serve with tortilla chips or crackers.

Creamy Mexican Party Dip

1 (14.5-ounce) can stewed
    tomatoes, well drained and
    chopped

2 cups sour cream

1 (7-ounce) can green chilies,
    chopped and drained

1 (1.1-ounce) package fiesta ranch
    dip mix

In mixing bowl, combine tomatoes, sour cream, chilies, and dip mix. Stir well to blend. Chill at least 1 hour. Serve with fresh veggies or chips.

Makes about 3½ cups

Spicy Sausage Dip

1 (8-ounce) package cream cheese

1 (14-ounce) can diced rotel
    tomatoes, undrained

1 (16-ounce) package bulk
    sausage, cooked and drained

1 (8-ounce) sour cream

Tortilla chips

In large electric skillet over medium-high heat, combine cream cheese and tomatoes, stirring until cheese melts. Add sausage and stir until blended. Stir in sour cream and serve warm with tortilla chips.

Serves 10

If you have dips to serve with the appetizers, try hollowing out a bell pepper or red cabbage to use as a container, or try a tea cup, ramekin, or small pottery bowl.

Try an all green crudité platter with this dip: cucumber and celery sticks, raw trimmed asparagus, snow peas, string beans and florets of broccoli can be attractively grouped in small white or silver dishes to great effects.

A frail chip won't stand up to this rich, thick delight. Serve with heavy, scooped corn chips, thicker crackers, or a spreader.

Hot and Cheesy Onion Dip

1 (12-ounce) package frozen
  chopped onions, slightly
  thawed

3 (8-ounce) packages cream
  cheese, softened

2 cups shredded Parmesan cheese

½ cup mayonnaise

Corn chips

Preheat oven to 425 degrees. In large mixing bowl, combine onion, cheeses, and mayonnaise, mixing well. Spoon mixture into prepared 9 x 11-inch dish. Bake 30 minutes, or until top is golden brown and bubbly. Serve with corn chips or assorted crackers.

If your frozen onions are icy, place them between paper towels and squeeze to remove excess moisture.

Avocado-Feta Salsa

1 (4-ounce) package crumbled
  feta cheese

3 tablespoons red wine vinegar

2 tablespoons olive oil

1 tablespoon freshly chopped
  parsley

½ teaspoon dried oregano

½ teaspoon salt

2 garlic cloves, minced

4 Roma tomatoes, chopped

2 tablespoons chopped red onion

2 chopped avocados

Tortilla chips

In mixing bowl, whisk together vinegar, oil, parsley, oregano, salt, and garlic. Add tomato and onion, tossing well to coat. Gently fold in avocado and sprinkle with feta just before serving. Serve with whole grain tortilla chips.

Serves 8

Equal parts varicolored tomatoes can be used to alter the taste and appearance of this lively salsa. Yellow, orange, and even green tomatoes combine quite nicely with Romas or other red, vine-ripened varieties.

Fresh Pico de Gallo with Roasted Poblano

Great as a dip or with any Latin-inspired food.

1 large poblano pepper, halved and seeded

9 to 10 large plum tomatoes, seeded and chopped

¾ cup finely chopped white onion

1 jalapeño pepper, seeded and finely chopped

Zest and juice of 2 large lemons

1 teaspoon olive oil

1 teaspoon salt

Dash of pepper

Preheat broiler on high. To roast, flatten poblano on foil-lined baking sheet. Place under broiler 8 to 10 minutes. Skin should darken and pull away. Immediately place poblano in plastic zip top bag or brown paper bag and seal. Allow to steam for 10 minutes. Remove from bag; peel and discard skin. Chop pepper. In large mixing bowl, combine poblano, tomato, onion, jalapeño, lemon zest and juice, and oil. Add salt and pepper. Season to taste. Serve at room temperature with tortilla chips. Add cilantro to taste.

Serves 6-8

This is also delicious as a condiment for baked fish or spread on a roast pork or chicken sandwich.

Raspberry Black Bean Dip

¼ cup chopped onion

1 (8-ounce) package cream cheese, softened

1 (15-ounce) can black beans, drained and mashed

⅓ cup raspberry preserves

1 cup medium-hot salsa

2 tablespoons chili powder

½ to ¾ cup shredded colby cheese

Preheat oven to 350 degrees. In large mixing bowl, combine onion, cream cheese and mashed beans, blending well. Spread on bottom of 8-inch glass casserole dish. In small mixing bowl, combine preserves and salsa, mixing well. Spread on top of cream cheese mixture. Sprinkle with chili powder. Top with thin layer of cheese. Bake 25 to 30 minutes. Let stand at least 30 minutes before serving. Serve with blue tortilla chips.

Serves 6-8

For a bean salad it's often necessary to rinse and drain canned black beans more than once to preserve their shape for appearance's sake. But in dips such as this one, where you're free to mash away, once is enough.

Bulldog Salsa

Great appetizer for a Georgia game, there is a lot of red and black in this salsa!

¼ cup extra virgin olive oil

½ cup fresh lime juice

½ cup fresh cilantro, chopped

½ cup fresh parsley, chopped

3 cloves garlic, crushed and minced

1½ teaspoons cumin

1 teaspoon crushed red pepper

1 teaspoon freshly ground black pepper

½ teaspoon salt

2 cans seasoned black beans, drained and rinsed

1 large can white shoepeg corn, drained

1 red bell pepper, diced

1 Vidalia onion, diced

In small mixing bowl, combine oil, lime juice, cilantro, parsley, garlic, cumin, red pepper, black pepper, and salt, whisking well. In large serving bowl, combine beans, corn, bell pepper, and onion. Pour marinade over bean mixture, tossing gently to coat. Chill overnight. Serve with tortilla chips.

Classic Cowboy Caviar

We love beluga as much as anyone, but blini can be time-consuming to make and sometimes you just can't lay hands on a horn spoon. Nevertheless, this "caviar" still goes well with the traditional accompaniment of sour cream.

1 (15-ounce) can black beans, drained

1 (11-ounce) can shoepeg corn, drained

¼ cup olive oil

¼ cup vinegar

¼ cup sugar

3 chopped green onions

¼ teaspoon garlic powder

Pepper to taste

½ cup crumbled feta cheese

In small mixing bowl, combine oil, vinegar, sugar, green onion, garlic powder, and pepper, whisking well to blend. In large mixing bowl, combine black beans and corn. Pour marinade over beans and corn, tossing gently to coat. Marinade at least 6 to 8 hours. Toss in feta just before serving. Serve with tortilla chips.

Serves 6-8

BLT Dip

1 cup sour cream

1 cup mayonnaise

Adobo seasoning

Salt and pepper to taste

½ head lettuce, shredded

8 slices bacon, cooked and broken
    into bits

1½ cups tomatoes, diced

1 bag large corn chips

In mixing bowl, combine sour cream and mayonnaise. Add Adobo seasoning, salt, and pepper to taste. Line a serving bowl with lettuce. Spoon sour cream mixture on top of lettuce. Sprinkle with bacon and tomato. Serve with corn chips.

Triangles of toasted white or wheat sandwich bread served with this dip complete the conversion of a lunch counter classic to a delectable appetizer. As with the namesake sandwich, extra bacon won't hurt a bit.

Sweet Potato Dip

1 pound sweet potatoes
    (about 1 large or 2 small)

1 whole head garlic

2 to 4 tablespoons extra virgin
    olive oil

2 tablespoons fresh lemon juice

Salt to taste

Hot pepper sauce to taste

Preheat oven to 375 degrees. Place sweet potatoes and garlic in baking dish. Drizzle with small amount of oil and bake 45 minutes, or until tender.

Peel sweet potatoes and place baked flesh in work bowl of food processor. Cut base off of garlic head and squeeze roasted garlic onto sweet potatoes. Discard sweet potato skin, garlic base, and garlic skin. Purée sweet potato and garlic mixture, adding oil, lemon juice, salt, and hot pepper sauce, processing until mixture reaches dip consistency. Serve at room temperature with crudités.

Makes about 2 cups

Noted low-country cookbook author and former UGA cinema student John Martin Taylor created this recipe and shared it with the submitter. "Hoppin' Johns" own line of stone-ground grits can be found in many an Athenian pantry.

Crisp vegetables with a lighter flavor, such as carrots or snow peas are best here or try tossing it into a salad with chow mein noodles and bamboo shoots.

Ginger Dip

1 cup mayonnaise

1 cup sour cream

½ cup chopped green onions

½ cup Italian parsley

1 (5-ounce) can sliced water chestnuts, drained

1 (2-ounce) jar crystallized ginger

1 tablespoon minced garlic

2 tablespoons soy sauce

In bowl of food processor, combine mayonnaise, sour cream, green onions, parsley, water chestnuts, ginger, garlic, and soy sauce and pulse 10 to 20 seconds, or until ginger is crushed and well mixed. For best results, prepare one to two days ahead.

FRUIT DIPPERS:

* Apple wedges

* Bananas

* Melon slices

* Grapes

* Mandarin oranges

* Pear wedges

* Pineapple slices

* Strawberries

Easy Fruit Dip

1 (8-ounce) package cream cheese, softened

1 (8-ounce) container frozen whipped topping, thawed

1 (14-ounce) can sweetened condensed milk

1 cup finely chopped pecans

½ teaspoon cinnamon

Zest of 1 orange

In large mixing bowl, beat cream cheese with electric mixture until smooth. Fold in whipped topping and milk, mixing until creamy. Fold in pecans, cinnamon, and orange zest. Cover and chill before serving with sliced fruit.

Serves 24

Cranberry Jewel

1 can whole cranberries in sauce

⅓ cup minced onion

2 tablespoons prepared
    horseradish

½ teaspoon salt

½ cup sugar

⅓ cup water

2 (8-ounce) packages cream
    cheese

Fresh rosemary sprigs

In large saucepan over medium heat, combine cranberries, onion, horseradish, salt, sugar, and water. Bring to a boil. Remove from heat and chill several hours or overnight. Spoon generously over blocks of cream cheese just before serving. Garnish with sprig of fresh rosemary and serve with butter crackers. This will keep in refrigerator for two weeks.

Basil Feta Dip with Pita Chips

1 (8-ounce) package cream
    cheese, softened

1 (6-ounce) package feta cheese,
    crumbled

2½ tablespoons fresh basil,
    chopped

2½ tablespoons sun-dried
    tomatoes, finely chopped

In mixing bowl, combine cream cheese, feta, basil, and tomatoes. Chill until ready to serve. Serve with crackers, pita chips or fresh vegetables.

Makes 1½ cups

PITA CHIPS

4 whole pitas
Olive oil

Cayenne pepper

Preheat oven to 375 degrees. Brush pitas with olive oil. Stack pitas and cut into wedges. Arrange wedges on baking sheet and sprinkle with cayenne. Top with second baking sheet to help keep chips flat. Place stacked baking sheets in oven and bake 12 to 15 minutes or until crisp.

This is pretty and colorful to use during the Thanksgiving and Christmas holidays. Also nice for Valentine parties and Fourth of July. Everyone wants this recipe after tasting it! Very quick and easy!

COCKTAIL PARTY PLEASERS

* Make appetizers small enough to be eaten in one bite for less mess.

* Garnish serving trays with kale, olives, parsley, or lemon peel and line bowls with cabbage leaves.

* Serve appetizers and dips in interesting containers such as hollowed out cabbage, bread, pumpkins, or watermelons.

* Place appetizers in multiple locations rather than having one table. This encourages your guests to move around.

* Serve cold foods such as vegetables, shrimp, and cubed cheese in a ring of ice.

* Stash fresh trays of appetizers in the kitchen so you can quickly refill.

* Provide easy-to-find receptacles for used napkins, skewers, etc.

Welsh Rabbit (Rarebit)

1 teaspoon butter or margarine

1 pound sharp Cheddar cheese, grated

1 cup stale beer

1 teaspoon salt

1 teaspoon prepared mustard

1 teaspoon paprika

Pinch of cayenne

Melt butter over slow heat and grease the bottom of the pan with it. It is best to use a chafing dish over hot water. Add grated cheese and beer, one tablespoon at the time. If stale beer is unavailable, bring fresh beer to a good boil, let cool, then measure. The mixture will thicken quickly, so add more beer and stir constantly and gently until mixture is satin smooth. All liquid may not be needed. Blend in remaining ingredients and serve on hot toast or crackers.

Serves 6

Cheese and Spinach Tartlets

6 slices firm white bread

1 (10-ounce) package frozen chopped spinach, thawed and squeezed dry

1 cup whipping cream

¾ cup crumbled blue cheese or mild Cheddar cheese

½ teaspoon salt

¼ teaspoon ground black pepper

⅛ teaspoon ground nutmeg

2 tablespoons pine nuts, toasted

The baked tartlets may be frozen in a tightly covered container; to reheat, place frozen tartlets on a pan in a 400 degree oven until hot, about 10 minutes.

Preheat oven to 400 degrees. Lightly oil 24 muffin cups, each 1¾ inches wide. With a 1½-inch cookie cutter, cut 4 rounds from each slice of bread. Place the 24 rounds on a cookie sheet; bake about 5 minutes or until pale gold, turning once. Gently press toasted rounds into the bottom of muffin cups; set aside.

In a medium bowl, combine spinach, cream, cheese, salt, pepper and nutmeg until blended. To toast pine nuts, place in a small dry skillet over medium heat until golden, stirring often. Spoon mixture into bread cups and sprinkle with pine nuts. Bake until filling is set, about 15 minutes. Remove to a wire rack to cool slightly.

Serve warm.

Pizza Crudités

2 (8-ounce) cans crescent rolls

2 (8-ounce) packages cream
   cheese, softened

½ cup mayonnaise

1 (1-ounce) package ranch
   dressing mix

1 cup shredded carrots

1 cup chopped broccoli

1 cup chopped golden pear

1 cup shredded cheese

Preheat oven to 375 degrees. Roll out crescent dough onto baking sheet. Pinch together seams of dough to form one large crust. Bake 7 to 10 minutes, or until golden brown. Remove from oven and cool completely. In mixing bowl, combine cream cheese, mayonnaise, and dressing mix. Spread over cooled crust. Arrange carrot, broccoli, and pear on top of dressing mixture. Sprinkle with cheese. Gently press vegetables and cheese into crust. Cut into squares and chill until ready to serve.

Serves 16-18

Hoisin Pork Wontons

24 round wonton wrappers

4 cloves garlic, minced

2 teaspoons ginger

4 tablespoons freshly chopped
   cilantro

2 teaspoons soy sauce

4 tablespoons orange juice

6 tablespoons hoisin sauce

2 teaspoons honey

1¼ pounds ground pork, cooked
   and drained

Preheat oven to 400 degrees. Place wonton wrappers a miniature muffin pan. In small mixing bowl, whisk together garlic, ginger, cilantro, soy sauce, orange juice, hoisin sauce, and honey, mixing well. Reserve half of mixture and set aside. Combine pork with remaining half of mixture. Spoon pork mixture into wonton wrappers. Bake 20 minutes. Transfer to serving plate and drizzle with reserved sauce.

Makes 24 appetizers

CRISPY CRUDITÉS

* Asparagus
* Yellow squash
* Red bell pepper
* Orange bell pepper
* Broccoli
* Baby bok choy
* Celery
* Portobello mushrooms
* Cauliflower
* Radishes, sliced
* Spring onions
* Cherry tomatoes
* Sugar snap peas

For decades UGA has been successful in attracting students from eastern and Asiatic cultures, and so the population of Athens is equally enriched and further diversified. Lighter than some dumplings you could serve, these appetizers will go over well even if Augusta, Georgia, is as "far east" as the person eating it has ever been.

Game Day Party Pleasers

Delicious even if it's not a game day, these can be made with smoked turkey as well, or add roasted pork and crisp dill pickles for miniature Cuban sandwiches.

4 (20-count) packages dinner rolls

16 tablespoons margarine, melted

3 tablespoons poppy seeds

3 tablespoons Dijon mustard

1 small onion, minced

1 teaspoon Worcestershire sauce

1 pound shaved deli ham

⅓ pound Monterey Jack cheese, shredded

Game day eve: Remove rolls from foil tray, being careful not to tear rolls apart. Using serrated knife, slice tops off of rolls. Repeat process for each tray. Return roll bottoms back to trays. In large mixing bowl, combine margarine, poppy seeds, Dijon mustard, onion, and Worcestershire. Spread mixture on inside tops and bottoms of each set of rolls, reserving a small amount. Place ham evenly across bottoms of rolls and sprinkle with Cheddar. Place top layers of rolls over ham and cheese and press down. Spread any remaining mixture over rolls. Cover with foil and chill overnight.

Game day morning: Preheat oven to 350 degrees. Bake, covered, 10 to 12 minutes. Serve immediately, or pack in a thermal bag and hurry to your favorite tailgating spot!

Serves 16

Sausage Poppers

1 package miniature smoked sausages

1 pound bacon (cut into 4-inch pieces)

1 (16-ounce) package light brown sugar

Preheat oven to 400 degrees. Spray glass baking dish with nonstick cooking spray. Wrap each sausage with one piece of bacon. Secure bacon with wooden toothpick and place into baking dish. Generously cover with brown sugar. Bake until golden brown. Cooking time will vary by oven. The bacon should be crisp, but not burnt.

Serves 10

Sausage Rolls

1 (16-ounce) package sage-
    flavored bulk sausage

1 (8-ounce) package cream cheese

2 (8-ounce) cans crescent rolls

Preheat oven to 375 degrees. Cook sausage and drain. Return sausage to skillet and add cream cheese, stirring over low heat until cheese melts. Remove from heat and set aside. Roll out dough onto baking sheet, being careful not to tear triangles apart (leave in two big sheets). Press seams together. Spoon half of sausage mixture onto each piece of dough. Roll dough lengthwise, jellyroll style. Bake 20 minutes, or until brown. Slice and serve warm.

Serves 8

Greek Bites

1 package refrigerated pizza
    crust, prepared according to
    package directions

½ jar sun-dried tomato pesto

1 (6-ounce) jar marinated
    artichokes, drained and
    chopped

1 (6-ounce) package crumbled
    feta cheese

¼ can pitted, sliced black olives,
    drained

Preheat oven to 400 degrees. Spread crust with pesto, covering entire crust. Sprinkle with artichokes, feta, and olives. Bake 6 to 8 minutes. Slice and serve.

Serves 12

Pastry Wrapped Mushrooms

1 container fresh mushrooms,
    washed, patted dry, and
    stemmed

1 container garlic and herb cheese
    spread

2 (8-ounce) cans crescent rolls

Preheat oven to 350 degrees. Fill mushroom caps with 1 teaspoon cheese spread. Wrap each filled mushroom with one crescent triangle. Arrange on baking sheet and bake 11 to 13 minutes. Serve immediately.

Serves 16

Caprese Tartlets

2 (15-count) packages prepared
    phyllo shells or any other
    prepared tartlet shell

¼ cup freshly grated Parmesan

15 grape tomatoes, halved

Freshly chopped basil

30 mozzarella cheese cubes

Salt and pepper

Olive oil

Preheat oven to 350 degrees. Place tartlet shells on baking sheet. Sprinkle inside of shells with Parmesan. Place tomato half in each shell and sprinkle with basil. Place mozzarella cube in each shell. Season with salt and pepper to taste. Drizzle with olive oil. Bake until cheese melts.

Serves 8-10

Asparagus Rolls

1 loaf white bread

16 tablespoons butter, melted

Parmesan cheese

1 can extra long asparagus,
    drained

Preheat oven to 350 degrees. On cutting board, remove and discard crust from bread. Flatten each piece of bread with rolling pin. Place asparagus piece on flattened bread and roll diagonally from corner to corner. Roll asparagus in butter, then in Parmesan cheese. Repeat process with remaining bread and asparagus. Place on baking sheet and bake 20 minutes, or until lightly browned.

Serves 8-10

Insalata Caprese is a simple salad of sliced fresh mozzarella, plum tomatoes, and basil. It is seasoned with salt, black pepper, and olive oil. The dish represents the colors of the Italian flag.

AMAZING ASPARAGUS

Choose firm stalks with tightly sealed tips. Asparagus can be peeled if you like, but it is not necessary. If you do decide to peel the stalks, stop peeling about 2 inches from the tips. Rinse the spears well then hold the spears in both hands and bend until they snap. The spears naturally break at the point where they begin to be tender. Steam or drizzle with olive oil and sea salt and roast them.

Artichoke Balls

2 tablespoons olive oil

4 tablespoons butter

2 cans artichoke hearts, chopped

2 teaspoons garlic powder

½ teaspoon lemon pepper

¼ teaspoon Worcestershire sauce

⅛ teaspoon celery salt

½ tablespoon chopped parsley

⅛ teaspoon oregano

Salt and pepper to taste

2 eggs, beaten

1 cup seasoned bread crumbs, divided

1 cup freshly grated Parmesan, divided

In large skillet over medium-low heat, heat olive oil and butter. Add artichoke, garlic powder, lemon pepper, Worcestershire, celery salt, parsley, oregano, salt, and pepper. Slowly add eggs, stirring often to avoid curdling. Add ½ cup bread crumbs and ½ cup Parmesan, mixing until heated through and of paste consistency. Set aside and cool. Combine remaining bread crumbs and Parmesan on plate and mix together. Roll artichoke mixture into 1 to 1½-inch sized balls. Roll in bread crumb mixture. Place on plate and chill. Serve chilled.

Makes approximately 40-50 balls

Sweet Potato Fries

1½ pounds sweet potatoes (2 to 3 medium-sized), rinsed and patted dry

1 teaspoon ground cumin

1 teaspoon coarse salt

¼ teaspoon freshly ground black pepper

1 tablespoon olive oil

Preheat oven to 425 degrees. Cut each potato in half lengthwise; quarter each half lengthwise. On large rimmed baking sheet lined with foil, toss potatoes with cumin, salt, pepper, and olive oil until coated. Arrange potatoes, cut sides down, in single layer. Roast about 30 minutes, turning potatoes halfway through cooking, or until tender and browned.

Serves 4

WHAT IS ANTIPASTO?

Antipasto means "before the meal" in Italian. So you can pretty much go with anything here. Traditionally antipasto is platters of food with various combinations of the following:

* Breads that have been prepared with fresh herbs and oils, along with dips and spreads.

* Boiled eggs, fish, cured meats, olives, and preserved vegetables.

* Fresh vegetables are also very common. You can use whatever you have on hand.

As an appetizer, serve these in individual paper cones with harissa sauce for dipping or drizzled with chestnut honey.

Cassi's Fried Dill Pickles

Great served with baked fish

1 sleeve crackers, crushed

1 cup all-purpose flour

1 teaspoon Old Bay Seasoning

1 teaspoon seasoned salt

1 jar dill pickle chips or slices, drained and dried

1 egg, beaten

Cooking oil for frying

Salt to taste

Combine crackers, flour, Old Bay, and seasoned salt into pie plate and mix thoroughly. Dip pickles into egg, then dredge in cracker mixture, shaking off excess. Pour oil into skillet and set to medium-high heat. Drop pickles into hot oil. Fry in single layers, turning after about 2 minutes. Fry until golden brown. Remove from oil and drain on paper towels. Allow to cool and sprinkle lightly with salt before serving.

Serves 4-6

Santa Fe Wraps

2 (8-ounce) packages cream cheese, softened

1 cup sour cream

1 (4½-ounce) can chopped green chilies, drained

1 (4¼-ounce) can chopped black olives, drained

1 cup shredded Cheddar cheese

3 green onions, chopped

1 jar salsa, divided

1 cup chopped, fresh spinach

12 large flour tortillas

In large mixing bowl, combine cream cheese, sour cream, chilies, olives, Cheddar cheese, onions, and 2 tablespoons salsa. Stir in spinach. Spread mixture evenly over each tortilla. Roll tightly, wrap in plastic wrap, and chill overnight until firm. Cut each roll into 1 to 2-inch slices with a serrated knife. Serve with remaining salsa for dipping.

Serves 10-12

Festive Cheese Ball

These make nice homemade gifts for the holidays!

4 (8-ounce) packages cream cheese, softened

¼ teaspoon baking soda

¼ teaspoon seasoned salt flavor enhancer

¼ teaspoon salt

⅛ teaspoon garlic salt

½ cup evaporated milk

1 pound Cheddar cheese, shredded

1 (4.25-ounce) can chopped black olives

1 cup chopped pecans

Paprika

In large mixing bowl, combine cream cheese, baking soda, salts, and milk. Fold in Cheddar, olives, and pecans, mixing well. Shape into a ball and sprinkle with paprika. Chill at least 2 hours. Serve with crackers.

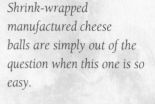

Shrink-wrapped manufactured cheese balls are simply out of the question when this one is so easy.

Tangy Cheese Ball

1 pound sharp Cheddar (New York sharp)

1 (8-ounce) package cream cheese

¾ cup chopped pecans

2 teaspoons garlic or garlic powder

4 tablespoons Durkee's dressing

2 tablespoons Worcestershire sauce

1 pinch salt

Paprika

Grate cheese, mix in cream cheese, pecans and garlic. Add all other ingredients. Make into a ball, roll in paprika, and refrigerate.

Calico Christmas Spread

6 ounces cream cheese, softened

1 cup shredded sharp Cheddar

1 tablespoon sherry

½ teaspoon curry powder

Sea salt to taste

1 (8-ounce) jar mango chutney, finely chopped

Chopped pecans

In mixing bowl, beat together cream cheese, Cheddar, sherry, curry, and salt until well blended. Stir in chutney.

Firmly pack into 3 to 4 (6-ounce) ramekins and sprinkle with pecans. Cover with plastic wrap and chill. These will keep in the refrigerator about 3 weeks.

WINE AND CHEESE PAIRINGS

* Asiago and Bardolino
* Baby Swiss and Asti Spumanti
* Brick and Chardonnay
* Brie and Merlot
* Camembert and Chenin Blanc
* Cheddar and Champagne
* Edam and Pinot Noir
* Feta and Beaujolais
* Fresh mozzarella and light red
* Gorgonzola and Bordeaux
* Gouda and Riesling
* Limburger and Beer
* Manchego and Rioja
* Muenster and Zinfandel
* Pecorino and Chianti
* Stilton and Port
* Tillamook Cheddar and dark beer

Cheese Torte

1 small package chopped pecan halves, toasted

1 (12-ounce) package shredded sharp Cheddar cheese, divided

2 (8-ounce) packages cream cheese, softened

1 (10-ounce) package chopped frozen spinach, thawed and drained

⅓ cup mayonnaise

1 teaspoon sugar

Salt and pepper to taste

1 jar mango chutney

1 teaspoon cayenne pepper

Divide pecans in half and place in single layer into bottoms of two (16-ounce) miniature loaf pans. Sprinkle ⅓ to ½ cup Cheddar over pecans in both pans. In mixing bowl, combine 1 package cream cheese and spinach; mix well and set aside. In separate mixing bowl, combine remaining Cheddar, mayonnaise, and sugar. Season with salt and pepper to taste and set aside. In third mixing bowl, combine remaining package cream cheese with chutney and cayenne pepper. Divide mixtures in half and layer in both loaf pans in order: mango chutney mixture pressed down well, spinach mixture pressed down well, and mayonnaise mixture pressed down well. Chill 4 hours before serving. Serve with crackers.

Cream Cheese and Amaretto Spread

1 (8-ounce) package cream cheese, softened

¼ cup amaretto

1 (2 or 4-ounce) package sliced almonds, toasted

Sliced apples

Pineapple juice

In mixing bowl, combine cream cheese and amaretto. Cover and chill until firm. Shape mixture into ball or ring. Cover with almonds. Marinate apples in pineapple juice at least 1 hour before serving. Serve spread with drained apple slices.

At Christmas, this is pretty shaped into a ring and surrounded with apple slices. Red and green apples are especially festive. It looks like a pinecone wreath.

Cheese Wafers

A tasty treat for cocktail hour!

2 cups shredded extra sharp
   Cheddar cheese

8 tablespoons butter or
   margarine, softened

1 cup all-purpose flour

¼ teaspoon cayenne pepper

⅛ teaspoon salt

½ cup sesame, caraway, or poppy
   seeds

In large mixing bowl, combine cheese and butter. Stir in flour, cayenne, and salt; mix well. Shape into two rolls. Roll dough in seeds. Wrap in wax paper and chill overnight.

Preheat oven to 350 degrees. Cut into thin slices and arrange on ungreased baking sheet. Bake 10 minutes. Allow to cool before serving.

These can be turned into that southern cocktail classic, the cheese straw, by piping the mixture through a pastry bag with a star-shaped tip.

Pepperoni Three Cheese Bread

1 loaf white yeast bread, frozen

2 egg whites, beaten

2 cups sliced pepperoni, divided

1 cup shredded Parmesan cheese,
   divided

1 cup shredded sharp Cheddar
   cheese, divided

1 cup shredded mozzarella
   cheese, divided

1 cup commercially prepared
   spaghetti sauce, divided

1 teaspoon black pepper

1 teaspoon garlic salt

Preheat oven to 350 degrees. Thaw yeast bread and let rise according to package directions. Divide dough in half after rising. Roll out each portion of dough to 14 x 8-inch oval shape and ¼-inch thickness. Brush tops of dough with egg white. Working one inch from edge of dough, create two vertical strips of layered ingredients on each side: ¼ cup Parmesan, Cheddar, and mozzarella; ½ cup pepperoni; ¼ teaspoon black pepper and garlic salt; and ¼ cup spaghetti sauce. Tuck in the ends of the dough. Pull outer edges of dough over each pepperoni strip and bring to the center of the oval, forming two tunnels of ingredients. Brush seams of dough with egg white so that no ingredients are loose. Press tunnels together so that there is one loaf. Flip bread onto lightly prepared baking sheet so that seam side is down. Brush top with egg white and sprinkle with Parmesan cheese. Repeat process for second loaf. Bake 20 minutes, or until top is golden brown. Baked bread may be frozen and reheated, but do not microwave.

Serves 6-8 (Makes 2 loaves)

NUTS AND BOLTS

1 pound assorted nuts

1 small box slim pretzels

1 small box Rice Chex
   cereal

1 small box Cheerios

3 sticks melted margarine

1 teaspoon seasoned salt

3 teaspoons garlic salt

Preheat oven to 250 degrees. Mix together margarine, season salt and garlic salt. Add to dry ingredients and stir well with wooden spoon. Bake for 2 hours, stirring every 15 minutes.

Back in the day when liquor was "illegal" for purchase in many southern counties, "Sherry Parties" began and cheese straws were always a favorite finger-food to have on hand for these and other impromptu get-togethers.

1-2-3 Cheese Straws

1 pound sharp cheese, grated

2 sticks margarine, softened

3 cups sifted flour

Several dashes red pepper

Preheat oven to 350 degrees. Combine cheese and margarine. Add flour and red pepper and mix thoroughly. Force through a cookie press with star design into long strips on a greased cookie sheet. Bake 12 to 15 minutes or until lightly browned. Cut into finger lengths and store in closed containers.

PUFF PASTRY PREP

Work with one sheet at a time, keeping the others in the refrigerator. Unfold pastry sheets on a lightly floured surface or on a pastry cloth. If the pastry becomes too soft, chill it in the refrigerator for a few minutes. Handle pastry as little as possible to ensure tenderness. Cut pastry with a sharp utensil such as a knife, pizza wheel, or pastry tool. Seal pastries by brushing a mixture of beaten eggs and water between layers, then pinching or pressing them together.

Herb-Cheese Pastry Puff

Looks difficult, but it's really easy!

1 teaspoon Dijon mustard

1 (12-ounce) package Havarti cheese

½ teaspoon dried parsley

½ teaspoon dried chives

¼ teaspoon dried whole dill

⅛ teaspoon dried whole basil

1 frozen puff pastry, thawed

1 egg, beaten

Preheat oven to 375 degrees. Spread mustard over top of cheese; sprinkle with parsley, chives, dill and basil. Place cheese, mustard side down, in center of pastry. Wrap package style, trimming excess pastry and seal seam. Place seam side down on lightly greased baking sheet. Brush with egg; chill 30 minutes. Bake 20 minutes. Brush with egg again and bake additional 10 minutes, or until golden brown. Serve warm with crackers or sliced apples.

Serves 12 to 15

Cheese Smackles

2 sticks butter, softened

1 (8-ounce) package shredded
   sharp Cheddar cheese

2 cups crispy rice cereal

2 cups all-purpose flour

½ teaspoon cayenne pepper

1½ teaspoons salt

Preheat oven to 350 degrees. In large mixing bowl, combine butter and Cheddar. Sift together flour, salt, and cayenne. Add flour mixture to cheese mixture, blending well. Add cereal and form into small balls. Arrange on prepared baking sheet. Press gently onto tops with fork. Bake 15 to 20 minutes.

Unforgettable Crab-Stuffed Mushrooms

2 (8-ounce) packages cream
   cheese, softened

4 tablespoons Worcestershire
   sauce

1 tablespoon horseradish, heaping

1 tablespoon garlic, heaping

2 (6-ounce) cans crabmeat,
   drained

1 pound white whole mushrooms,
   rinsed, patted dry, and
   stemmed

Old Bay seasoning

Preheat oven to 350 degrees. In mixing bowl, combine cream cheese, Worcestershire, horseradish, and garlic. Fold in crabmeat and mix well. Stuff mushroom caps with heaping tablespoon of crab mixture. Place in prepared baking dish and sprinkle with Old Bay seasoning. Bake 35 minutes.

Double this recipe and use it to "stuff" marinated Portobello caps for an unforgettable first course. Any reserved crab mixture makes an excellent dip as well.

DEVEINING SHRIMP

The black vein running down the back of shrimp is the digestive tract. It is harmless, so to devein or not to devein is up to you. To devein: Grasp the tail in one hand and gently remove the shell. Pull off the tail. Make a shallow slit along the shrimp's back with a sharp paring knife and lift the vein out with the tip of the knife.

INSTANT APPETIZER

On a large platter, place fresh marinated mozzarella cheese, imported provolone, marinated roasted peppers and artichoke hearts, prosciutto, sopressata, Genoa salami, and specialty olives, accompanied by crusty Italian bread.

Cajun Shrimp

2 cups cooking oil
¼ cup hot sauce
1 tablespoon olive oil
1 tablespoon minced garlic
1½ teaspoons salt
1½ teaspoons seafood seasoning
1½ teaspoons dried whole basil
1½ teaspoons dried whole oregano
1½ teaspoons dried whole thyme
1½ teaspoons minced fresh parsley
5 pounds large shrimp, boiled, peeled and deveined

In mixing bowl, whisk together cooking oil, hot sauce, olive oil, garlic, salt, seafood seasoning, basil, oregano, thyme, and parsley. Pour over shrimp in large bowl, tossing well to coat. Cover and chill 8 hours. Drain shrimp before serving and serve in lettuce-lined bowl.

Serves 25 (appetizer servings)

Grilled Shrimp Skewers

2 pounds uncooked, fresh jumbo shrimp, deveined and rinsed
½ pound bacon
Skewers
Lemon wedges

Place shrimp in bag and marinate at least 30 minutes. Remove shrimp, wrap in bacon, and thread on skewers. If using wooden skewers, be sure to soak in water before grilling. Place on preheated grill and cook about 1 minute per side, or until shrimp is no longer translucent. Use marinade to brush on shrimp during grilling. Discard remaining marinade. Serve with lemon wedges. Enjoy!

MARINADE

¼ cup fresh lemon juice
¼ cup ketchup
3 dashes hot sauce
1 garlic clove crushed or minced
½ cup canola oil

In plastic zip top bag, combine lemon juice, ketchup, hot sauce, garlic, and oil.

Shrimp á la Cuff
So easy and a crowd pleaser!

2½ pounds large shrimp, peeled
    and deveined

¼ cup chopped parsley

¼ cup chopped green onions

¼ cup tarragon vinegar

¼ cup red wine vinegar

½ cup olive oil

5 heaping tablespoons Dijon
    mustard

1 teaspoon crushed red pepper

1 teaspoon kosher salt

Cook shrimp in boiling, salted water until pink. Drain shrimp and dry on paper towels. Set aside. In large mixing bowl, whisk together parsley, green onion, vinegars, oil, mustard, red pepper, and salt. Pour over shrimp, tossing gently to coat. Cover and chill overnight.

Serves 8

Meatballs in Sweet BBQ Sauce
Try adding salsa or jalapeños to the meatballs for more zip!

MEATBALLS

1½ pounds ground beef

2 eggs, beaten

1 tube crackers, finely crushed

1 finely chopped onion

1 (15-ounce) can diced tomatoes,
    drained and crushed

1 (28-ounce) can finely chopped
    banana peppers, drained

Preheat oven 350 degrees. In large mixing bowl, combine ground beef, eggs, crackers, onion, tomatoes, and peppers. Form meatballs and place on baking sheet in rows. Cook 30 minutes, or until centers are no longer pink. Serve with Sweet BBQ Sauce.

SWEET BBQ SAUCE

3 tablespoons butter

1 bottle chili sauce

3 teaspoons prepared mustard

¼ cup white vinegar

¾ cup brown sugar

¾ cup barbecue sauce

In saucepan over medium heat, combine butter, chili sauce, mustard, vinegar, and brown sugar. Bring to a simmer. Add barbecue sauce (or more to taste). Reduce heat to low and simmer 10 minutes.

We love a meatball that doesn't require leaving a crockpot sitting out in plain sight. These can also easily transition to other favorites with marinara sauces over spaghetti or in a hero-sandwich with Parmesan.

Spicy Party Weenies

1 onion, chopped

2 tablespoons butter or margarine

1½ cups ketchup

½ cup vinegar

2 teaspoons dry mustard

2 teaspoons paprika

2 teaspoons chili powder

2 teaspoons Worcestershire sauce

1 teaspoon Tabasco sauce

½ cup brown sugar

1 teaspoon pepper

2 packages cocktail wieners or hot dogs, sliced

In small skillet, sauté onion in butter until tender. In large mixing bowl, whisk together ketchup, vinegar, mustard, paprika, chili powder, Worcestershire, Tabasco, brown sugar, and pepper. Stir in onion. Transfer mixture to slow cooker and add cocktail wieners. Set slow cooker to low temperature and cook 2 hours.

Little E's Duck Bites

1 bottle Catalina salad dressing

¼ cup Worcestershire sauce

1 tablespoon garlic powder

1 onion, sliced

1 pound dove, duck, or goose breasts, cut into 1-inch pieces

1 cup jalapeño peppers, sliced

1 pound bacon, uncooked

In large mixing bowl, combine dressing, Worcestershire, and garlic powder. Mix well and set aside. Place onion slice on one side of breast and jalapeño slice on other side. Wrap with bacon and skewer with toothpick. Place in shallow baking dish and cover with dressing mixture. Chill and marinate at least 1 hour. Cook over hot grill until bacon is done. Remove toothpicks before serving.

Makes 12-14 pieces

Ernie's Gator Nuggets

1 pound alligator tail meat, cut
    into 1-inch cubes

Cornmeal

Cajun seasoning to taste

Cooking oil

Tenderize alligator with meat mallet. In large mixing bowl, combine cornmeal and Cajun seasoning. Dredge gator in cornmeal mixture. In large skillet, heat oil to 350 degrees. Fry gator about 4½ minutes. To test for doneness, pick up and check milk drippings from gator cube. If there is large amount of milk, return cube to oil and cook another 30 seconds. Drain on paper towels.

Smoked Crabmeat Pizza

2 (8-ounce) packages cream
    cheese, softened

2 tablespoons liquid smoke

1 (6-ounce) bottle cocktail sauce

2 tablespoons Worcestershire
    sauce

1 tablespoon prepared
    horseradish

2 cans lump crabmeat, drained

Parsley

Pepper

In small mixing bowl, combine cream cheese and liquid smoke. Spread on bottom of serving dish. In separate bowl, combine cocktail sauce, Worcestershire, and horseradish. Spread over cream cheese mixture. Sprinkle crabmeat over cocktail sauce mixture. Sprinkle with parsley and pepper and serve with crackers.

Serves 10-12

The contributor's husband prepares this for their church's annual springtime wild game banquet. Nobody likes a "gator on the gridiron" but this delicacy is an easily acquired taste. Ernie warns against overcooking, and cautions, "it's tough as shoe leather. There is nothing worse than overcooked gator unless it's undercooked."

TOMATO TEA SANDWICHES

Take two packages of your favorite dinner rolls and slice each roll in half, set the top halves of the rolls to the side. Use a spatula to spread a thin layer of mayonnaise on the bottom halves, lightly pepper, and add a thin layer of garden fresh tomatoes, and a few fresh basil leaves. Replace the top half. Use a sharp knife to slice the dinner rolls into bite-sized sandwiches. This recipe is great for tea parties and showers. It can be prepared in 10 minutes and is best if made just prior to serving.

WHITE PARTY MIX

4½ cups bite-size, crispy-corn cereal squares

4½ cups bite-size, crispy-rice cereal squares

2 cups pretzels

2 cups dry roasted peanuts

1 cup plain M&Ms

1 pound white baking chocolate

In large mixing bowl, combine cereals, pretzels, peanuts, and M&Ms and set aside. Microwave white chocolate on high for 90 seconds, stirring every 30 seconds. Stir chocolate until smooth and pour over cereal mix. Toss with wooden spoon and spread on waxed paper to cool. Break into pieces before serving.

Spiced Pecans

1 (18-ounce) package pecan halves

2 teaspoons sea salt (or kosher salt)

¾ teaspoon freshly ground black pepper

½ teaspoon cayenne pepper

1½ teaspoons cinnamon

1½ teaspoons light brown sugar

4 tablespoons unsalted butter, melted

Preheat oven to 350 degrees. Spread pecans on baking sheet and toast 10 minutes, or until fragrant. In small mixing bowl, combine salt, black pepper, cayenne pepper, cinnamon, brown sugar, and butter Transfer toasted pecans to large mixing bowl and add spice mixture, tossing well to coat. Return pecans to baking sheet and toast 3 to 4 minutes. Remove from oven and cool.

Ranch Oyster Crackers

1 (10-ounce) box of oyster crackers

¼ teaspoon cayenne pepper

1 teaspoon lemon pepper

1 teaspoon dill weed

1 teaspoon Beau Monde seasoning

2 (1-ounce) dry Ranch salad dressing

1 cup vegetable oil

Heat oil, add spices, and mix. Toss with crackers. Store in closed container to retain crispness.

Breads & Brunch

Hazel Caldwell

Ashford Manor Crème Brûlée French Toast

1 stick unsalted butter

1 cup packed brown sugar

2 tablespoons corn syrup

Grated peel of 1 orange

1 (8 to 9-inch) round country-style loaf (baguette or Hawaiian Bread is best)

6 large eggs

2 cups half-and-half

1 teaspoon vanilla

1 teaspoon Grand Marnier™ or Triple Sec

¼ teaspoon salt

1 (8-ounce) package cream cheese, cut into cubes and softened

In small, heavy saucepan over medium heat, melt butter with brown sugar and corn syrup, stirring until smooth. Pour into prepared 9 x 13-inch baking dish. Sprinkle with orange peel. Cut bread in ¾-inch thick slices. Arrange bread in one layer in baking dish, squeezing slices slightly to fit. Cover with layer of cream cheese.

In large mixing bowl, whisk together eggs, half-and-half, vanilla, Grand Marnier™ or Triple Sec, and salt until well combined and pour evenly over bread. Cover and chill at least 8 hours or up to 24 hours.

Place oven rack in middle of oven and preheat oven to 350 degrees. Bring soaked bread to room temperature. Bake, uncovered, until toast is puffed and edges are golden pale, or about 35 to 40 minutes. Using a spatula, invert French toast onto plates, turning slices syrup side up.

Serves 8

Sometimes, before cutting the French toast, we turn the whole thing over by placing a baking sheet over the pan and flipping it over and cutting it. We also use a "Brûlée" torch to put the final crystallized touch to the topping.

In the world of Bed and Breakfast recipes, there are many versions of a stuffed, French Toast-type casserole dish. We took several of our favorite recipes and combined them into this very unique, very Ashford Manor recipe. Important to this recipe is the "garnish." We dust the finished servings with confectioners' sugar and in the Spring, we sprinkle fresh wisteria petals over the top. We use many edible flower blossoms from our gardens, rose petals for instance, but use them only if you use organic fertilizers and insecticides. We like to serve this breakfast for room service at Ashford Manor. The consistency of this dish, like a crème brûlée, does not require a knife, and thus can easily be eaten on a tray in bed.

Ashford Manor Herbed Eggs

We have served these eggs alone or on puff pastries or crescent roll dough that is shaped into cups.

4 to 6 tablespoons butter, at room temperature

1 small garlic clove, minced

1 teaspoon freshly chopped herbs—parsley, oregano, rosemary, thyme, chives

2 to 3 eggs per person, at room temperature and whisked

1 teaspoon dry vermouth, white wine, or flat champagne, or stale beer per 3 eggs, at room temperature

Salt and freshly ground pepper

Minced parsley

In small saucepan over low heat, combine butter, garlic, and 1 teaspoon of each herb you plan to use. Cook slowly about 5 to 10 minutes. (Adjust the amount of butter and herbs according to the number of eggs being cooked.)

In saucepan or skillet over medium heat, scramble eggs with herbed butter, wine, salt, and pepper. Add minced parsley and cook to desired consistency.

There are a few secrets to the success of this dish.

Secret 1—We use only fresh herbs that come out of our herb garden. Even during a Georgia winter, we have rosemary, parsley, thyme, and sometimes chives. You can use any combination of these with parsley, but rosemary and oregano are too strong to use together. We often make the herb butter the night before, in quantity, as we have many guests for breakfast. Made the evening before, the butter "ripens" and becomes more flavorful. Parsley stays greener than other herbs that are cooked and make the dish look fresher.

Secret 2—Our eggs are 2 to 3 day old, farm fresh eggs from our neighbor, Al Cuming, but store-bought eggs also work well. Leave the eggs out overnight, or warm then in a bowl of warm water before breaking them.

Secret 3—The booze. We use any white wine or champagne that may be leftover from the night before. If no wine is available, vermouth works. On several occasions I have used stale beer that has gone flat, or I take fresh beer and put about ¼ cup in the microwave for a minute. This also works very well when making omelets.

Classic City Chef Sweet Potato Biscuits

3½ cups self-rising flour

1 teaspoon salt

1 cup shortening

2 cups mashed, cooked sweet
    potatoes, warmed

½ cup sugar

¼ cup milk

Preheat oven to 400 degrees. In large mixing bowl, sift together flour, and salt. Cut in shortening with fork or pastry cutter. In separate bowl, combine warm sweet potatoes and sugar, mixing well. Stir in milk. Add sweet potato mixture to flour mixture and blend well. Place dough on floured surface and roll out to ½-inch thickness, or to desired thickness. Cut dough with biscuit cutter and place on lightly greased baking sheet. Bake 10 minutes, or until lightly browned.

Makes about 2½ dozen

Classic City Chef had the honor to serve these sweet potato biscuits to former President Jimmy Carter and the members of his White House staff at a private event wrapping up the Carter Conference in January 2007. You can imagine their surprise (and delight) when they realized that everyone had stopped talking about the events of the weekend and had begun talking about the wonderfully delicious biscuits! We think they are a perfect accompaniment to ham and are best served warm, slathered with butter.

Coach Hartman's Favorite Baked Cheese Grits

Ruth, Laura, and Barbara Hartman

3 cups water

1 cup quick-cooking grits

1 teaspoon salt

1 cup sharp or extra-sharp
    shredded Cheddar cheese

3 tablespoons butter

1 cup milk

3 eggs, beaten

Paprika

Preheat oven to 350 degrees. In large saucepan over medium-high heat, bring water to a boil. Reduce heat to medium. Add grits and salt. Cook until slightly firm. Remove from heat. Stir in cheese (or more, if desired) and butter, stirring until cheese melts. Add milk and eggs, mixing well to combine. Pour into prepared casserole. Sprinkle with paprika. Bake 45 minutes to 1 hour.

Serves 6

Coach Bill Hartman was a running back for both the Georgia Bulldogs and the Washington Redskins before World War II. He graduated from the University of Georgia in 1937, where he was a member of the Chi Phi Fraternity. Coach Hartman was admitted into the College Football Hall of Fame in 1984 and the Georgia Sports Hall of Fame in 1981.

The Hoyt House Vegetarian Benedict

2 portabella mushrooms
    marinated in balsamic
    vinaigrette

2 cups baby spinach, wilted

1 sprig Daikon sprouts

2 eggs, poached

2 tablespoons Roasted Red
    Pepper Hollandaise

2 tablespoons Parmesan

2 tomatoes, sliced ½-thick and
    grilled

Place portabella mushroom on serving plate. Top with layers of
spinach, sprouts, and egg. Spoon Roasted Red Pepper Hollandaise over egg
and sprinkle with Parmesan. Serve immediately with grilled tomatoes.

ROASTED RED PEPPER HOLLANDAISE

4 egg yolks

½ cup butter, melted and cooled

1 tablespoon freshly squeezed
    lemon juice

1 teaspoon Tabasco

Red Pepper Reduction

In stainless steel mixing bowl, whisk yolks until frothy and pale yellow.
(The eggs should have a ribbon effect when pulling the whisk through the
eggs.) Slowly incorporate butter into eggs. Mixture may need to be warmed
slightly so that eggs can accept butter. Add lemon juice, Tabasco, and Red
Pepper Reduction, stirring gently to combine. Keep at room temperature.

RED PEPPER REDUCTION

3 red bell peppers, seeded and
    minced

2 shallots, minced

2 tablespoons peppercorn
    medley, crushed

2 tablespoons balsamic vinegar

In small saucepan over medium heat, combine peppers, shallots,
peppercorn, and vinegar. Reduce until all liquid has evaporated. Remove
from heat and cool to room temperature. Use the reduction sparingly—
just enough to add flavor to the hollandaise sauce.

Banana-Stuffed French Toast

2 tablespoons cream cheese

4 slices cinnamon raisin bread

1 ripe medium banana, sliced

¼ cup milk

1 large egg, beaten

¼ teaspoon vanilla

1 teaspoon butter

Maple syrup

Fresh fruit slices

Spread cream cheese on bread slices. Place banana slices on 2 slices of bread and top with remaining bread slices. In small, shallow bowl, combine milk, egg, and vanilla; mix well. In sauté pan over medium heat, melt butter. Briefly dip individual sandwiches into egg mixture. Cook sandwiches in sauté pan until golden brown (about 3 to 4 minutes per side). Before serving, top with maple syrup and garnish with fruit.

Serves 2

Fabulous French Toast

Make it ahead and bake in the morning!

4 tablespoons butter or
   margarine, softened

1 French baguette, cut into 1-inch
   slices

6 large eggs, beaten

1½ cups milk

1½ cups half-and-half

¼ cup sugar

1 teaspoon vanilla

⅛ teaspoon cinnamon

⅛ teaspoon nutmeg

Confectioners' sugar

Warm maple syrup

Sliced fruit (optional)

Thoroughly coat a 9-inch square baking dish with butter. Fill dish to top with bread slices. Combine eggs, milk, half-and-half, sugar, vanilla, cinnamon, and nutmeg. Pour over bread slices. Cover and chill overnight. Preheat oven to 350 degrees. Bake, uncovered, 40 to 45 minutes, or until puffed and golden. Let stand 5 minutes. Cut and serve. Sprinkle with confectioners' sugar, drizzle with syrup, and garnish with fruit, if desired.

Serves 4-6

French toast originated as a way to use day-old or stale bread (some breads, especially French bread, become stale after one day). Whereas a stale, crunchy bread might seem unappetizing, soaking the bread in eggs and frying it solves that problem. The name "French toast" is claimed to be from English soldiers serving on campaign in France during the 100 Year War. Upon being provided rations consisting solely of stale bread and tea, the soldiers combined the ingredients to make it more palatable. The precise origins of the recipes are unknown, but similar dishes have existed in many countries and under many names.

BAKING APPLES

* Fuji
    Sweet and juicy, firm, red skin
* Granny Smith
    Moderately sweet, crisp flesh, green skin
* Jonathan
    Tart flesh, crisp, juicy, bright red on yellow skin
* McIntosh
    Juicy, sweet, pinkish-white flesh, red skin
* Rome Beauty
    Mildly tart, crisp, greenish-white flesh, thick skin
* Winesap
    Firm, very juicy, sweet-sour flavor, red skin

Austrian Apple Strudel

¼ cup raisins

2 tablespoons rum

3 Granny Smith apples, peeled and thinly sliced

Lemon juice

½ cup sugar

1 teaspoon cinnamon

½ teaspoon vanilla

1 roll frozen puff pastry, thawed 40 minutes at room temperature

1 stick butter, divided and melted

2 bread slices, toasted and crumbled in food processor

1 egg, beaten

Confectioners' sugar

Preheat oven to 350 degrees. In small bowl, soak raisins in rum and set aside. In large mixing bowl, sprinkle apples with lemon juice; add sugar, cinnamon, and vanilla, tossing gently to coat. In small sauté pan, melt 4 tablespoons butter and sauté bread crumbs until crisp. Roll out puff pastry on well-floured surface to 15 x 10 inches. Sprinkle bread crumbs over pastry. Spoon apple mixture lengthwise atop dough and sprinkle with rum-soaked raisins. Roll up dough, jellyroll style. Transfer to prepared baking sheet and brush with egg. Using sharp knife, carefully cut several slits in strudel. Bake 30 to 35 minutes, or until golden brown. While baking, brush occasionally with remaining 4 tablespoons melted butter. Dust with confectioner's sugar and slice. Best served warm.

Serves 8

Butterscotch Sticky Buns

½ cup sugar

1 teaspoon cinnamon

½ cup chopped pecans

1 (10-ounce) package biscuits

4 tablespoons melted butter

1 (3-ounce) package butterscotch morsels

⅓ cup evaporated milk

Preheat oven to 400 degrees. In small bowl, combine sugar and cinnamon; set aside. Sprinkle pecans into prepared 9-inch cake pan. Separate biscuits and completely dip in melted butter. Dip into sugar mixture. Place on top of nuts. Bake 9 to 11 minutes or according to package directions.

In small saucepan over medium heat, combine butterscotch morsels and evaporated milk, stirring constantly until smooth. Pour over hot biscuits. Let stand 5 minutes. Turn out of pan onto serving plate.

Serves 6

Honey Bun Cake

This recipe is great as a dessert or coffee cake.

1 package yellow pudding cake
    mix

4 eggs

⅔ cup cooking oil

⅓ cup water

1 (8-ounce) container sour cream

½ cup firmly packed brown sugar

1 teaspoon ground cinnamon

⅔ cup chopped pecans

1 cup sifted confectioners' sugar

2 tablespoons milk

½ teaspoon vanilla

Preheat oven to 350 degrees. Combine cake mix, eggs, oil, water, and sour cream in large mixing bowl and mix until smooth. In separate bowl, combine brown sugar, cinnamon, and pecans and set aside. Pour half of batter into greased and floured 13 x 9-inch baking pan. Sprinkle half of sugar mixture over batter. Pour remaining batter into pan. Top with remaining sugar mixture. Gently swirl with knife. Bake 30 to 35 minutes. To make glaze, combine confectioners' sugar, milk, and vanilla in small bowl with electric mixer. Drizzle over cake when cool.

Serves 15

Sticky Buns

¼ cup sugar

1 teaspoon cinnamon

16 large marshmallows

3 tablespoons butter, melted

2 (8-ounce) cans crescent rolls

1½ cups confectioners' sugar

3 tablespoons milk

¼ cup chopped pecans (optional)

Preheat oven to 375 degrees. In small mixing bowl, combine sugar and cinnamon. Dip marshmallows in butter and roll in sugar-cinnamon mixture. Separate crescent rolls into 16 triangles. Wrap marshmallow in triangle, pinching edges to seal. Repeat with remaining marshmallows and triangles. Place each roll in lightly greased muffin cup. Bake 10 to 15 minutes, or until golden. Combine milk and confectioners' sugar, stirring well to form smooth glaze. Drizzle over warm rolls and sprinkle with pecans.

Serves 16

Sticky buns are a dessert or breakfast pastry that generally consist of rolled pieces of leavened dough, sometimes containing brown sugar or cinnamon, which are then compressed together to form a kind of flat loaf corresponding to the size of the baking pan. Prior to placement of the dough within the pan, the pan is lined with the "sticky" ingredients like maple syrup, honey, or both, as well as nuts and perhaps more sugar and sometimes butter. After the buns are baked, they are inverted so that the pan-lining ingredients become a topping.

These make a great dessert in the evening or a great treat for breakfast, especially on Christmas morning!

Surprise Apple Dumplings

2 large Granny Smith apples,
    cored and cut into 8 wedges

2 (8-ounce) cans crescent rolls

1 stick butter

1¼ cups sugar

1 teaspoon vanilla

1 teaspoon cinnamon

1 can Mountain Dew

Preheat oven to 350 degrees. Wrap each wedge in an individual crescent triangle. Transfer to 9 x 13-inch baking dish and set aside. Melt butter in saucepan over medium heat. Stir in sugar, vanilla, and cinnamon, heating until smooth; pour over wrapped apples. Pour Mountain Dew over apples. Bake 30 minutes, or until brown and bubbly.

Serves 16

Overnight Coffee Cake

1⅓ sticks butter, softened

1 cup sugar

2 large eggs, lightly beaten

1 cup sour cream

2 cups biscuit baking mix

¾ cup firmly packed dark brown
    sugar

½ cup pecans, chopped

1 teaspoon cinnamon

¼ cup butter, melted

Preheat oven to 350 degrees. Lightly spray a 9 x 13-inch pan with nonstick cooking spray. In large mixing bowl, combine softened butter and sugar, beating with electric mixer until light and fluffy. Add eggs and sour cream, beating well. Stir in baking mix. Transfer dough to prepared pan. Combine brown sugar, pecans, and cinnamon; sprinkle over dough. Using the end of a wooden spoon, press holes in into dough. Drizzle with melted butter. Bake 30 to 45 minutes, or until toothpick inserted near center comes out clean. Dough may be covered with plastic wrap and chilled overnight before baking, if desired.

Cranberry Apple Bake

1 bag fresh cranberries

2 cans sliced pie apples
  (NOT apple pie filling)

1 cup sugar

Preheat oven to 350 degrees. Combine cranberries, apples, and sugar, mixing well. Pour into 3-quart deep-dish casserole and bake 45 minutes. Remove from oven and cover with topping. Bake an additional 15 minutes.

TOPPING

½ cup brown sugar

1 teaspoon cinnamon

1 package apple cinnamon instant oatmeal

In small mixing bowl, combine brown sugar, cinnamon, and oatmeal.

Banana Tea Bread

2½ cups all-purpose flour

1 cup sugar

3½ teaspoons baking powder

1 teaspoon salt

3 tablespoons cooking oil

¾ cup milk

1 large egg, beaten

1 cup mashed ripe banana (about 2 to 3 medium bananas)

1 cup pecans, finely chopped and toasted

Preheat oven to 350 degrees. In mixing bowl, combine flour, sugar, baking powder, and salt. In large mixing bowl, combine oil, milk, egg, and banana. Add flour mixture to banana mixture. Mix with electric mixer on medium speed about 30 seconds. Spread mixture into a greased and floured 9-inch baking pan. Bake 55 minutes to 1 hour, 5 minutes, or until center is puffed, and toothpick inserted in center comes out clean. Let cool in pan 5 minutes. Remove from pan and cool completely before serving.

Cranberries are one of the few fruits native to North America. In fact, long before the Pilgrims landed at Plymouth Rock, cranberries were a staple in the diets of American Indians. Wild cranberries ripened in such abundance that they were eaten fresh, ground, or mashed with cornmeal and baked into bread. Maple sugar or honey was used to sweeten the berries' tangy flavor.

EASY CHRISTMAS MORNING BREAKFAST BREAD

20 unbaked frozen dinner rolls

1 cup brown sugar

¼ cup instant vanilla pudding mix

2 teaspoon ground cinnamon

⅓ cup butter, melted

Lightly grease a 10-inch Bundt pan. Place frozen rolls in pan and sprinkle with brown sugar, pudding mix and cinnamon. Pour the melted butter over the top. Cover with a clean, damp cloth and leave overnight at room temperature to rise. The next morning, preheat oven to 350 degrees. Bake for 25 minutes, until golden brown. Turn rolls out onto a serving plate and serve.

Coffee Cake Banana Bread

½ cup margarine, softened

1 (8-ounce) package cream cheese, softened

1¼ cups sugar

2 eggs

1¼ cups mashed bananas (about 3 to 4 bananas)

1 teaspoon vanilla

2¼ cups all-purpose flour

1½ teaspoons baking powder

½ teaspoon baking soda

2½ tablespoons brown sugar

2½ teaspoons cinnamon

Preheat oven to 350 degrees. Grease and flour two (8 x 4-inch) loaf pans. In large mixing bowl, cream together margarine and cream cheese with electric mixer on medium speed. Gradually add sugar and beat until light and fluffy. Add eggs one at a time, beating well after each addition. Stir in bananas and vanilla. In separate mixing bowl, combine sift together flour, baking powder, and baking soda. Add flour mixture to batter, mixing until batter is just moist. In small bowl, combine brown sugar and cinnamon. Divide and pour half of batter evenly between both loaf pans. Sprinkle half of cinnamon mixture on top of batter. Pour remaining batter in and top with the rest of the cinnamon mixture. Bake 45 minutes, or until toothpick inserted near center comes out clean.

Pumpkin Bread

4 eggs, beaten

⅔ cup cold water

2 cups pumpkin

1 cup cooking oil

3½ cups all-purpose flour

2 teaspoons baking soda

1½ teaspoons salt

1 teaspoon nutmeg

1 teaspoon cinnamon

2½ cups sugar

Raisins (optional)

Nuts (optional)

Preheat oven to 350 degrees. In large mixing bowl, beat together eggs, water, pumpkin, and oil with electric mixer. Sift together flour, baking soda, salt, nutmeg, and cinnamon; add to pumpkin mixture, beating well. Add sugar, beating until smooth. Fold in raisins and nuts, if desired. Pour into 3 prepared loaf pans until half full. Bake about 1 hour, or until knife inserted near center comes out clean. Serve slices with butter or cream cheese.

Serves 8-10 per loaf

Nutty Zucchini Bread

Makes great Christmas gifts!

3 cups all-purpose flour	2 cups sugar
1½ teaspoons cinnamon	1 cup cooking oil
1 teaspoon baking soda	1½ tablespoons vanilla
1 teaspoon salt	2 cups grated zucchini
¼ teaspoon baking powder	½ cup nuts
3 eggs, well beaten	

Preheat oven to 350 degrees. In mixing bowl, combine flour, cinnamon, baking soda, salt, and baking powder; set aside. In large mixing bowl, cream together eggs, sugar, and oil; stir in vanilla. Add flour mixture and mix well. Stir in zucchini and nuts. Pour into two prepared loaf pans. Bake about 1 hour, or until toothpick inserted near center comes out clean.

Serves 12

Zucchini is the basis for all sorts of dishes, from pasta sauces and breads to main courses. As a general rule, you should select the smallest possible zucchini that can be used for the recipe, because larger zucchini are less flavorful and can have bitter overtones.

Peach Muffins

5⅓ tablespoons butter, softened	¼ teaspoon ground nutmeg
1 cup sugar, divided	½ cup milk
1 egg	¾ cup peeled, chopped peaches (about 2 medium peaches)
1½ cups all-purpose flour	
1½ teaspoons baking powder	1 teaspoon cinnamon
½ teaspoon salt	4 tablespoons butter, melted

Preheat oven to 350 degrees. In large mixing bowl, cream softened butter and ½ cup sugar with electric mixer. Add egg and beat well. In separate mixing bowl, combine flour, baking powder, salt, and nutmeg. Stir flour mixture into butter mixture alternately with milk. Gently fold in peaches. Fill prepared muffin cups two-thirds full. Bake 20 to 25 minutes. Combine remaining ½ cup sugar and cinnamon. Remove muffins from oven and immediately dip tops into melted butter, then into cinnamon-sugar mixture.

As near and dear as peaches are to our hearts, they become dearer when late frosts and other weather maladies affect the local harvest. If it's an off year for Georgia's official state fruits then the addition of a few teaspoons of Grand Marnier™ to the muffin batter will supply the "zing" that trucked-in peaches sometimes lack.

A to Z Bread

3 cups all-purpose flour

1 teaspoon salt

1 teaspoon baking soda

3 teaspoons cinnamon

½ teaspoon baking powder

3 eggs, beaten

1 cup cooking oil

2 cups sugar

2 cups A to Z mix (if using something sweet, reduce sugar to 1½ cups)

3 teaspoons vanilla

1 cup nuts (optional)

Preheat oven to 350 degrees. Sift together flour, salt, baking soda, cinnamon, and baking powder and set aside. In large mixing bowl, cream together eggs, oil, and sugar with electric mixer. Add A to Z mix and vanilla. Slowly add flour mixture, mixing well. Add nuts, if desired. Pour into prepared Bundt pan or two loaf pans. Bake 50 minutes, or until toothpick inserted near center comes out clean.

A-to-Z mix: Use one of the following ingredients or a combination to equal 2 cups (except as indicated): grated apples, applesauce, chopped apricots, mashed bananas, grated carrots, pitted and chopped cherries, freshly ground coconut, pitted and chopped dates, ground eggplant, finely chopped figs, seedless grapes, honey (omit sugar in recipe), ½ cup lemon juice, marmalade (omit 1 cup sugar in recipe), mincemeat, chopped oranges, fresh or canned chopped peaches, ½ cup chopped peppermint leaves, chopped pears, drained crushed pineapple, 1 cup chopped pitted prunes, canned pumpkin, raisins, chopped rhubarb, fresh or frozen and drained strawberries, cooked tapioca, grated sweet potatoes, chopped tomatoes (add an extra ½ cup sugar), cooked and mashed yams, plain or flavored yogurt.

Banana Bread Muffins

1 stick margarine, softened

1½ cups sugar

2 eggs

1¾ cups all-purpose flour

1 teaspoon baking soda

4 tablespoons buttermilk

4 bananas, mashed

1 cup pecans, chopped

2 teaspoons vanilla

Preheat oven to 350 degrees. In large mixing bowl, combine margarine and sugar, beating with electric mixer until light and fluffy. Add eggs, beating well. Add flour and baking soda alternately with buttermilk. Add bananas, pecans, and vanilla, combining well. Pour mixture into muffin pans. Bake 15 to 20 minutes, or until toothpick inserted in each muffin comes out clean.

Serves 24

Banana bread first became a standard feature of American cookbooks with the popularization of baking soda and baking powder in the 1930s. The home baking revival of the 1960s and the simplicity of its recipe led to an explosion in banana bread's popularity. The cookbooks of the 1960s added to its popularity because they commonly listed multiple variations of bread that added fruits and nuts.

Pumpkin Muffins

1¼ cups all-purpose flour

2 cups sugar

1½ tablespoons baking powder

1 teaspoon salt

¾ tablespoon cinnamon

1 (16-ounce) can pumpkin

2 tablespoons butter, melted

4 eggs, beaten

1 tablespoon vanilla

½ cup milk

Preheat oven to 375 degrees. In mixing bowl, combine flour, sugar, baking powder, salt, and cinnamon; set aside. In large mixing bowl, beat together pumpkin, butter, eggs, and vanilla. Add flour mixture to pumpkin mixture. Slowly add milk, stirring constantly. Pour batter into prepared muffin pans and bake 30 minutes, or until golden brown.

Serves 12-18 (24 mini muffins)

If cooler breezes and a sweater around your neck haven't brought on that welcome feeling of "it's fall, y'all," the taste of a pumpkin muffin will complete the sensations of the season. Pungent preserves may overshadow the delicate taste of pumpkin so enjoy these with butter or honey.

GEORGIA SPICED PEACHES

1 large can peach halves

½ cup vinegar

½ cup sugar

12 whole cloves

1 cinnamon stick

Drain peaches, reserving ½ cup peach syrup; set peaches aside. In large saucepan over medium heat, combine peach syrup, vinegar, sugar, cloves, and cinnamon stick, stirring constantly until slightly thickened. Add peaches and heat 2 minutes. Transfer to container, let cool, seal, and chill. Peaches may also be served hot. Remove cloves and cinnamon stick before serving.

Spiced peaches are a delicious and beautiful accompaniment to a meal. Before serving, place a clove on each peach.

Mini Cream Cheese Muffins

1 stick butter, softened

1 (8-ounce) package cream cheese, softened

1 cup self-rising flour

Preheat oven to 400 degrees. In large mixing bowl, cream butter and cream cheese for 2 minutes with electric mixer. Add flour, mixing until smooth. Spoon dough into mini muffin pans. Bake 15 minutes.

Serves 18-24

Fresh Apple Muffins

2 cups all-purpose flour

2 teaspoons cinnamon

1 teaspoon baking soda

½ teaspoon salt

2 eggs, beaten

1 cup sugar

1 cup cooking oil

2 teaspoons vanilla

½ cup chopped nuts

4 large apples, peeled, cored and chopped

Preheat oven to 350 degrees. In medium mixing bowl, sift together flour, cinnamon, baking soda, and salt. In large mixing bowl, combine eggs and sugar, mixing well. In separate bowl, combine oil and vanilla; fold in nuts and apple. Alternately add flour mixture and oil mixture to egg mixture. When mixture gets too difficult for electric mixer, use wooden spoon. Spoon batter into paper-lined muffin pans. Bake 15 to 20 minutes. These freeze well.

Serves 12

It will seem like too many apples, but after baking them, you will realize that it is just right!

Healthy Oatmeal Muffins

2 cups all-purpose flour

2 cups quick-cooking oats,
    uncooked

1 cup firmly packed brown sugar

2 teaspoons baking powder

2 teaspoons ground cinnamon

1 teaspoon salt

1 teaspoon baking soda

2 eggs, beaten

2 cups buttermilk

⅔ cup cooking oil or shortening

Pecans (optional)

Blueberries (optional)

Preheat oven to 400 degrees. In large mixing bowl, combine flour, oats, brown sugar, baking powder, cinnamon, salt, and baking soda. Make a well in center of mixture. In separate mixing bowl, combine eggs, buttermilk, and oil thoroughly. Stir into flour mixture until combined. Fold in pecans and blueberries, if desired. Pour into muffin cups and bake 18 to 20 minutes. (Before baking, you can top with additional brown sugar and oats.)

Serves 12

The contributor's mother often made these with blueberries added, and in Athens we are fortunate that several area farms offer these in season, and a few will even allow you to pick your own.

Bran Muffins

1¼ cups all-purpose flour

1 tablespoon baking powder

½ teaspoon salt

½ cup sugar

2½ cups bran flakes

1¼ cups milk

1 egg

¼ cup vegetable oil

Preheat oven to 400 degrees. Stir together flour, baking powder, salt and sugar. Set aside. Measure bran flakes and milk into a large bowl and stir to combine. Let stand 1 to 2 minutes or until softened. Add egg and milk. Beat well. Add flour mixture to flake mixture, stirring only until combined. Portion the batter evenly into 12 greased muffin cups. Bake for 18 to 20 minutes.

Serves 12

Biscuits do not have to be eaten just for breakfast— they are great for dinner with a hearty soup or stew.

Easy Sour Cream Biscuits

2 cups self-rising flour　　　**1 (8-ounce) container sour cream**
2 sticks margarine, melted

Preheat oven to 400 degrees. In large mixing bowl, combine flour, margarine, and sour cream, blending well. Spoon mixture into prepared muffin tins. Bake 12 to 15 minutes.

Serves 12

Mouth-watering and yet so simple, this recipe comes to us courtesy of a League member's mother-in-law. Be sure to reach past the mass-produced strawberry and grape options in the jam safe and grab that homemade muscadine or mayhaw jelly.

Ma's Biscuits

These are wonderful with homemade muscadine jelly!

3 cups self-rising flour　　　**Milk**
¾ cup butter-flavored shortening

Preheat oven to 350 degrees. In large mixing bowl, cut shortening into flour and mix. Add small amount of milk, mixing and adding milk as necessary for dough consistency. Transfer dough to floured surface and lightly knead. Roll out dough to ½-inch thickness and cut with biscuit cutter. Place biscuits on baking sheet. Bake 10 to 15 minutes, or until golden brown.

Serves 16

Muscadine Jelly

5 pounds freshly picked
   muscadines, stemmed and
   washed

1 box commercially prepared fruit
   pectin (such as Sure-Jell)

½ teaspoon butter

7 cups sugar

Place muscadines in large boiler, adding enough water to just cover muscadines. Bring to a boil, continuing to cook until muscadines burst open. Remove from heat, cover, and allow to cool. Drain fruit and juice through colander; drain again through smaller sieve and cheesecloth until juice is clear of pulp. In 6-quart stockpot over medium heat, combine pectin and 5 cups juice, stirring until smooth. Add butter (this will reduce foaming). Bring mixture to a rolling boil. Stir in sugar. Bring to full rolling boil for exactly 1 minute, stirring constantly. Remove from heat and let stand 10 minutes.

Skim off any foam with metal spoon. Pour mixture in clean sterilized jars, leaving about ½-inch space from top. Cover with sterilized lids and tops. Turn jars upside down on wooden board for 5 minutes. Turn jars right side up and, wipe off jars before labeling and storing.

This recipe makes about 4 pints of jelly.

HOW TO EAT A MUSCADINE:

Scuppernongs, like all muscadines, have thick skins and contain seeds. To eat a scuppernong, hold the grape stem side up and squeeze the grape. The juicy pulp will squirt into your mouth. Be careful to spit out the seeds and discard the bitter skin.

You won't even need to spray your muffin tin or line it with cupcake papers since this dough is so moist. Bake in mini-muffin tins and they are perfect alongside a large dinner salad.

Rich Cheese Biscuits

2 sticks butter, melted

2 cups self-rising flour

2 cups shredded sharp Cheddar cheese

1 (8-ounce) container sour cream

Preheat oven to 350 degrees. Allow butter to cool in large mixing bowl. Add flour, cheese, and sour cream. Thoroughly combine with hands. Spoon mixture into two 12 cup muffin pans. Bake for 20 minutes.

Serves 24

Willie Mae Barber of Monticello, Georgia made this for the contributor's family, and we are happy to hand it down to the readers of this generation. The use of cast iron cookware is crucial for its even heating properties and the light outer crust it gives this skillet bread.

The Best Southern Cornbread

1 tablespoon bacon drippings or olive oil

1 cup self-rising buttermilk cornmeal mix

1 tablespoon self-rising flour

1 tablespoon sugar

¼ cup cooking oil

1 egg, beaten

1 cup buttermilk

Preheat oven to 425 degrees. Pour bacon droppings or olive oil into 8-inch black cast iron skillet and place in oven. In mixing bowl, combine cornmeal mix, flour, sugar, cooking oil, egg, and buttermilk and mix thoroughly with hands. Pour batter into hot, greased skillet and bake 15 minutes on lower rack and additional 5 minutes on upper rack.

Serves 8

Broccoli Cornbread

2 sticks butter

2 (8½-ounce) boxes corn muffin
    mix

2 sticks butter, melted

4 large eggs

1 large onion, finely chopped

1 (10-ounce) container cottage
    cheese

1 (10-ounce) package frozen
    broccoli, thawed, but not
    drained

1 (8-ounce) package shredded
    Mexican cheese

Preheat oven to 375 degrees. Melt 2 sticks butter in 9 x 13-inch baking dish and set aside. In large mixing bowl, combine corn muffin mix, remaining 2 sticks melted butter, and eggs. Fold in onion, cottage cheese, and broccoli. Pour into baking dish over melted butter. Top with shredded cheese. Bake 30 to 35 minutes.

Mexican Cornbread

½ cup cornmeal

½ cup bacon drippings

1 egg, beaten

½ cup milk

1 small can cream style corn

1 large onion, chopped

¼ pound cheese, shredded

1 jalapeño pepper, seeded and
    chopped

Cornmeal

½ pound ground beef, cooked and
    drained

Preheat oven to 350 degrees. In large mixing bowl, combine cornmeal, drippings, egg, milk, and corn; set aside. In separate bowl, combine onion, cheese, and pepper. Sprinkle prepared 9 x 13-inch baking pan with cornmeal. Layer cornmeal mixture, beef, and cheese mixture in pan. Bake 45 minutes.

Thomas Jefferson, often called the "Farmer President," was an avid gardener and collector of new seeds and the plants of fruits and vegetables that arrived in the United States. In 1766 he began keeping detailed notes of any seeds or seedlings planted in his extensive garden at Monticello, his home near Charlottesville, Virginia. He recorded his planting of broccoli, along with radishes, lettuce, and cauliflower on May 27, 1767.

Place a cooked, boneless, skinless chicken breast atop a large square of this hearty cornbread, then add a thick slice of Pepper Jack cheese and run under the broiler for a fabulous pre-plated main course. Garnish with fresh cilantro in season, or ground coriander.

Bacon Wrapped Bread Sticks

1 large package grissini-style
    bread sticks

1 (16-ounce) package high quality
    sliced bacon

Dark brown sugar

Break bread sticks into 4-inch pieces and set aside. Cut bacon slices in half and place on cutting board. Press brown sugar onto one side of bacon, coating completely until sugar no longer adheres.

Preheat oven to 325 degrees. Place baking rack over foil-lined baking sheet. Roll bacon strips, sugar side in, around bread sticks in spiral fashion. (Begin close to bread stick edge and roll tightly.) Place seam side down on rack. Bake about 20 minutes, watching carefully so that sugar does not burn. Remove from oven and let rest 1 hour on rack until firm.

Traditional Irish soda bread has caraway seed and currants, and a superstitious crosscut across the top to "ward off the man downstairs." Here raisins are used, but if you're a particularly "devil-may-care" baker go ahead and try any dried fruit you like.

Irish Soda Bread

3 cups all-purpose flour

2/3 cup sugar

1 tablespoon baking powder

1 teaspoon baking soda

1 teaspoon salt

2 eggs, beaten

1¾ to 2 cups buttermilk

1½ cups raisins

Preheat oven to 350 degrees. In large mixing bowl, combine flour, sugar, baking powder, baking soda, and salt, blending well. Add eggs and milk, stirring until thoroughly combined. Pour into prepared loaf pan. Bake 1 hour.

Old-Fashioned Ice Box Rolls

1 quart milk

1 cup shortening

1 cup sugar

1 package yeast

4 cups all-purpose flour

1 tablespoon salt

1 teaspoon baking soda

1 teaspoon baking powder

All-purpose flour

Preheat oven to 400 degrees. In saucepan over low heat, combine milk, shortening, and sugar, stirring until shortening melts. Remove from heat and cool to room temperature.

When cooled, transfer to large mixing bowl. Add yeast and flour, mixing until it is the consistency of cake batter. Let rise in warm place for 2 hours. Punch dough down.

Sift together salt, baking soda, and baking powder and mix into dough, adding enough flour to form stiff dough. Roll dough into balls and let rise.

Bake about 10 minutes. Dough will keep in refrigerator about one week.

Yeast Biscuits

1 package yeast

1 tablespoon sugar

⅓ cup lukewarm water

3 cups sifted all-purpose flour

4 teaspoons baking powder

1 teaspoon salt

⅔ cup shortening

⅔ cup milk

Preheat oven to 450 degrees. In small mixing bowl, combine yeast, sugar and water; let stand until ready to use. In large mixing bowl, sift together flour, baking powder, and salt two times. Cut in shortening and mix well. In separate bowl, add yeast mixture to milk. Add milk mixture to flour, mixing well until dough has formed.

Turn out dough on floured surface and knead. Roll out to ¼-inch thickness and cut with biscuit cutter. Place on baking sheet and allow to rise at least 1 hour. Bake about 15 minutes.

Makes 2 dozen

There are two types of dry yeast: Regular Active Dry and Instant Yeast or Rapid-Rise. The two types of dry yeast can be used interchangeably. The advantage of the rapid-rise is the rising time is half that of the active dry and it only needs one rising.

You can speed up standard yeast bread recipes by changing the yeast in the recipe. Substitute one package instant or fast-acting yeast for one package regular active dry yeast. Instant yeast is more finely ground and thus absorbs moisture faster, rapidly converting starch and sugars to carbon dioxide, the tiny bubbles that make the dough expand and stretch.

Supper Club Bread

1 small can of mushrooms, drained

1 small can sliced ripe olives, drained

1 stick butter, melted

¾ to 1 cup mayonnaise

1½ cups shredded mozzarella cheese

1 loaf of French bread, cut in half lengthwise

Preheat oven to 350 degrees. In mixing bowl, combine mushrooms, olives, butter, mayonnaise, and cheese. Spread on lower half of bread and top with upper half. Cut into slices and wrap sub-sandwich style in heavy foil. Bake about 25 to 30 minutes. Serve warm.

Herb and Onion Focaccia

1 (1¼-ounce) package active dry yeast

1 tablespoon sugar

1 cup warm water

3 cups all-purpose flour, divided

2 teaspoons salt

4 tablespoons extra virgin olive oil, divided

1 medium onion, finely chopped

2 tablespoons minced garlic

½ medium onion, sliced

1 teaspoon pepper

1 tablespoon dried basil

1 tablespoon dried parsley

In small glass bowl, sprinkle yeast and sugar over warm water; let stand 10 minutes. Meanwhile, combine 2½ cups flour and salt in large bowl of electric stand mixer. Make a well in flour and slowly add yeast mixture. Attach dough hook and knead for 10 minutes; scrape down sides of bowl. Add remaining flour and knead until dough forms a soft ball and is no longer sticky. Cover with oiled plastic wrap and let rise in warm place for 30 minutes. Punch dough down; cover and let rise an additional 30 minutes. Preheat oven to 450 degrees; oil a baking sheet and set aside. In small skillet, sauté chopped onion in 1 tablespoon olive oil for 2 minutes; add garlic and sauté an additional 2 minutes. Remove from heat and spread on small plate to cool. Add remaining oil to skillet and sauté sliced onion until tender and set aside to cool. Knead onion and garlic mixture, pepper, basil, and parsley into dough. With floured hands, transfer dough to baking sheet and shape. Arrange sliced onions on top of loaf and bake 20 to 25 minutes. Remove from oven and cool on wire rack.

Spicy Sausage Bread

1 box bread dough mix

1 (12-ounce) package shredded mozzarella cheese

5 to 6 sweet Italian or turkey sausage links, cooked and crumbled

¼ to ½ cup shredded Parmesan cheese

Oregano and Italian spices to taste

Preheat oven to 350 degrees. Prepare dough according to package directions. Roll out dough to thin rectangle, adding more flour as needed. Cover dough with mozzarella. Sprinkle with sausage, Parmesan, oregano, and Italian spices. Roll up dough, jellyroll style. Transfer to baking sheet and form into a "U" shape. Bake 25 to 30 minutes. Slice and serve warm or cold. Dip slices in marina sauce.

Prepackaged pizza dough may be used instead of boxed dough mix.

These savory pinwheels are amazing dipped in marinara sauce or artichoke dip and can be served hot or cold.

Cheesy Artichoke Bread

Super easy and super yummy!

1 (14-ounce) can artichoke hearts, drained and chopped

1 cup mayonnaise

1 cup shredded Parmesan cheese

¼ teaspoon garlic powder

1 loaf French or Italian bread, split in half lengthwise

Preheat oven to 350 degrees. In small mixing bowl, combine artichokes, mayonnaise, Parmesan, and garlic powder. Spread mixture on lower half of bread and cover with upper half. Transfer to baking sheet. Bake 20 minutes, or until golden and thoroughly heated.

Serves 8

Any soup would be enhanced by serving these toasts with it, or consider using a narrower baguette sliced perpendicularly for cheese dollars that are right on the money when tossed into a garden salad.

Souper Cheese Toast
Perfect with vegetable beef soup.

1 cup shredded mozzarella cheese
¾ cup shredded carrot
¼ cup mayonnaise

½ teaspoon dried Italian seasoning
2 green onions, chopped
8 (1-inch thick) slices French bread

In small mixing bowl, combine cheese, carrot, mayonnaise, Italian seasoning, and green onion; set aside. Place bread slices on ungreased baking sheet. Broil until bread is lightly browned (about 2 minutes). Turn bread slices over and spread cheese mixture evenly on the untoasted sides. Broil again until topping melts (about 2 minutes). Serve immediately.

Serves 4

No amount of noise can make this wonderful, foolproof souffle "fall," and it is to-die-for served with crisp bacon and a side of fresh fruit.

Easy Egg Soufflé

1 stick butter
3 (5-ounce) jars sharp, processed cheese spread

16 slices Italian or French bread, crusts removed
8 eggs, beaten
1 quart milk

In saucepan over medium heat, combine butter and cheese. Spread mixture on bread slices. Place bread in thoroughly buttered 9 x 13-inch baking dish and set aside. In mixing bowl, combine eggs and milk. Pour over bread, breaking up bread with spoon. Cover with foil and chill at least 24 hours. Bake uncovered at 350 degrees for 1 hour.

Serves 8-12

Three Cheese Puff

6 eggs, beaten

½ cup all-purpose flour

1 teaspoon baking powder

1 cup milk

1 pound Monterey Jack cheese, cubed

1 (8-ounce) container cottage cheese

1 (3-ounce) package cream cheese, cubed

6 tablespoons margarine, cubed

Preheat oven to 350 degrees. In large mixing bowl, combine eggs, flour, and baking powder, beating well. Stir in milk, beating until smooth. Stir in cheeses and margarine. Pour into prepared 12 x 8 x 2-inch baking dish. Bake 45 minutes, or until set and lightly browned.

Serves 6

The recipe may be doubled and baked in a larger rectangular glass baking dish.

Yancey's Impossible Quiche

12 slices bacon, cooked and crumbled

1 cup shredded Swiss cheese

½ cup finely chopped onion

2 cups milk

⅓ cup biscuit baking mix

4 eggs

Salt and pepper to taste

Preheat oven to 350 degrees. Sprinkle bacon, cheese, and onion into prepared 10-inch pie plate and set aside. Combine milk, baking mix, eggs, salt, and pepper in blender. Cover and blend on high for 1 minute. Pour into pie plate. Bake 50 to 55 minutes, or until golden brown. Let stand 5 minutes before cutting.

Serves 4-6

Brunch Chicken Casserole

Don't forget to make ahead!

8 slices white bread, crusts removed

4 cups cooked and shredded chicken breasts (3 whole breasts)

½ pound fresh mushrooms, sliced

1 stick butter

½ cup mayonnaise

8 slices sharp Cheddar cheese

4 eggs, well beaten

2 cups milk

1 teaspoon salt

1 (10¾-ounce) can cream of mushroom soup

1 (10¾-ounce) can cream of celery soup

1 tablespoon lemon juice

1 (2-ounce) jar pimento, drained and sliced

Preheat oven to 350 degrees. Place bread in bottom of prepared 9 x 13-inch baking dish. Spread chicken over bread and set aside. In small skillet over medium heat, sauté mushrooms in butter; sprinkle over chicken. Dot with mayonnaise. Place cheese slices on top of mayonnaise. In small mixing bowl, combine eggs, milk, and salt; pour over cheese. Using same mixing bowl, combine soups, lemon juice, and pimentos. Pour over layers. Cover and chill overnight. Bake for 1 hour, 30 minutes.

Serves 12-16

Quick and Easy Breakfast Casserole

1 (8-ounce) can crescent rolls

1 (16-ounce) package hot ground pork sausage, cooked and drained

4 large eggs, beaten

¾ cup milk

⅛ teaspoon salt

⅛ teaspoon pepper

2 cups shredded mozzarella cheese

Preheat oven to 425 degrees. Line a 13 x 9 x 2-inch baking dish with crescent rolls, pressing seams together. Cover with sausage, then cheese. In small mixing bowl, combine eggs, milk, salt, and pepper; pour over sausage and cheese. Bake 20 minutes.

Serves 6-8

Salmon Quiche with Almond Crust

CRUST

1 cup whole wheat flour

½ teaspoon salt

¼ teaspoon paprika

6 tablespoons cooking oil

⅔ cup shredded sharp Cheddar cheese

¼ cup slivered almonds

Preheat oven to 400 degrees. In large mixing bowl, sift together flour, salt, and paprika. Add oil, mixing well. Fold in cheese and almonds and press into 9-inch pie plate. Bake 10 minutes.

QUICHE

1 (14¾-ounce) can salmon, boned and skinned

3 eggs, beaten

1 cup sour cream

¼ cup mayonnaise

Reduce oven temperature to 325 degrees. Drain salmon and reserve liquid. Add enough water to liquid to equal ½ cup. Combine salmon, liquid, eggs, sour cream, and mayonnaise. Pour into baked crust. Bake 45 minutes.

Salmon is a popular food, and consuming salmon is considered to be reasonably healthy due to its high protein and low fat levels and to its high Omega-3 fatty acid content.

Breakfast Pizza

1 (8-ounce) can crescent rolls

1 (16-ounce) package pork sausage, cooked and drained

1 cup frozen hash browns, thawed

1 cup shredded sharp Cheddar cheese

5 eggs

¼ cup milk

½ teaspoon salt

⅛ teaspoon pepper

2 tablespoons shredded Parmesan cheese

Preheat oven to 375 degrees. Separate crescent rolls into 8 triangles. Transfer crescents to ungreased 12-inch pizza pan with points facing center. Press dough into bottom and up sides to form crust, sealing seams. Spoon sausage over crust. Sprinkle with hash browns and top with Cheddar.

In mixing bowl, beat together eggs, milk, salt, and pepper. Pour into crust and sprinkle with Parmesan. Bake 25 to 30 minutes.

UNUSUAL BREAKFAST IDEAS:

* A banana dog (peanut butter, banana, and raisins in a long whole-grain bun)

* A breakfast taco (shredded cheese on a tortilla, folded in half and microwaved; top with salsa)

* A fruit and cream cheese sandwich (use strawberries or other fresh fruit)

* A sandwich — grilled cheese, peanut butter and jelly, or another favorite

* Leftovers (they're not just for dinner anymore!)

Continental Cheesebake

Ham or shrimp may be substituted for sausage.

1 onion, chopped

1 tablespoon butter

1 (10¾-ounce) can cream of
mushroom soup

1 cup milk

½ teaspoon dry mustard

1 teaspoon dill weed

1 (16-ounce) package sausage,
cooked and drained

4 cups shredded sharp Cheddar
cheese

1 to 2 celery stalks, chopped
(optional)

8 hard-boiled eggs, sliced

Cocktail pumpernickel bread,
buttered

Preheat oven to 350 degrees. In sauté pan over medium heat, cook onion in butter until caramelized and set aside. In large mixing bowl, combine soup, milk, mustard, and dill weed, mixing well. In 9 x 13-inch baking dish, layer sausage, onions, celery, and eggs. Top with soup mixture. Sprinkle with cheese and cover with bread. Bake 25 to 30 minutes. Place under broiler for 5 minutes to toast bread.

Brunch Biscuits

1 pound ground beef

1 pound ground sausage

1 (16-ounce) box processed
cheese loaf, cubed

3 packages small dinner rolls, cut
in half lengthwise

In large skillet over high heat, cook ground beef and sausage together; drain and set aside. Wipe pan clean and add cheese cubes, cooking over medium-low heat. Return meat to skillet, mixing well until cheese melts. Divide mixture into thirds. Spread evenly over bottom halves of rolls in aluminum foil pans. Top with upper halves of rolls and place in warm oven to heat bread slightly. Serve immediately.

Serves 15-18

Brunches are quite popular for entertaining, especially in the springtime. Whether you're gathering for Easter, Mother's Day, or a neighborhood get-together, you can make the experience extra-special and easy!

Soups, Salads,
& Sandwiches

Marti's at Midday Pimento Cheese

*One of the staples at Marti's at Midday—if I am ever famous,
please let it be for my pimento cheese!*

½ medium sweet white onion
(such as Vidalia), grated

1 cup diced pimentos with juice

1 teaspoon cayenne pepper
(or to taste)

4 ounces cream cheese, softened

¾ cup real mayonnaise

6 cups shredded sharp white
Cheddar cheese
(about 1 pound)

In a medium bowl, combine onion, pimentos, and cayenne. Add cream cheese and mayonnaise, stirring until smooth and all ingredients are incorporated. Add Cheddar and mix until just combined, keeping texture somewhat chunky.

The pimento cheese will keep in the refrigerator for up to 2 weeks ... if it lasts that long!

Mama's Boy Poppy Seed Chicken Salad

1 to 2 tablespoons poppy seeds

½ onion, chopped (optional)

4 celery stalks, minced

½ cup mayonnaise

4 boneless, skinless chicken
breasts, cooked and chopped

1 cup seedless red grapes,
chopped

Salt and pepper to taste

In large mixing bowl, combine poppy seeds, onion, celery, and mayonnaise. Fold in chicken and grapes, stirring gently to combine. Season with salt and pepper to taste. Serve this chicken salad atop mixed field greens with toast points and fresh fruit.

For nearly forty years, Barbara Dooley has been Athens' 'First Lady of Football,' and although it's difficult to think of her without also thinking of her husband, long-time head football coach and former UGA Athletic Director Vince Dooley, she has had many accomplishments in her own right. She has been a motivational speaker, author, college lecturer, businesswoman, humorist, and broadcast personality, in addition to being a wife and mother. We are thrilled to have some of her favorite recipes to include in our cookbook. As one of our most recognizable and beloved Athenians, if anyone understands the essence of a championship-level tailgate party, Barbara most certainly does.

Creamy Apple Salad
Barbara Dooley

1 cup water
½ cup dried cranberries
¼ cup golden raisins
½ cup mayonnaise
3 tablespoons plain yogurt
2 tablespoons sugar
2 teaspoons lemon zest

1 tablespoon freshly squeezed lemon juice
1 Granny Smith apple, cored and chopped
3 Gala apples, cored and chopped
1 cup chopped celery
½ cup chopped pecans, toasted

In medium saucepan over medium-high heat, bring water to a boil. Remove from heat and stir in cranberries and raisins. Let stand 10 minutes and then drain.

In large mixing bowl, combine mayonnaise, yogurt, sugar, zest, and lemon juice. Stir in apples, celery, cranberries, and raisins. Cover and chill. Sprinkle with pecans just before serving. Enjoy!

Serves 8

Barbara's Pumpkin Soup
Barbara Dooley

6 cups chicken stock
1½ teaspoons salt
4 cups pumpkin purée
1 cup chopped onion
½ teaspoon freshly chopped thyme

1 garlic clove, minced
5 whole black peppercorns
½ cup heavy whipping cream
1 teaspoon freshly chopped parsley

In large saucepan over medium high heat, combine stock, salt, pumpkin, onion, thyme, garlic, and peppercorns. Bring to a boil, reduce heat to low, and simmer 30 minutes, uncovered.

Purée the soup in small batches (about 1 cup at a time) using a food processor or blender.

Return to saucepan and return to a boil. Reduce heat to low and simmer additional 30 minutes, uncovered. Stir in cream. Pour in soup bowls and garnish with fresh parsley.

The Hoyt House's Shrimp Bisque

1 pound mirepoix (onions, carrots, celery), diced

2 pound rock shrimp/shells (½ pound shrimp, 1½ pounds shells)

3 ounces butter

2 ounces garlic cloves

2 ounces tomato paste

4 ounces brandy

12 ounces white wine

1 gallon fish stock

Sachet of bay leaf, dried thyme, crushed peppercorns, and flat leaf parsley

16 ounces heavy whipping cream

Salt and white pepper to taste

½ teaspoon cayenne pepper

2 ounces rock shrimp, sautéed for garnish

In large saucepan, sweat the mirepoix and shrimp shells in butter. Add garlic and tomato paste and sauté lightly. Add brandy and flambé, cooking out all liquor. Add wine and simmer until reduced by half.

Add fish stock and sachet; simmer on low heat 1 hour, skimming occasionally.

Remove and discard sachet. Strain liquids and reserve solids. Purée solids in food processor or blender and return to liquid; cook 10 minutes.

Strain soup through mesh colander lined with cheesecloth. Return soup to heat and stir in cream. Season with salt, white pepper, and cayenne pepper. Serve in individual bowls or cups and garnish with 3 rock shrimp per serving.

Mama's Boy Cole Slaw

1 finely julienned head of cabbage
   (cut out the bitter heart)

1 medium-sized carrot, finely
   julienned

10 chives, minced

1½ teaspoons celery seed

1 tablespoon tarragon

2 tablespoons white vinegar

1 cup mayonnaise

½ teaspoon Worcestershire sauce

1 teaspoon sugar

1 teaspoon ketchup

1 tablespoon fresh parsley, finely
   chopped

½ of 1 small fresh jalapeño,
   stemmed, seeded, and
   minced

Salt and pepper to taste

In large mixing bowl, whisk together chives, celery seed, tarragon, vinegar, mayonnaise, Worcestershire, sugar, ketchup, parsley, and jalapeño. Season with salt and pepper to taste. Pour over cabbage and carrot, tossing well to coat. Chill several hours. Slaw will keep up to 3 days.

This unusual slaw was runner-up in a cole slaw competition conducted by the Southern Foodways Alliance—the authority on all things concerning Southern food. There were over 300 entries from all over the country at this competition held in Oxford, Mississippi. It was also featured in the brilliant cookbook Taming the Flame *by Elizabeth Karmel whom Al Roker of* The Today Show *calls the "Queen Bee of Bar-Bee-Que."*

Marti's at Midday Blue Cheese Coleslaw

1 medium head of green cabbage,
   cored and finely shredded

2 medium carrots, shredded

¼ cup finely chopped sweet white
   onion

¼ cup chopped green onion

2 Roma tomatoes, diced

1 English cucumber, diced

½ cup cider vinegar

3 tablespoons sugar

2 tablespoons kosher salt, divided

½ cup mayonnaise

½ cup sour cream

½ cup crumbled mild blue cheese

Freshly ground black pepper to
   taste

In large mixing bowl, combine cabbage, carrots, onion, tomato, and cucumber. Set aside. In small saucepan over medium heat, combine vinegar, sugar, and 1 teaspoon salt. Bring to a boil. Pour mixture over cabbage, tossing well to coat. Let stand 15 minutes. Drain cabbage well in colander. Return to mixing bowl. Stir in mayonnaise, sour cream, blue cheese, remaining salt, and pepper to taste. Toss well to combine. Cover and chill at least 30 minutes.

Serves 8-10

Marti's at Midday Luxembourg Dressing

2 cups olive oil

2 cups canola oil

2 small shallots, chopped

3 tablespoons freshly minced herbs (we use tarragon, dill, and parsley)

½ cup balsamic vinegar

½ cup white wine vinegar or champagne vinegar

3 tablespoons whole-grain mustard

¼ cup sugar

2 teaspoons kosher salt

1 teaspoon freshly ground black pepper

In large mixing bowl, combine oils and set aside. In bowl of food processor or blender, combine shallots, herbs, vinegars, mustard, sugar, salt, and pepper. Process until well combined. Slowly pour in oil in a steady stream.

Makes 6 cups

Our house vinaigrette is loaded with fresh shallots and herbs. It will last up to five days and is good as a dressing, marinade, or dip for crudités.

Hallie Jane's Indies Balsamic Vinaigrette

¾ cup balsamic vinegar

1 cup olive oil

¼ cup sugar

1 teaspoon country-style Dijon mustard

1 teaspoon Worcestershire sauce

1 teaspoon kosher salt

Nutmeg

Tabasco

Paprika

White onions, thinly sliced

Chopped green olives

In large mixing bowl, whisk together vinegar, oil, sugar, mustard, Worcestershire, and salt. Gently stir in nutmeg, Tabasco, and paprika. Fold in onions and olives. Keep refrigerated for up to two weeks.

Great on a spring mix with crumbled blue cheese, spiced pecans, and sliced strawberries or pears.

Mama's Boy Balsamic Vinaigrette

1 cup balsamic vinegar	2 tablespoons honey
2 tablespoons lemon juice	2 tablespoons Dijon mustard
½ teaspoon thyme	¼ cup extra virgin olive oil
½ teaspoon dried basil	1¾ cups blended oil
1 tablespoon sugar	

In bowl of food processor or blender, combine vinegar, lemon juice, thyme, basil, sugar, honey, and mustard. Process until well combined. Slowly pour in oils in a steady stream. Continue to mix until well blended.

According to local legend, this favorite was first served at Central Grocery on New Orleans' Decatur Street in 1906. The "dressing" for the sandwich is called "olive salad."

Muffuletta

1 (7-ounce) jar Spanish olives with pimentos, chopped	Juice of ½ lemon
1 (6½-ounce) can sliced black olives	2 loaves Italian or French bread
½ cup extra virgin olive oil	¾ pound thinly sliced salami
1 tablespoon freshly chopped oregano	1 pound thinly sliced ham
1 teaspoon freshly chopped basil	12 slices provolone
2 tablespoons parsley flakes	12 slices mozzarella
2 tablespoons capers, chopped	Shredded lettuce
	Sliced tomatoes

In small bowl combine green and black olives, olive oil, oregano, basil, parsley, capers, and lemon juice. Cover and chill at least 8 hours. (Mixture can also be coarsely chopped in food processor.)

Preheat oven to 400 degrees. Split loaf in half horizontally and remove most of inner bread, creating a cavity inside each half. Fill bottom cavity with one-third of olive mixture. Layer with salami, ham, and cheeses. Top with upper loaf. Repeat process with remaining loaf. Spread remaining one-third olive mixture on top of loaves. Wrap sandwich tightly in foil. Toast in oven 15 minutes, or until cheese melts. Remove from oven and foil; cut into slices. Serve with lettuce and tomatoes.

Serves 12

Spinach and Artichoke Pinwheels

1 (10-ounce) package frozen
  chopped spinach, thawed
  and drained

1 (14-ounce) can artichoke hearts,
  drained and chopped

½ cup mayonnaise

½ cup grated Parmesan

1 teaspoon onion powder

1 teaspoon garlic powder

½ teaspoon pepper

1 (17.3-ounce) package frozen
  puff pastry

Preheat oven to 400 degrees. In large mixing bowl, combine spinach, artichoke hearts, mayonnaise, Parmesan, onion powder, garlic powder, and pepper. Thaw puff pastry at room temperature for 30 minutes. Unfold pastry and place on lightly floured surface. Spread half of spinach mixture on pastry sheet. Roll up jellyroll style, pressing seam to seal. Wrap in plastic wrap and repeat process with remaining pastry and mixture. Freeze 30 minutes. Remove plastic wrap and cut into ½-inch slices. Transfer to nonstick baking sheet. Bake 20 minutes.

Serves 48

The green artichoke (Cynara scolymusis) is actually a type of thistle. Just watch to see which of your cocktail party guests get "prickly" should you run out of these!

Spinach Chicken Round

1 (10-ounce) package frozen
  chopped spinach, thawed
  and drained

1 (10¾-ounce) can cream of
  chicken soup

½ cup sour cream

1 cup shredded Cheddar cheese

¼ cup chopped bell pepper

2 cooked, boneless skinless
  chicken breasts, chopped

2 (8-count) packages crescent
  rolls, divided

In large mixing bowl, combine spinach, soup, and sour cream. Add cheese, bell pepper, and chicken, mixing well to combine; set aside.

Roll out crescent rolls and separate into twelve triangles. Arrange triangles in a circle, overlapping each other on baking sheet. Spoon mixture onto middles of crescents. Fold outer tip of crescent rolls inside over mixture to middle of ring. Bake according to crescent roll directions. Remove from oven and cool. Transfer to round serving platter and cut into slices.

Serves 8

Herb Chicken Crescents

Makes a wonderful brunch or luncheon entrée!

2 tablespoons margarine, softened

2 (3-ounce) packages cream
    cheese, softened

1½ cups cooked cubed chicken

1 (8-count) package crescent
    rolls, separated

1½ sticks margarine, melted

1 cup herb-seasoned stuffing mix

Preheat oven to 375 degrees. In mixing bowl, cream together margarine and cream cheese, mixing well to combine. Add chicken and mix well. Spoon ¼ cup chicken mixture onto each crescent. Wrap dough around mixture and pinch edges to seal. Dip each roll into melted margarine and coat with stuffing. Place on baking sheet and bake 20 minutes.

Serves 4

Chili Blanco con Pollo

1 tablespoon cooking oil

2 pounds chicken breast, cut into
    bite-sized pieces

2 cups chopped onion

2 garlic cloves, minced

2 teaspoons cumin

½ teaspoon dried oregano

1 teaspoon coriander

2 (4½-ounce) cans chopped green
    chilies, undrained

2 (15½-ounce) cans cannelloni
    or navy beans, rinsed and
    drained

1 (14-ounce) can chicken broth

1 cup water

½ teaspoon hot pepper sauce

1 cup shredded Monterey Jack
    cheese

½ cup freshly chopped cilantro

½ cup chopped green onions

Heat oil in large nonstick skillet over medium high heat. Add chicken and cook 10 minutes, or until chicken is no longer pink; stir frequently. Remove from heat and set aside. Coat large saucepan with nonstick cooking spray and heat over medium high heat. Add onion and sauté 6 minutes or until tender, stirring frequently. Add garlic and sauté 2 minutes, stirring frequently. Stir in cumin, oregano, and coriander; sauté 1 minute. Stir in chilies; reduce heat to low and cook 10 minutes, partially covered. Add chicken, beans, broth, and water; bring to a simmer. Cover and simmer 10 minutes. Stir in hot pepper sauce. Serve in individual bowls and sprinkle with cheese, cilantro, and green onion.

Serves 8

Rumpus Chili

So named because a wild "rumpus" begins when kids help make this tasty chili!

1 pound ground turkey or ground beef

1 (1¼-ounce) packet chili seasoning mix

1 (28-ounce) can diced tomatoes

1 (15½-ounce) can dark red kidney beans

1 (15-ounce) can black beans

1 (15½-ounce) can light red kidney beans

1 (15¼-ounce) corn, drained

1 (12-ounce bottle) high quality beer, divided

Sour cream, shredded Cheddar cheese, and chives, for garnish

In Dutch oven over medium heat, brown meat. Drain and return meat to pot. Add chili seasoning packet and stir. Add tomatoes, beans, and corn. Simmer 20 minutes. Add ¾ bottle of beer. Simmer 5 minutes. Serve in individual bowls and garnish with sour cream, Cheddar, and chives.

The small amount of alcohol from the beer cooks off as this chili heats, so do serve it to your little ones in good conscience (and with supreme confidence)!

But be sure to drink the remaining beer while stirring the chili!

Best Damn Chili

2 pounds ground beef or ground sirloin

1 tablespoon cooking oil

2 cups chopped onion

1 quart water

1 quart canned tomatoes

½ (4-ounce) can green chilies

2 (15-ounce) cans pinto beans

3 tablespoons chili powder

2 teaspoons salt

1 teaspoon pepper

½ teaspoon dry mustard

¼ teaspoon cayenne

¼ teaspoon celery salt

Sliced jalapeño peppers to taste (optional)

Cooked rice (optional)

Shredded Cheddar cheese and sour cream, for garnish

In Dutch oven over medium high heat, brown ground beef in oil and drain well. Add onion and sauté until tender. Add water, tomatoes, green chilies, and beans. Stir in chili powder, salt, pepper, mustard, cayenne, celery salt, and jalapeños, if desired. Bring to a boil and simmer 3 hours. Serve in individual bowls or over rice. Garnish with Cheddar cheese and sour cream.

A combination of half pinto beans and half kidney beans may also be used.

Hollowed sourdough rounds make excellent "bowls" for serving this crowd-pleaser. After cutting a circle on the top of each individual loaf and carefully tearing it away, scoop out the insides and then toast lightly to ensure sturdiness.

Melba rounds spread with a paste of grated Gruyère and butter, then toasted until brown, make attractive garnishes that are also flavorful enough to go with such a hearty chili. Float a few atop each serving alongside a dollop of sour cream or with a jalapeño slice.

Turkey Barley Chili

3 cups water

1 (16-ounce) jar salsa or tomato sauce (or mixture of both)

1 (14½-ounce) can diced tomatoes, undrained

1 (14½-ounce) can chicken broth

1 cup quick cooking barley

1 tablespoon chili powder

1 teaspoon cumin

1 (15-ounce) can black beans, rinsed and drained

1 (15-ounce) can corn

1½ pounds cooked ground turkey or chopped, cooked chicken breast (3 cups)

Shredded cheese and sour cream (optional)

In large saucepan over medium heat, combine water, salsa, tomatoes, broth, barley, chili powder, and cumin. Bring to boil. Cover and reduce heat to low. Simmer 20 minutes, stirring occasionally. Add beans, corn, and turkey. Bring to a boil. Cover and reduce heat to low. Simmer another 5 minutes, or until barley is tender. Add additional broth or water if chili is too thick. Garnish with cheese and sour cream, if desired.

Ideally, the delicate flavor of crab roe is what makes this coastal tradition special. You may opt to add more sherry to each bowl before ladling as consolation for living further inland.

Simple She Crab Soup

¾ cup chopped onion

6 tablespoons butter, divided

1 tablespoon extra virgin olive oil

1½ pounds crabmeat (real, imitation, or combination)

2 (12-ounce) cans evaporated milk

4 tablespoons Worcestershire sauce

Juice of ½ lemon

3 tablespoons sugar

⅛ cup sherry

1 teaspoon onion powder

1 teaspoon salt

1 teaspoon white pepper

½ teaspoon celery salt

¼ teaspoon black pepper

4 cups milk

In 6-quart stockpot, sauté onion in 1 tablespoon butter and olive oil until transparent. Reduce heat to low and add remaining 5 tablespoons butter. When butter melts, add crabmeat and stir well. Add evaporated milk, Worcestershire sauce, lemon juice, sugar, sherry, onion powder, salt, white pepper, celery salt, and black pepper; stir well to combine. Add milk and simmer over low heat, stirring often. Serve immediately with oyster crackers.

Serves 8

Spicy Oyster Stew

Great for a Christmas Eve supper.

2 pints oysters (with liquid)

1 stick butter

1 tablespoon minced garlic

1 medium onion, finely chopped

1 medium carrot, finely chopped

2 tablespoons Cajun seasoning

1 quart seafood stock

1 (10-ounce) can tomatoes with green chilies, puréed

1 quart half-and-half

¼ cup white wine

Paprika to taste

Parsley, green onion, and paprika, for garnish

Drain oysters and reserve liquid. Set oysters and liquid aside. In 2-gallon stockpot over medium heat, melt butter. Add garlic, onion, and carrot. Sauté, constantly stirring, until onion is translucent. Add Cajun seasoning, stirring to combine. Add reserved oyster liquid, seafood stock, and tomatoes and simmer. Add oysters and cook until edges begin to curl. Add half-and-half and wine. Season with paprika to taste. Serve immediately in individual bowls. Garnish with parsley, green onion, and paprika.

Serves 8

Be sure and check through oysters carefully for tiny pieces of shell. Even professional shuckers can have an off day, as will you if a guest or loved one says, "That last spoonful had something extra to it!"

Hearty Corn Chowder

2 tablespoons unsalted butter

18 baby carrots, finely chopped

3 celery stalks, finely chopped

1 onion, finely chopped

3 (14-ounce) cans vegetable broth

½ tablespoon freshly chopped basil

1 teaspoon thyme

1 teaspoon paprika

3 garlic cloves, chopped or ⅜ teaspoon garlic powder

4 medium potatoes, peeled and diced

2 pounds frozen corn

2 cups whipping cream

¼ cup cornstarch

¼ cup dry white wine

1½ teaspoons salt

In Dutch oven over medium heat, melt butter. Add carrot, celery, and onion and sauté 10 minutes. Add broth, basil, thyme, paprika, and garlic. Bring to a boil. Add potatoes and corn. Bring to a boil. Add cream. Simmer 15 minutes, or until vegetables are tender. In small mixing bowl, whisk together cornstarch and wine until smooth. Add small amount of soup to cornstarch mixture to thin. Pour mixture into chowder and add salt, stirring until thickened (about 1 minute).

Chowders get their name from the French word chaudière, a caldron used by fisherman for stews made from fresh catches. For this 'landlubbers' variety you'll merely need your favorite soup pot and a good appetite.

Chicken and Corn Chowder

3 slices bacon, chopped

1 pound boneless skinless
    chicken breasts, cubed

¾ cup chopped onion

¾ cup chopped celery

2 cups whole kernel corn

2 cups Mexican style corn

4 cups chicken broth, divided

2 cups potatoes, peeled and
    cubed

1 teaspoon Worcestershire sauce

Salt to taste

1 cup whipping cream

2 cups shredded Cheddar cheese

Freshly ground pepper to taste

In Dutch oven over medium heat, cook bacon until crisp. Remove bacon and drain on paper towels. Set bacon aside. Reserve 2 tablespoons drippings and return to Dutch oven; discard remaining drippings. Add chicken, onion, and celery to skillet and cook until tender (about 15 minutes).

Combine Mexican style corn and 1 cup broth in blender. Process until smooth. Add puréed corn, remaining chicken broth, whole kernel corn, potatoes, Worcestershire, and salt to chicken mixture. Bring to a boil and reduce heat. Simmer 30 minutes or until potatoes are tender. Stir in whipping cream and cheese. Simmer 5 minutes. Add bacon; season with salt and pepper.

A confetti of red onion makes a colorful garnish for this chowder, as do halved grape or cherry tomatoes. Pierce the side of each tomato along the center with a sharp knife, then slice through the exact same spot, keeping each half intact and juicy.

World's Easiest Vegetable Soup

1 pound ground beef, cooked

3 cans diced tomatoes

2 cans mixed vegetables

1 bay leaf

Dash of marjoram

1 (12-ounce) can tomato paste

1 can beef broth

1 celery stalk

2 onions, finely chopped

In a large stockpot over medium heat, combine ground beef, tomatoes, mixed vegetables, bay leaf, marjoram, tomato paste, broth, celery, and onion. Simmer at least 1 hour. Add water to thin, if desired. Remove and discard bay leaf before serving.

Serves 12

No Stir Chicken Soup

This soup freezes well.

6 chicken breasts	1 cup fresh button mushrooms
Light Italian dressing	3 carrots, sliced
½ cup chopped onion, divided	3 celery stalks, sliced
2 garlic cloves, minced	1 (15-ounce) jar pearl onions
Olive oil	1 (14-ounce) can diced tomatoes
2 (32-ounce) packages organic chicken broth	¼ cup rosemary, chopped
	Salt and pepper to taste

Place chicken in zip top plastic bag. Pour dressing over chicken and seal. Chill and marinate 30 minutes. Preheat oven to 350 degrees. Transfer chicken and marinade to baking pan; discard bag. Bake 1 hour. Remove from oven and slice chicken into bite-sized pieces and set aside.

In large skillet over medium heat, sauté ¼ cup onion and garlic in extra virgin olive oil for 15 minutes, stirring occasionally.

Add chicken, onion and garlic, broth, mushrooms, carrot, celery, pearl onions, tomatoes, and rosemary. Combine all ingredients in a crock pot on low for 6 hours. Season with salt and pepper to taste.

Serves 6-8

Cooked pastas such as orecchiette or farfalle ("ears" and "butterflies," known to us as shells and bowties respectively) are a wonderful addition, but leave them out if you intend to freeze this soup, as the reheating causes a chewiness beyond the desired al dente.

Tomato and Okra Stew

1 pound ground chuck	1½ pounds fresh okra, sliced
1 medium onion, chopped	1 teaspoon chili powder
1 green bell pepper, seeded and chopped	Salt and pepper to taste
1 (24-ounce) can diced tomatoes	1 (15-ounce) can Great Northern beans, drained

In Dutch oven over medium heat, brown ground chuck with onion and bell pepper. Stir in tomatoes, okra, and chili powder. Season with salt and pepper to taste. Reduce heat and cook, covered, for 30 minutes. Add beans and simmer until thoroughly heated.

Traditionally used as a thickener for gumbo, okra is a Southern favorite and supplies us with vitamins A and C.

Cheeseburger Soup

Croutons made from cubed sesame-seed buns are a clever thematic garnish for Cheeseburger Soup, or try serving fried pickles as an accompaniment.

¾ cup chopped onion

¾ cup chopped celery

¾ cup chopped carrots

1 teaspoon dried basil

1 teaspoon dried parsley flakes

4 tablespoons butter, divided

3 cups chicken broth

4 cups peeled and diced potatoes

½ pound ground beef, cooked and drained

¼ cup all-purpose flour

8 ounces processed cheese loaf

1½ cups milk

¾ teaspoon salt

Freshly ground pepper to taste

¼ cup sour cream

In 3 quart saucepan over medium high heat, sauté onion, celery, carrot, basil, and parsley in 1 tablespoon butter until tender (about 10 minutes). Add broth, potatoes, and beef. Bring to a boil. Reduce heat, cover, and simmer approximately 15 minutes, or until potatoes are tender.

In small skillet over medium heat, melt remaining 3 tablespoons butter. Add flour and cook 3 to 5 minutes, stirring constantly. Add to soup and bring to a boil. Cook and stir 2 minutes. Reduce heat to low. Add cheese, milk, salt, and pepper, gently stirring until cheese melts. Remove from heat and stir in sour cream.

Serves 6-8

Zuppa di Verdura

Crusty slices of ciabatta brushed with olive oil and sprinkled with grated asiago, then lightly toasted, are delightful served straight from the oven with this Italian vegetable soup.

1 pound ground beef, cooked and drained

1 cup chopped onion

1 cup sliced celery

1 cup sliced carrots

2 garlic cloves, minced

1 (15-ounce) can diced tomatoes

1 (15-ounce) can tomato sauce

1 (15-ounce) can red kidney beans, undrained

1 tablespoon dried parsley

5 cups beef broth

2 cups water

1 teaspoon salt

½ teaspoon oregano

½ teaspoon sweet basil

¼ teaspoon pepper

2 cups shredded cabbage

1 cup frozen Italian green beans

½ cup miniature penne pasta

In large stockpot over medium heat, combine beef, onion, celery, carrot, garlic, tomatoes, tomato sauce, kidney beans, parsley, broth, water, salt, oregano, basil, and pepper. Stir well to combine. Bring to a boil and reduce heat. Cover and simmer 20 minutes. Add cabbage, green beans, and pasta. Bring to a boil, reduce heat, and simmer until vegetables are tender.

Elinor's Tomato Aspic

For a special treat, serve with shrimp mayonnaise.

1 large can tomato juice	5 envelopes unflavored gelatin
1 (11½-ounce) can V-8 juice	1 bay leaf
Juice of 1 lemon	2 tablespoons vinegar
2 ribs of celery (broken)	2 tablespoons sugar
½ medium onion, sliced	1 tablespoon horseradish
1 tablespoon Italian seasoning	Salt and pepper to taste
3 dashes Worcestershire sauce	Dill weed (optional)

Soften gelatin in V-8 juice. Squeeze and quarter the lemon into the tomato juice, and add the remaining ingredients. Bring to a simmer and stir occasionally for 5 to 6 minutes. Add the V-8 gelatin mixture to the tomato juice. Stir well then strain the juice into an oiled mold. Add ¼ cup chopped onion and ¼ cup chopped celery. Add 2 tablespoons dill weed if desired.

Serves 10-12

Creamy Broccoli Soup

1 box frozen chopped broccoli	1 cup sour cream
1 (14½-ounce) can chicken stock	1 (10¾-ounce) can cream of mushroom soup
1 medium onion, chopped	
Dash of nutmeg	

In saucepan over medium high heat, cook broccoli and onion in chicken stock. Stir in nutmeg. Remove from heat and cool. Pour into blender and purée until smooth. Add sour cream and soup and pulse until mixed. Chill or reheat to serve.

Serves 6

SHRIMP MAYONNAISE

1 quart peeled raw shrimp

2 onions, sliced

1 cup vegetable oil

1 cup olive oil

1 cup vinegar

Grated peel of 1 lemon

Juice of 1 lemon

3 cups mayonnaise

Boil shrimp in salted water for 12 minutes. Combine onions, lemon, oils, and vinegar. Add the shrimp to this mixture and marinate for 24 hours in refrigerator. Before serving, drain and chop all ingredients into small pieces. Mix with 3 cups mayonnaise.

Serve with congealed salads.

Cold Cucumber Soup

Hothouse or seedless cucumbers make this one a snap. Perfect for any warm day, this soup can be attractively garnished with a few thin slices of cucumber and a sprig of fresh dill or parsley.

2 medium cucumbers, peeled and quartered

1½ cups milk

2 (10¾-ounce) cans cream of celery soup

Dash of hot sauce

1 (16-ounce) container sour cream

Thin cucumber slices, for garnish

Combine cucumbers, milk, soup, and hot sauce in blender and pulse until smooth. Pour into large mixing bowl. Whisk in sour cream with wire whisk. Cover and chill. Serve in individual bowls and garnish with thin cucumber slices.

Serves 6

Twice Baked Potato Soup
Serve with hot cornbread on a cold winter night!

Garnish this soup exactly as you would a baked potato- with sour cream, chives, bacon bits, or shredded cheese (or all of them)!

4 chicken bouillon cubes

5 cups water

1 cupped chopped celery

¾ cup chopped onion

1 cup chopped carrots

2 (10¾-ounce) cans cream of chicken soup

5 cups cubed potatoes

1 (16-ounce) package processed cheese loaf, cubed

Salt and pepper to taste

Chives, sour cream, bacon bits, and shredded cheese, for garnish

In Dutch oven over medium high heat, dissolve bouillon cubes in water. Add celery, onion, and carrot and cook 20 minutes. Add soup and potatoes. Cook 20 minutes. Add cheese cubes, stirring until cheese melts. Season with salt and pepper to taste. Serve in individual bowls and garnish with chives, sour cream, bacon bits, and shredded cheese.

Serves 4-6

Lentil Minestrone

1 bacon slice, chopped

1 medium onion, chopped

2 carrots, chopped

2 garlic cloves, minced

½ teaspoon dried rosemary

Salt and pepper to taste

1 tablespoon tomato paste

2 (15-ounce) cans navy or cannelloni beans, rinsed and drained

2 (14½-ounce) cans chicken broth

4 cups water

¾ cup ditalini pasta

¼ cup freshly chopped parsley

Shredded Parmesan

In large saucepan over medium heat, cook bacon 8 minutes, or until crisp. Add onion and carrot; cook 5 minutes, or until tender. Add garlic and rosemary and cook 1 minute, or until fragrant. Season with salt and pepper to taste. Stir in tomato paste, beans, broth, and water. Bring to a boil and reduce heat. Simmer 10 minutes, partially covered, or until soup has thickened slightly. Mash some beans in pot with large spoon or potato masher in order to thicken soup. Add pasta and simmer 10 minutes, or until pasta is al dente; stir constantly. Serve in individual bowls and sprinkle with parsley and Parmesan.

Serves 6

The ditalini called for in this recipe are really just miniature versions of our old favorite macaroni. Topped with Parmesan and served with buttered brown bread, this potful is substantial enough for a meal in and of itself. It's no wonder that minestrone literally means "big soup."

Spicy Pumpkin Soup

4 tablespoons unsalted butter

1 small yellow onion, chopped

2 teaspoons minced garlic

⅛ teaspoon crushed red pepper flakes

1 teaspoon curry

½ teaspoon coriander

Dash of cayenne

3 (15-ounce) cans 100% pumpkin

5 cups chicken broth

½ cup brown sugar

2 cups milk

¾ cup whipping cream

In 4-quart saucepan over medium high heat, melt butter. Add onions and garlic and sauté, stirring frequently, until tender. Add red pepper, curry, coriander, and cayenne. Cook 1 minute, stirring well. Add pumpkin and chicken broth and stir well. Bring to a boil, reduce heat, and simmer 15 minutes. Remove from heat and cool slightly.

Pour soup in blender and purée until smooth. Return soup to saucepan. Set heat to low and stir in brown sugar. Slowly add milk, stirring constantly. Slowly add whipping cream, stirring constantly. Adjust seasonings to taste.

Serves 6

Additional cream balances a soup that's too spicy. Use a strainer to make a smoother soup if pieces of onion remain after blending. Serve this in small cups as an appetizer at parties or in bowls for a warming first course.

Lucy's Santa Fe Soup

1½ to 2 pounds ground turkey or beef

1 onion, chopped

2 (.5-ounce) packages ranch style dressing mix

2 (1 ½-ounce) packages taco seasoning mix

1 (16-ounce) can black beans, undrained

1 (16-ounce) can kidney beans, undrained

1 (16-ounce) can pinto beans, undrained

1 (16-ounce) can diced tomatoes with chilies, undrained

1 (16-ounce) can tomato wedges, undrained

2 (16-ounce) cans white corn, undrained

2 cups water

Tortilla chips

In large saucepan over medium heat, brown meat with onion. Add ranch dressing mix and taco seasoning, stirring well to combine. Add beans, tomatoes, corn, and water. Simmer 2 hours. Serve in individual bowls with tortilla chips.

Serves 6 to 8

Aunt Kathy's Tortilla Soup

8 corn tortillas, chopped

6 garlic cloves, minced

½ cup freshly chopped cilantro

1 medium onion, chopped

6 tablespoons olive oil

1 (28-ounce) can diced tomatoes

2 tablespoons cumin

½ tablespoon chili powder

1 teaspoon salt

¼ teaspoon cayenne

3 bay leaves

6 cups chicken stock

4 to 6 cooked chicken breasts, cubed

2 corn tortillas, sliced into strips and fried

Shredded Monterey Jack cheese (optional)

Cubed avocado (optional)

Sour cream (optional)

In large saucepan over medium heat, sauté 8 tortillas, garlic, cilantro, and onion in oil 2 to 3 minutes. Stir in tomatoes and bring to a boil. Add cumin, chili powder, salt, cayenne, bay leaves, and stock; bring to a boil. Reduce heat and simmer 30 minutes. Remove and discard bay leaves; add chicken. Serve in individual bowls and top with fried tortilla strips (or tortilla chips). Garnish with cheese, avocado, and sour cream, if desired.

Serves 6

Healthy Black Bean Soup

Perfect comfort food for those cold fall and winter nights!

1 medium onion, finely chopped

4 medium garlic cloves, minced

3 (15-ounce) cans black beans, undrained

½ teaspoon red pepper flakes

1 teaspoon cumin

1 (14.5-ounce) can low sodium, fat-free chicken broth

1 (10-ounce) can tomatoes with green chilies

1 (11-ounce) can whole kernel corn, drained

Green onions, low-fat cheese, and low-fat sour cream, for garnish

Coat bottom of large stockpot with nonstick cooking spray. Add onion and garlic; sauté over medium heat, stirring frequently, until onion is tender, but not brown (about 7 minutes).

Pour 1 can of beans in blender; add sautéed onion mixture, red pepper flakes, and cumin. Cover and blend on high until smooth (about 30 seconds). Pour mixture into stockpot.

Pour 1 can of beans and broth in blender and blend until smooth. Pour mixture into stockpot.

Add remaining beans, tomatoes, and corn to stockpot. Bring to a boil. Reduce heat to medium and simmer 20 minutes. Serve in individual bowls and garnish with green onions, low-fat cheese, and low-fat sour cream, if desired.

Serves 8

 # Woodlawn Chicken Mull

1 small hen (about 4 pounds)

4 large onions, chopped

1 quart milk

1 stick butter or margarine

Catsup

Worcestershire sauce

Red pepper

Saltine crackers (crumbled)

Cook hen in a small amount of water. Debone and cut into small pieces. Cook down in stock (add water if necessary) with about 4 large onions, chopped. Add milk, butter, catsup, Worcestershire sauce, red pepper. Add saltine crackers gradually until mull reaches desired consistency—it is easier if you season hen and stock a little and then add crackers and finish seasoning.

Serves 10

Garnishing this soup with green onions, reduced fat sour cream, or shredded skim milk cheese helps keep it healthy without sacrificing flavor.

This dish originated as a Northeast Georgia stew made of meat, broth, butter, vegetables and seasonings thickened with soda cracker crumbs.

Popular for being a cold-weather dish, during winter months, mulls can be found served in local rural restaurants or hunters' camps and are always a favorite for special events such as church socials, community gatherings or fundraisers.

Serve with large onion rings, tomatoes, and cucumbers which have been marinated in vinegar and chilled for an hour.

Right On Chicken Vegetable Stew

Only 2 grams of fat per serving.

48 ounces fat-free chicken broth (6 cups)

6 boneless skinless chicken breasts

1 cup chopped onion

4 celery stalks, chopped

1 (28-ounce) package frozen white corn

2 (16-ounce) packages frozen baby lima beans

2 (14½-ounce) cans chopped tomatoes with green pepper and onions

½ cup ketchup

8 ounces chopped ham

2 tablespoons sugar

6 tablespoons red wine vinegar

2 teaspoons Worcestershire sauce

2 teaspoons hot sauce

In large Dutch oven over medium heat, bring broth to a boil. Add chicken, onion, and celery and return to a boil. Reduce heat to low and simmer 40 minutes. Remove chicken and cool. Shred and set aside.

Add corn, beans, tomatoes, ketchup, ham, sugar, vinegar, Worcestershire, and hot sauce. Gently stir in chicken. Bring to a boil, reduce heat to low and simmer, stirring occasionally, 40 minutes to 1 hour.

Serves 12 to 16

Kielbasa Gulasz

Delicious on cold days.

Flavorful and filling, serve this stew with crusty peasant bread and add a small dollop of coarse stone-ground mustard to each bowl before serving.

Instead of cooking vegetables in water, use chicken or beef stock for extra flavor.

1 large head of cabbage, sliced into thick wedges

1 large onion, chopped

4 large potatoes, cut into chunks

1 small package baby carrots

1 large package Polish sausage, cooked

8 tablespoons margarine

Salt and pepper to taste

Tabasco sauce to taste

Garlic powder to taste

1 tablespoon sugar

In large stock pot, combine cabbage, onion, potato, and carrot and cover with water. Bring to a boil over medium high heat. Add sausage. Reduce heat to low and add margarine, salt, pepper, Tabasco, garlic powder, and sugar. Simmer until vegetables are tender. Serve in individual bowls.

Traditional Brunswick Stew

2 quarts water

3 pounds chicken

2 (15-ounce) cans baby lima beans, undrained

2 (28-ounce) cans diced tomatoes, undrained

1 (16-ounce) package frozen baby lima beans

3 medium potatoes, peeled and chopped

1 large yellow onion, chopped

2 (15-ounce) cans cream-style corn

¼ cup sugar

1 stick unsalted butter or margarine

2 tablespoons salt

2 teaspoons pepper

2 teaspoons hot sauce

2 tablespoons garlic powder

1 teaspoon cayenne

1 cup ketchup

2 tablespoons apple cider vinegar

2 tablespoons Worcestershire sauce

¼ cup barbecue sauce

In stockpot over medium heat, bring water and chicken to a boil. Reduce heat, and simmer 40 minutes, or until chicken is tender. Remove chicken, and set aside. Reserve 3 cups broth, discarding remaining broth. Transfer reserved broth to Dutch oven. Pour canned lima beans and liquid through wire-meshed strainer into Dutch oven. Reserve beans and set aside. Add tomatoes and bring to a boil over medium-high heat. Cook, stirring often, for 40 minutes or until liquid is reduced by one-third. Debone and shred chicken. Mash reserved beans with potato masher. Add chicken, mashed beans, frozen beans, potato, and onion to Dutch oven. Simmer over low heat 3 hours, 30 minutes, stirring often. Stir in corn, sugar, butter, salt, pepper, hot sauce, garlic powder, cayenne, ketchup, vinegar, Worcestershire, and barbecue sauce. Cook over low heat, stirring often. Simmer 1 additional hour.

Brunswick stew is a traditional southeastern accompaniment to barbecue. Our variety seems to go especially well with barbecued ribs!

Although salinity may be kept in check by adding water, do so cautiously, as thickness makes the difference between soups and stews. A hot, thick wedge of buttered rye bread goes well with this.

Take a Bite Out of the Bitter Cold Stew

2 to 2½ pounds stew beef

Olive oil

1 teaspoon Kosher salt

1 teaspoon coarsely ground black pepper

½ teaspoon sage

½ teaspoon tarragon

½ teaspoon thyme

5 carrots, peeled and coarsely chopped

2 large potatoes, peeled and coarsely chopped

2 large onions

5 to 6 celery stalks

2 cups chopped white mushrooms

4 cloves garlic, finely chopped

2 cups low sodium beef broth

4 tablespoons butter, cut into pieces

4 tablespoons cornstarch

Rough cut stew beef into bite-sized pieces. In heavy skillet over medium heat, cook beef in oil until browned on outside, being careful not to overcook. Season with salt, pepper, sage, tarragon, and thyme. Remove from heat, drain half of accumulated liquid. Set aside beef and remaining liquid.

Coat bottom of large crock pot with oil. Add carrot, potatoes, onion, celery, mushrooms, and garlic. Pour in beef broth and add stew beef with reserved liquid; stir gently. Add any additional salt, pepper, and spices to taste. Add butter and fill crock pot to top with cold water; stir gently. Cover and simmer on high 6 to 8 hours.

In small mixing bowl, combine cornstarch and warm water, mixing slowly to dissolve. Make about ½ to 1 cup. Slowly add cornstarch mixture to stew. Stir in a little at a time and wait 10 to 15 minutes before adding more. Stew should start to thicken quickly. Season with salt to taste. Serve with lots of buttered, crusty bread.

Serves 6-8

Tomato Basil Tortellini Salad

2 cups canned corn, drained

1 cup chopped tomatoes

¼ cup freshly chopped basil

2 tablespoons freshly chopped
    parsley

3 tablespoons olive oil

1 tablespoon red wine vinegar

1 garlic clove, minced

Salt and pepper to taste

1 (16-ounce) package cheese
    tortellini, cooked al dente

2 tablespoons shredded Parmesan

In large mixing bowl combine corn, tomatoes, basil, and parsley; set aside. In small mixing bowl, whisk together oil, vinegar, and garlic. Season with salt and pepper to taste. Drizzle over corn mixture. Add tortellini and toss gently. Sprinkle with Parmesan.

Serves 2-4

For a different presentation, use the large filled pasta tortellone and use quartered Roma tomatoes, tossing a few whole fresh basil leaves in before serving.

Spinach and Tomato Pasta Toss

1½ cups sliced fresh mushrooms

1½ tablespoons olive oil

1 (6-ounce) package baby spinach
    leaves

1 (14½-ounce) can diced
    tomatoes with basil, garlic,
    and oregano

½ cup shredded mozzarella
    cheese

4 tablespoons grated Parmesan

Salt and pepper to taste

2 cups penne pasta, cooked
    according to package
    directions

In large saucepan over medium high heat, sauté mushrooms in oil until tender. Add spinach and tomatoes. Cook 2 minutes, or until spinach wilts, stirring occasionally. Season with salt and pepper to taste. Remove from heat and keep warm. Place pasta in large serving bowl. Add tomato mixture and cheese, tossing gently to combine.

Serves 4

This is excellent with cooked chicken or shrimp added to make it a main dish, or with antipasta platter favorites, such as artichoke hearts, olives, or roasted red peppers thrown into the mix.

Artichoke and Olive Tortellini Salad

2 bags frozen cheese tortellini, thawed

1 (6-ounce) jar artichoke hearts, drained

1 jar green or Kalamata olives, drained

Grape tomatoes, halved

1 envelope dry Italian dressing mix (prepared according to package directions)

1 (8-ounce) package shredded Italian blend cheese

Freshly cracked black pepper

In large bowl, combine tortellini, artichoke hearts, olives, and tomatoes. Add dressing and toss well to coat. Sprinkle with cheese and toss. Top with freshly cracked black pepper.

Serves 8-10

Chorizo Pasta Salad

1 (12-ounce) package cooked chorizo (about 3 to 4 links)

3 garlic cloves, minced

1 poblano pepper, seeded and chopped

2 tablespoons white wine vinegar or apple cider vinegar

⅓ cup extra virgin olive oil

Juice of 1 lime

1 (15-ounce) can black beans, drained and rinsed

1 (12-ounce) jar roasted red peppers, drained

½ cup salsa (optional)

1 (8-ounce) package pasta, cooked al dente

1 cup cilantro, chopped

1 cup queso fresco, crumbled

Remove chorizo from casings. In sauté pan over medium heat, cook chorizo 5 to 6 minutes. Add garlic and poblano; cook 2 additional minutes. Remove from heat and drain mixture on paper towels.

In large mixing bowl, whisk together vinegar, oil, and lime juice. Fold in chorizo mixture, beans, roasted red peppers, and salsa. Toss with pasta, gently stirring to combine. Just before serving, add cilantro and crumbled queso and toss gently.

Serves 8

Shrimp and Feta Pasta Salad

1 (9-ounce) package angel hair pasta, cooked al dente

1 cup sliced carrots, steamed

½ pound asparagus, steamed and cut

4 green onions with tops, chopped

½ cup sliced black olives

½ to ¾ pound cooked shrimp, peeled

4 tablespoons olive oil

½ teaspoon oregano

Salt and pepper to taste

½ cup feta

¾ cup olive oil

6 tablespoons red wine vinegar

¼ teaspoon garlic salt

Basil and oregano to taste

In large serving bowl, combine pasta, carrots, asparagus, green onion, olives, shrimp, oil, and oregano. Season with salt and pepper to taste. In small mixing bowl, whisk together, oil, vinegar, garlic salt, basil, and oregano. Just before serving, drizzle with the dressing, tossing gently to coat. Sprinkle with feta.

Serves 6-8

This can be chilled overnight, but we suggest leaving the shrimp out and adding it the next morning to prevent an overly maritime flavor from pervading the whole salad.

Fresh Pasta Pesto Salad

Great to serve at bridal or baby showers!

⅓ cup red wine vinegar

1 tablespoon sugar

1 teaspoon pepper

½ teaspoon salt

1 teaspoon Dijon mustard

1 garlic clove, minced

½ cup olive oil

1 (16-ounce) package small pasta, cooked al dente

1 cup freshly chopped fresh basil

Shredded Parmesan cheese

½ cup toasted pine nuts

Grape tomatoes, halved, for garnish

In a mixing bowl, whisk together vinegar, sugar, pepper, salt, mustard, and garlic. Gradually whisk in olive oil. Pour over pasta, tossing to coat. Add basil, cheese, and pine nuts. Toss gently to combine. Garnish with tomato.

Serves 8-10

A tricolor rotini adds color to this salad, and its spirals are perfect for conveying fresh pesto in every biteful.

Quick-As-A-Flash Chicken Pasta Salad

A great quick lunch to serve while at the beach!

3 cups chopped, cooked chicken

1 package corkscrew pasta,
   cooked al dente

1 cucumber, chopped

1 to 2 celery stalks, chopped

1 small jar sliced green olives,
   drained

1 medium onion, chopped

1 (8-ounce) bottle zesty Italian
   dressing

½ cup mayonnaise

1 tablespoon prepared mustard

In large mixing bowl, combine chicken, pasta, cucumber, celery, olives, and onion. In small mixing bowl, whisk together dressing, mayonnaise, and mustard. Pour over pasta mixture while pasta is still hot, tossing gently to coat.

Serves 8

Romaine and Noodle Salad

3 tablespoon margarine

2 packages chicken-flavored
   ramen noodles, coarsely
   crumbled

½ cup slivered almonds, toasted

1 head of Napa cabbage, thinly
   sliced

1 head of romaine lettuce, thinly
   sliced

1 red bell pepper, seeded and
   chopped

1 orange bell pepper, seeded and
   chopped

6 green onions, chopped

1 cup oil

⅓ cup red wine vinegar

¼ teaspoon pepper

⅔ cup sugar

1 teaspoon salt

In sauté pan over medium heat, melt margarine. Sauté noodles. Add almonds and seasoning packets, gently stirring to combine. Remove from heat and cool. In large mixing bowl, combine cabbage, lettuce, bell peppers, and onion. Just before serving, sprinkle with noodle mixture. In small mixing bowl, whisk together oil, vinegar, pepper, sugar, and salt. Chill until ready to prepare and serve salad. Drizzle with dressing, tossing gently to coat.

Virtually anything can be substituted for chicken here, allowing for endless variations: smoked salmon, sliced ham, or wedges of buffalo mozzarella.

This vegetarian chameleon can change colors with each new basketful of summer garden bounty that finds its way into your kitchen.

Three Cheese Pasta Salad

1 (14-ounce) mini or small pasta shells, cooked al dente

2 (8-ounce) cans artichoke hearts, drained and chopped

1 (8-ounce) package Monterey Jack cheese, cubed

1 (8-ounce) package Muenster cheese, cubed

Salt and pepper to taste

1 (8-ounce) container grated Parmesan

Italian seasoning to taste

Olive oil

4 to 6 small avocados, pitted, peeled, and cubed

White vinegar to taste

In large mixing bowl, combine pasta, artichokes, Monterey Jack, and Muenster, tossing well to combine. Season with salt and pepper to taste. Add Parmesan cheese and Italian seasoning to taste. Add enough olive oil to coat well. Add avocado. Drizzle with vinegar to taste. Chill until ready to serve. More oil and vinegar may need to be added after chilling.

Serves 8-10

Busy Mom's Pasta

1 (16-ounce) package bow-tie pasta

1 pound asparagus, ends trimmed and cut into 2-inch pieces

1 packet garlic and herb dressing packet

1 pint grape tomatoes, halved

Grilled chicken slices (optional)

Black olives (optional)

Cook pasta in salted water according to package directions. Add asparagus to pasta during last 2 minutes of cooking time. Drain and rinse under cool water. Prepare garlic and herb dressing according to package directions. Mix dressing with pasta and asparagus according to taste. Stir in tomatoes. Add chicken and olives and toss gently, if desired.

Serves 4

Should you refrigerate this overnight, you may want to add additional oil and vinegar before serving.

Other cheeses may be used such as Swiss, Colby Jack, or Gouda. Goes great with French bread or crackers.

Crunchy Cabbage Salad
Great with pork, fish, or seafood!

Pork entrees and seafood are especially enhanced by this simple side salad. Dressing the salad components immediately before serving ensures its namesake crunchiness.

1 (16-ounce) package slaw mix

2 bunches green onions, chopped

1 cup sunflower seeds

½ cup sliced almonds

2 packages beef-flavored ramen noodles, coarsely crumbled

1 cup cooking oil

½ cup sugar

½ cup vinegar

2 seasoning packets from ramen noodles

In large mixing bowl, combine slaw and green onions. Cover with plastic wrap and chill. Just before serving, add seeds, almonds, and noodles. In a small mixing bowl, whisk together oil, sugar, vinegar, and seasoning packets. Drizzle with dressing, tossing gently to coat.

Serves 6

Great German Slaw

Use this as the side for grilled sausages or roasted pork with apples for a complement of flavor and texture. Refrigerate and store safely for up to three days.

1 medium head of cabbage, shredded

1 large onion, finely chopped

1 large green bell pepper, seeded and finely chopped

1 cup sugar

½ cup white vinegar

⅓ cup cooking oil

1 teaspoon salt

½ teaspoon pepper

In large serving bowl, combine cabbage, onion, and bell pepper. In mixing bowl, whisk together sugar, vinegar, oil, salt, and pepper. Drizzle with dressing, tossing well to coat. Chill until ready to serve.

Sweet Broccoli Salad

2 pounds broccoli florets, cut into
    small pieces
2 cups shredded Cheddar cheese
1 cup cooked and crumbled bacon
1 medium red onion, chopped

1 cup raisins
1½ cups mayonnaise
¾ cup sugar
6 tablespoons red wine vinegar

In large mixing bowl, combine broccoli, cheese, bacon, onion, and raisins. In separate mixing bowl, combine mayonnaise, sugar, and vinegar, whisking until smooth. Pour over broccoli mixture, tossing well to combine. Chill at least 4 hours before serving.

Serves 20

With some salads, preparing a day ahead is an option. Here, it is an imperative, as it gives the broccoli time to absorb the salad's dressing.

Black-Eyed Pea Salad

2 (15½-ounce) black-eyed peas,
    rinsed and drained
1 medium purple onion, chopped
1 medium tomato, seeded and
    chopped
1 green bell pepper, seeded and
    chopped
3 tablespoons red wine vinegar

2 tablespoons cooking oil
½ tablespoon Tabasco sauce
2 tablespoons freshly chopped
    cilantro
1 garlic clove, minced
½ teaspoon salt
Curly leaf lettuce, for decoration

In large mixing bowl, combine peas, onion, tomato, and bell pepper. In small mixing bowl, whisk together vinegar, oil, Tabasco, cilantro, garlic, and salt. Drizzle with dressing, tossing well to coat. Cover and chill at least 2 hours. Serve on lettuce-lined serving platter.

Serves 6

Native to Asia, the black-eyed pea is a Southern staple both in wintertime for lentil soups and Hoppin' John and in the summer for salads like these. Serve on a platter lined with curly leaf lettuce.

Tart Cherry Salad

1 head of iceberg lettuce, chopped

1 head of red leaf lettuce,
   chopped

5 green onions, chopped

⅓ cup cherry vinegar

⅓ cup cooking oil

⅓ cup sugar

2 tablespoons dried parsley

2 tablespoons sesame seeds

½ teaspoon salt

1 teaspoon Worcestershire sauce

1 (4-ounce) package crumbled
   feta cheese

1 (4-ounce) package dried tart
   cherries

1 (2-ounce) package slivered
   almonds

In large serving bowl, combine iceberg lettuce, red leaf lettuce, and green onion. In mixing bowl, whisk together vinegar, oil, sugar, parsley, sesame seeds, salt, and Worcestershire. Just before serving, drizzle with the dressing, tossing well to coat. Sprinkle with feta, cherries, and almonds.

Raspberry vinegar may be substituted for the
"often hard-to-find" cherry vinegar.

Marinated Vegetable Salad
Great to make a day ahead!

1 avocado, pitted, peeled, and
   cubed

1 pound asparagus, steamed and
   cut into bite-sized pieces

1 can artichoke hearts (not
   marinated), and chopped

1 can hearts of palm, drained and
   chopped

Lemon juice

1 bunch green onions, chopped

1 packet dry Italian dressing
   mix, prepared according to
   package directions

Dip avocado cubes in lemon juice. In large mixing bowl, combine avocado, asparagus, artichoke hearts, hearts of palm, and green onion. Drizzle with prepared dressing, tossing gently to coat. Chill at least 1 hour.

Serves 8

Romaine, Avocado, and Corn Salad

½ head of romaine lettuce, cut into ½-inch strips

2 cups fresh corn kernels, steamed

1 cup cherry tomatoes, halved

1 avocado, pitted, peeled, and cubed (divided)

⅓ cup water

2 to 3 tablespoons fresh lime juice

½ teaspoon chili powder

Coarsely ground salt and pepper to taste

In large mixing bowl, combine lettuce, corn, and cherry tomatoes. Add three-quarters of avocado to bowl; set aside. Purée remaining avocado with water, lime juice, and chili powder, blending until smooth. Season with salt and pepper to taste. Pour over salad, tossing gently to coat.

Serves 4 to 6

Avocados ripen happily in a brown paper bag on your kitchen counter and help make this dressing so irresistible you may, in fact, want to double it.

Simple Summer Spinach Salad

1 bag spinach leaves

½ cup blueberries, rinsed and drained

½ cup raspberries, rinsed and drained

¾ cup toasted pecans

Blueberry vinaigrette

⅓ cup crumbled feta

10 small red onion rings

In large serving bowl, combine spinach, berries, and pecans. Toss with a blueberry-flavored vinaigrette. Top with feta and onion rings.

TARRAGON VINAIGRETTE DRESSING

½ cup sugar

1 cup canola oil

½ cup tarragon vinegar

1 teaspoon paprika

1 teaspoon celery seed

1 teaspoon dry mustard

1 teaspoon salt

1 garlic clove, peeled and split

In mixing bowl, whisk together sugar, oil, vinegar, paprika, celery seed, mustard, salt, and garlic. Pour into plastic container with lid, seal tightly, and chill. Remove and discard garlic and mix well before serving.

This is a great dressing on a simple salad of Boston Bibb lettuce, red onions, crumbled blue cheese, and toasted pecans.

Spinach Salad with Savory Dressing

1 pound fresh spinach leaves

5 hard-boiled eggs, chopped

6 slices bacon, cooked and crumbled

1 cup pine nuts

1 cup cooking oil

½ cup sugar

¼ cup apple cider vinegar

⅓ cup ketchup

3 tablespoons Worcestershire sauce

Rinse and pat dry spinach leaves. Remove and discard stems. In large serving bowl, combine spinach, eggs, and bacon. Sprinkle with pine nuts. In large mixing bowl, whisk together oil, sugar, vinegar, ketchup, and Worcestershire. Just before serving, drizzle with dressing. For a prettier salad, do not toss before serving.

Serves 8

Dress this salad immediately before serving to ensure crispness of the greens, or go the other route altogether: brown slivered bacon and add (also immediately before serving) along with pan drippings for a truly wilted and delicious result.

Sweet and Spicy Rice Salad

1 box wild rice, prepared according to package directions

1½ cups chopped broccoli florets

1 package dried cranberries

3 green onions, chopped

1 cup honey-roasted peanuts

½ (8-ounce) bottle poppy seed dressing

In large serving bowl, combine rice, broccoli, cranberries, and green onion. Just before serving drizzle with dressing and add nuts, tossing gently to combine.

Quartered fresh figs in season can be substituted for the dried cranberries, as can chopped sugared dates year-round.

Easy Fall Salad

10 ounces fresh spinach leaves

2 tablespoons sliced green onions

1½ cups red apples, finely chopped

½ cup dried sweetened cranberries

½ cup dry roasted peanuts

In large mixing bowl, combine spinach, green onion, apple, cranberries, and peanuts. Drizzle with dressing, tossing gently to coat.

HONEY MANGO DRESSING

¼ cup white wine vinegar

¼ cup cooking oil

2 teaspoons sugar

¼ teaspoon salt

1½ teaspoons curry

1 teaspoon dry mustard

½ teaspoon honey

2 tablespoons mango chutney

In mixing bowl, whisk together vinegar, oil, sugar, salt, curry, mustard, and honey. Stir in chutney. Chill until ready to prepare and serve salad.

Either Winesaps or plain old Granny Smith apples suit this tailgate favorite. If your apple corer's gone missing since last fall, the melon baller you used all summer will do in a pinch for removing apple seeds quickly and neatly.

Super Veggie Caesar Salad

1 can quartered artichoke hearts, drained

1 can hearts of palm, drained

2 cups sliced carrots

1 small can ripe olives, drained

10 green olives, sliced

15 cherry tomatoes, sliced

1 cucumber, peeled and sliced

1 bottle Italian dressing

2 bags romaine lettuce

1 box Caesar style croutons

2 avocados, pitted and sliced

Caesar dressing

In large bowl, combine artichoke hearts, hearts of palm, carrots, olives, tomatoes, and cucumber. Pour Italian dressing over vegetables. Chill and marinate at least 2 hours. Before serving, drain marinated vegetables and spoon over romaine lettuce. Add Caesar dressing and toss well to coat. Just before serving, add avocado and croutons and toss gently.

Serves 10-14

As customarily prepared, Caesar dressing contains raw egg and as such might be avoided. Although we tend to think of the salad as Italian, its legendary origins in a Tijuana restaurant are license enough, we think, to use any bottled dressing you like.

Green Bean and Fennel Salad with Champagne Vinaigrette

If champagne vinaigrette eludes you while marketing, an equal amount of any dry champagne will do if allowed to sit a minute after pouring—a perfect salad for either "surf or turf."

Use purple-skinned potatoes to add color.

1 pound green beans

1 fennel bulb base, thinly sliced

½ cup grape tomatoes

½ cup cubed potatoes, cooked

¼ cup chopped walnuts

1½ tablespoons high quality Dijon mustard

1 medium shallot, finely chopped

Salt and pepper to taste

¼ cup champagne vinegar

¼ cup apple cider

¾ to 1 cup olive oil

1 (6-ounce) container crumbled blue cheese

In large saucepan over medium high heat, bring water to a boil. Add green beans and cook until tender crisp. Remove from heat and drain. Set aside and cool. In large mixing bowl, combine green beans, fennel, tomatoes, potatoes, and walnuts. In mixing bowl, combine mustard, shallot, salt, and pepper. Add vinegar and cider. Slowly whisk in olive oil to create an emulsion. Drizzle with dressing, tossing gently to coat. Sprinkle with blue cheese.

Serves 8-10

Curried Chicken Salad

Use an ice cream scoop to dollop this salad onto individual toast rounds or leafy greens, then sprinkle a tiny bit of curry powder atop each.

1 cup mayonnaise

2 teaspoons curry

6 boneless skinless chicken breasts, cooked and chopped

3 celery stalks, chopped

1 medium onion, chopped

2 apples, peeled, cored, and coarsely chopped

1 small bunch seedless grapes, halved

1 cup coarsely chopped pecans

In large mixing bowl, combine mayonnaise and curry. Fold in chicken, celery, onion, apple, grapes, and pecans; gently stir to combine. Cover and chill until ready to serve.

Grilled Chicken and Vegetable Orzo Salad

3 boneless skinless chicken
    breasts

1 bell pepper, seeded and
    chopped

1 red bell pepper, seeded and
    chopped

1 zucchini, chopped

1 onion, chopped

1 cup orzo pasta, cooked
    according to package
    directions

½ cup shredded Romano cheese

Save time—grill chicken and vegetables at the same time if your grill allows!

Place chicken breasts in large zip top plastic bag and pour half of dressing in bag. Seal and chill at least 2 hours. Set aside remaining dressing. Preheat grill. Remove chicken from bag and grill on medium high heat, 6 minutes per side, or until center of chicken is no longer pink. Chop chicken into bite-sized pieces and set aside.

Place vegetables in grill basket and grill, stirring often, until onions are tender (about 15 to 20 minutes).

Place pasta in large serving bowl. Add chicken and vegetables, tossing gently to combine. Toss with remaining dressing and sprinkle with Romano cheese. Serve warm.

BALSAMIC DRESSING

½ cup balsamic vinegar

½ cup extra virgin olive oil

2 teaspoons lemon juice

1 teaspoon dried basil

1 teaspoon dried tarragon

½ teaspoon salt

In mixing bowl, whisk together vinegar, oil, lemon juice, basil, tarragon, and salt.

Krista's Favorite Chicken Salad

1 (8-ounce) can pineapple chunks or tidbits, drained

⅔ cup mayonnaise

1 tablespoon Dijon mustard

¾ teaspoon curry

¼ teaspoon salt

4 to 5 cups cooked, cubed or shredded chicken

¼ cup thinly sliced celery

2 tablespoons chopped green onion

½ cup slivered almonds, toasted

⅓ cup golden raisins (optional)

Drain pineapple and reserve 2 tablespoons juice. Set pineapple aside. In mixing bowl, combine reserved juice with mayonnaise, mustard, curry, and salt; set aside. In separate mixing bowl, combine chicken, celery, green onion, almonds, pineapple, and raisins. Add mayonnaise mixture, tossing well to coat. Chill at least 1 hour. Serve on lettuce leaves or in pastry cups.

We all try to outdo one another with our chicken salad, using homemade mayonnaises and adding bacon or chopped egg to raise the "richness" quotient. But this lighter version is a winner both nutritionally and taste-wise.

Chicken and Apple Salad

A chunky chicken salad!

2 cups cubed, cooked chicken breasts

1 cup chopped Granny Smith apple

½ cup chopped celery

¼ cup raisins

2 tablespoons chopped green onions

⅓ cup low fat mayonnaise

1 tablespoon reduced fat sour cream

1 teaspoon lemon juice

¼ teaspoon salt

¼ teaspoon pepper

⅛ teaspoon cinnamon

In large mixing bowl, combine chicken, apple, celery, raisins, and green onion; set aside. In small mixing bowl, whisk together mayonnaise, sour cream, lemon juice, salt, pepper, and cinnamon. Add mayonnaise mixture to chicken mixture, tossing well to coat.

Serves 4

Savory Shrimp Salad

⅓ cup mayonnaise

2 tablespoons French dressing

1 tablespoon lemon juice

1 tablespoon minced onion

½ teaspoon salt

1 cup cooked rice, cooled

1 cup cooked, peeled, deveined shrimp

¾ cup chopped celery

½ cup chopped green bell pepper

1 tablespoon chopped olives

In small mixing bowl, whisk together mayonnaise, French dressing, lemon juice, minced onion, and salt. In large mixing bowl, combine rice and mayonnaise mixture, mixing until just moist. Fold in shrimp, celery, bell pepper, and olives. Cover and chill for at least 1 hour.

Serves 4

Shrimp's worst enemy is a heavy or lingering hand over heat, so be sure not to overcook them whether boiling or sautéing, and remember to store cooked shrimp no more than three days before using.

Graciously Good Grape Salad

8 cups green or red seedless grapes

1 (8-ounce) package cream cheese, softened

1 (8-ounce) container sour cream

½ cup sugar (or equivalent sugar substitute)

1 teaspoon pure vanilla

¾ cup brown sugar

1 cup chopped pecans

In large mixing bowl, cream together cream cheese, sour cream, and sugar with electric mixer on medium speed. Add vanilla, beating well. Add grapes, tossing gently to combine. Transfer to a large serving bowl and sprinkle with brown sugar and pecans just before serving.

Take this bridal-shower classic out of the refrigerator a few minutes before serving to allow the grapes' flavor a moment to "open up."

Congealed salads are classic indeed! Gaining popularity in the 1950s and 60s there weren't many dinners that didn't include a congealed salad of some sort, adding color, flavor and a unique texture to any meal.

Pickled Peach Salad

1 package orange gelatin

1 jar pickled peaches

1 cup fresh orange juice

1 (8-ounce) package cream cheese, softened

½ cup crushed pecans

Remove seed from pickled peaches, tearing peaches as little as possible. Bring the pickled peach juice and fresh orange juice to a boil; add the orange gelatin. Soften the cream cheese with a little of the combined juices and add the pecans. Fill the hollows made in peaches by removal of seeds with cream cheese mixture. Place a peach in each individual salad mold. Fill remainder of the mold with the gelatin mixture and allow to congeal. Serve on a bed of lettuce and garnish with slivers of orange peel.

Serves 6 to 8

Double this recipe for eight servings, triple it for twelve, and no matter the size of your dinner party, you won't need to make room in the freezer for chilling salad plates, as it's best served room temperature.

Fig, Parmesan, and Pecan Salad

½ cup balsamic vinegar

6 cups mixed salad greens

1 cup dried figs, chopped

½ cup pecan halves, toasted

½ cup celery, thinly sliced

¼ cup shaved Parmesan

3 tablespoons extra virgin olive oil

Sea salt

Freshly ground black pepper

In small saucepan over medium heat, bring vinegar to a boil. Simmer, watching closely, until reduced by half. Remove from heat and cool; set aside. In large serving bowl, combine greens, figs, pecans, celery, and Parmesan. Gently toss with oil. Divide among four salad plates and drizzle with reduced vinegar. Sprinkle with sea salt and freshly ground pepper.

Serves 4

Fluffy Mandarin Orange Salad

Children love this salad!

1 cup water

1 (3-ounce) package lemon
flavored gelatin mix

1 (3-ounce) package orange
flavored gelatin mix

2 (11-ounce) cans Mandarin
oranges, undrained

1 (20-ounce) can crushed
pineapple, undrained

1 bag miniature marshmallows

1 container frozen whipped
topping, thawed

1½ cups shredded mild Cheddar
cheese (optional)

In large saucepan over medium high heat, bring water to a boil. Dissolve gelatin mixes in boiling water, stirring well. Add oranges and pineapple. Pour into 9 x 13-inch glass dish. Top with marshmallows and chill. When firm, spread with the whipped topping. Sprinkle with Cheddar and chill.

A tried and true standard, this congealed salad is a welcome addition to any summer table and is suitable for dessert too, especially after heavier fare.

Mema's Cherry Salad

2 cups crushed pineapple,
undrained

½ cup sugar

2 tablespoons gelatin mix

¼ cup water

Juice of ½ lemon

1 (8-ounce) package cream
cheese, softened

12 maraschino cherries

2 tablespoons cherry juice

1 cup frozen whipped topping,
thawed

In saucepan over medium heat, combine pineapple and sugar. In small mixing bowl, dissolve gelatin mix in water. Add to pineapple, stirring well to combine. Stir in lemon juice. Remove from heat and cool. Stir cream cheese and cherry juice into pineapple mixture. Fold in cherries. Cool until slightly thickened. Fold in frozen whipped topping. Pour mixture into serving dish. Cover and chill until ready to serve.

Serves 4

While named for a League member's husband's great-aunt, this heavenly take on holiday cranberries "Mayberry" well have you begging for seconds.

Aunt Bea's Cranberry Salad
This is a great side dish for holiday meals!

2 cups water

1 package whole cranberries

½ cup sugar

2 (3-ounce) packages cherry gelatin mix

1 cup pineapple juice

1 cup chopped pecans

1 cup frozen whipped topping, thawed

½ package miniature marshmallows

1 (8-ounce) package cream cheese, softened

In large saucepan over medium high heat, bring water to a boil. Reduce heat to medium. Add cranberries, sugar, and gelatin mix. Stir in pineapple juice and pecans. Pour into glass dish and chill. In mixing bowl, combine frozen whipped topping and marshmallows; chill overnight. In small mixing bowl, beat cream cheese until smooth. Fold in marshmallow mixture. Spoon on top of cranberry mixture and chill until ready to serve.

Serves 12-15

Entrées

Hazel Caldwell

Entrées

Dooley's Meat Pies
Barbara Dooley

1 pound ground meat

1 medium onion, finely chopped

¼ cup pine nuts

Juice of 3 lemons

1 tablespoon Laban or plain
   yogurt

1 teaspoon salt

⅓ teaspoon pepper

Unbaked biscuit dough
   (homemade or canned)

Preheat oven to 400 degrees. In skillet over medium-high heat, cook meat and onions lightly. Remove from heat and drain off liquid. Add pine nuts, lemon juice, yogurt, salt, and pepper, stirring well to combine. Spoon meat mixture into center of each biscuit. Fold in half, pinching edges together to seal. Place on prepared baking sheet and bake 20 minutes, or until lightly browned.

Coach Richt's Favorite Manicotti
Katharyn Richt

1 box manicotti shells, cooked
   according to package
   directions

1 pound ground beef or turkey

1 large jar spaghetti sauce

1 (16-ounce) container cottage
   cheese

1 egg, beaten

1 tablespoon chopped parsley

1 teaspoon garlic salt

1 teaspoon minced onion

Preheat oven to 350 degrees. In large skillet over medium-high heat, brown ground beef or turkey. Add sauce to meat and set aside. In large mixing bowl, combine cottage cheese, egg, parsley, garlic salt, and onion. Stuff cheese mixture into manicotti shells. Spoon sauce into bottom of 9 x 13-inch baking pan. Arrange shells in single layer in baking pan. Pour remaining sauce over shells and bake 35 minutes.

Katharyn Richt, mother of four, has shown every bit as much class as the coach to whom she is married. As her husband stands on the sidelines leading our beloved Bulldogs, she's right there with him. No, not up on the front lines with husband Mark Richt, but somewhere back behind the bench, in between the linemen and the kickers, handing out water and cheering our "Dawgs" on to victory.

5 & 10 Pan Roasted French-Cut Pork Chops with Baked Beans and Roasted Pepper Agrodolce

For this wintery dish, you need to start soaking the beans the day before, brine the pork chops, and make the agrodolce. That means, for a presentation that will dazzle your guests, you only have to cook the beans and roast the pork chops the day of your dinner. Brining makes the pork much more tender and succulent. If you can find a heritage breed pork, like a Berkshire or Red Wattle, then go for it. The taste is really superior.

BAKED BEANS

2 cups white beans	1 tablespoon orange zest
Water to cover by 2 inches	2 garlic cloves, minced
4 bacon slices	½ teaspoon dry mustard
1 tablespoon fresh thyme, pulled and chopped	2 tablespoons maple syrup
	2 cups chicken stock

Soak beans in water overnight. Cook beans according to package directions the next day at least 5 hours prior to dinner. Drain beans, reserve water, and set aside.

Preheat oven to 300 degrees. Line pot with bacon slices. Combine reserved water, thyme, orange zest, garlic, dry mustard, and maple syrup. Add beans and water mixture to pot. Add enough chicken stock to bring liquid level up to one inch above beans. Bring beans to a boil.

Turn off heat and cover with lid. Place in oven and cook about 2 hours, or until beans are tender. Remove from oven and reheat when ready to serve.

ROASTED PEPPER AGRODOLCE

2 large red bell peppers	2 tablespoons water
1 tablespoon olive oil	1 tablespoon chopped parsley
¼ cup raisins	1 tablespoon balsamic vinegar
¼ cup port	Salt and pepper to taste

Preheat oven to 450 degrees. Gently rub peppers with olive oil. Roast in oven about 15 minutes, until blistering. Remove peppers from oven and, using tongs, transfer peppers to large bowl. Cover immediately with plastic wrap and let cool. This will help the skin come off easily. Remove and discard skin from peppers; discard seeds and stalk. Chop roasted pepper flesh into rough ½-inch dice, place in clean bowl, and set aside.

In small saucepan over medium heat, combine raisins, port, and water and gently plump raisins about 5 minutes.

Add raisins, parsley, and balsamic vinegar to bell pepper. Season with salt and pepper and toss gently to combine. The agrodolce can be made up to 48 hours in advance.

PORK CHOPS

2 cups apple juice
3 cups water
¼ cup kosher salt
¼ cup maple syrup
3 tablespoons coarsely ground
    black pepper

1 teaspoon cinnamon
6 (1½-inch thick) center-cut
    pork loin chops, trimmed of
    excess fat
1 tablespoon olive oil
Salt and pepper to taste

In large saucepan over medium-high heat, combine apple juice, water, salt, maple syrup, black pepper, and cinnamon and bring to a simmer. As soon as salt has completely diluted into liquid, turn off heat, and allow to cool. Place pork chops in brine for 24 hours. After 24 hours, remove pork chops from brine and pat dry.

Preheat oven to 400 degrees. In large cast iron skillet over medium-high heat, heat olive oil until warm, but do not let it smoke. Season pork chops with salt and pepper and carefully place in skillet. Sear 3 minutes per side, or until pork chops begin to caramelize. If all pork chops do not fit in the pan, then cook three at a time. Place seared chops on baking sheet and transfer to oven. Cook 8 minutes.

To plate, place a small amount of beans on each plate. Place pork chop on top of the beans and spoon about 1 tablespoon of Agrodolce on each pork chop. Drizzle with high quality olive oil and eat away!

Serves 6

Famed chef Hugh Acheson has brought gourmet to Athens with his establishments 5 &10 Restaurant in Five Points, his Gosford Wine shop at Alps and his newest restaurant, The National, located in the heart of downtown Athens.

Known for incorporating locally grown food into his dishes, he succeeds in "merging soul food with Old World Cuisine." His food has been featured in some prominent gourmet magazines and his dishes have been labeled "Contemporary American with influences from France and Italy."

How wonderful it is that he offers Athenians and visitors the opportunity to experience such a wonderful culinary delight.

DePalma's has been serving Athens for 20 years and is a favorite eatery for three generations of Athenians. While pasta dishes, like homemade lasagna, are this restaurant's specialty, their homemade breadsticks and pizza are also wonderful. You can enjoy a wide range of wines from their mostly Italian list or opt for one of their unique microbrew beer selections.

DePalma's Penne Charmaine

This recipe goes great with garlic bread and a Caesar salad.

½ cup chopped fresh spinach

½ heaping cup chopped vine-ripened tomatoes

⅛ cup sun-dried tomatoes

1 (8-ounce) can chopped tomato fillets

⅓ cup grated Parmesan

⅛ cup chopped scallions

1 tablespoon seeded and chopped jalapeño

1 tablespoon lime juice

1 tablespoon freshly chopped garlic

¼ cup fresh basil, chopped

⅓ cup extra virgin olive oil

Salt and pepper to taste

1 quart whipping cream

1½ pounds fresh penne or other similar pasta, cooked according to package directions and drained

In large saucepan over medium-high heat, combine spinach, tomatoes, tomato fillets, Parmesan, scallions, jalapeños, lime juice, garlic, basil, olive oil, salt, pepper, and whipping cream. Bring sauce to a gentle boil and simmer 15 minutes, or until sauce is reduced by almost half. Toss pasta in sauce to coat. This sauce has a moderate heat—use more or less jalapeños to your taste.

Serves 6

On February 14, 1986, Harry Bissett's New Orleans Café and Oyster Bar first opened its doors for business, offering a variety of traditional Cajun/Creole fare along with original dishes inspired by the rich culinary traditions of Louisiana. Many of Harry Bissett's original menu items are still offered today, dishes such as, Oysters Rockefeller, Oysters Bienville, Seafood Gumbo, Shrimp Creole, Filet Mignon Au Poivre, Trout Almondine, and Blackened Fish.

Harry Bissett's Shrimp Rémoulade

1 celery stalk

2 green onions

¼ cup freshly chopped parsley

¼ cup prepared horseradish

1 tablespoon Creole mustard

2 teaspoons chopped garlic

1 teaspoon paprika

¼ cup red wine vinegar

1 cup mayonnaise

1 tablespoon ketchup

2 cups olive oil

2 pounds large shrimp, boiled and cooled

Chopped iceberg lettuce

Lemon, quartered

Combine celery, onion, parsley, horseradish, mustard, garlic, paprika, vinegar, mayonnaise, and ketchup in bowl of food processor; process until smooth. Add olive oil slowly until completely incorporated. Pour over shrimp in large mixing bowl, tossing well to coat. Serve over lettuce and garnish with lemon wedges.

Fire and Flavor Planked Salmon with Asian Marinade

2 tablespoons minced garlic, about 2 cloves

2 tablespoons soy sauce

2 tablespoons finely chopped fresh parsley

1 tablespoon freshly grated ginger

¼ cup extra virgin olive oil

Freshly ground black pepper to taste

1½ pounds salmon fillets or 4 (6-ounce) salmon fillets

1 large cedar grilling plank, soaked in water

1 small orange, thinly sliced, for garnish

2 tablespoons finely chopped scallions

1 tablespoon sesame seeds, toasted

Combine garlic, soy sauce, parsley, ginger, olive oil, and black pepper in plastic zip top bag, shaking well to combine. Add salmon to marinade, seal bag, and chill 15 minutes, turning once. Heat grill to 350 degrees and place soaked plank on grill. Close lid and heat 3 minutes. Remove salmon from marinade and discard marinade. Using tongs, flip plank; place salmon on plank and arrange orange slices on top of salmon, overlapping slightly. Grill with lid closed 12 to 15 minutes, or until medium rare. Remove plank and salmon from grill and allow to rest 3 minutes. Sprinkle with scallions and sesame seeds just before serving.

Serves 4

Cedar planks infuse salmon with a delicious smoky flavor and keep fish moist and tender. You can find grilling planks in the seafood department or charcoal aisle of most grocery stores.

Mama's Boy Salmon Cakes

¾ pound grilled skinless salmon

1 teaspoon chopped capers

3 celery stalks, minced

¾ cup minced yellow onion

1 teaspoon dry dill weed

1 teaspoon dry English mustard

½ cup cornmeal

¾ cup mayonnaise

Salt and pepper to taste

Cornmeal

Allow salmon to cool after grilling. Gently flake salmon with fork and set aside. In large mixing bowl, combine capers, celery, onion, dill weed, mustard, and ½ cup cornmeal. Fold in flaked salmon. Slowly mix in mayonnaise. Gently shape mixture into 6 equal-portioned cakes. Roll cakes in bowl of cornmeal seasoned with salt and pepper, until thoroughly coated and cake holds its shape, but is not stiff. Heat cooking oil in skillet over medium-high heat. Carefully place cakes in hot oil (in batches, if necessary) and cook until golden brown on each side.

Mama's Boy is a locally owned Athens restaurant. They offer freshly prepared meals at affordable prices and are conveniently located near downtown, the Classic Center, and the North Oconee Greenway. New versions of old timey Southern dishes like Buttermilk Fried Chicken Breast, Salmon Croquettes, and Mama's Boy Meatloaf take on a whole new attitude. And their Cheese Grits and Georgia Peach Stuffed French Toast are out of this world.

R.E.M.'s Veggie Lasagna

Lasagna noodles, prepared according to package directions

3 cups shredded mozzarella cheese, divided

Sauce

Filling

Preheat oven to 350 degrees. Spoon thin layer of sauce over bottom of 9 x 13-inch baking dish. Layer noodles lengthwise, covering entire surface. Spoon more sauce over noodles and cover with one-third of spinach mixture. Sprinkle with 1 cup mozzarella. Repeat layering of sauce, spinach mixture, and mozzarella two more times. Bake 45 minutes.

SAUCE

2 (15-ounce) cans Italian diced tomatoes

1 (28-ounce) can tomato purée

¼ cup fresh parsley, chopped

2 teaspoons minced garlic

½ teaspoon oregano

½ teaspoon basil

½ teaspoon salt

½ teaspoon cracked black pepper

In stockpot over medium-high heat, combine tomatoes, purée, parsley, garlic, oregano, basil, salt, and pepper. Simmer 20 minutes.

FILLING

1 (15-ounce) container ricotta cheese

2 eggs

Salt and pepper to taste

Pinch of red pepper flakes

2 pounds fresh mushrooms, cleaned and sliced

1 bag baby spinach

In large mixing bowl, combine ricotta, eggs, salt, pepper, and red pepper flakes. Fold in mushrooms and spinach, mixing well to combine.

Secret ingredient: 2 splashes of red wine over lasagna to keep moist.

Coach Butts' Favorite Country Captain

2 Spanish onions, finely minced

2 green bell peppers, finely minced

¼ bunch parsley, finely minced

1 tablespoon butter

3 tablespoons cooking oil

1 (4 to 5-pound) chicken fryer, cut into pieces

¾ cup all-purpose flour

1 (28-ounce) can whole peeled tomatoes, undrained

1 garlic clove, mashed

1 teaspoon salt

½ tablespoon curry powder

¼ teaspoon dried thyme

¼ pound slivered almonds

½ cup currants (or raisins)

2 cups uncooked rice, prepared according to package directions

In pan over medium-high heat, sauté onions, peppers, and parsley in butter.

In large skillet over medium-high heat, heat cooking oil. Dredge chicken pieces in flour and carefully fry in hot oil. Add onion mixture to chicken. Add tomatoes, garlic, salt, curry, and thyme; cook 2 to 3 hours, or until chicken falls from bone. Add water as needed. Add currants and almonds. Serve chicken in center of cooked rice.

This is a recipe from the kitchen of Mrs. Wallace Butts.
This was one of her husband's favorite dishes.

Creamy Southern Chicken

1 (8-ounce) package cream cheese, softened

1 (10¾-ounce) can cream of chicken soup

1 tablespoon poppy seeds

1 tablespoon pepper

1 cup shredded Cheddar cheese

3 cups cooked chicken, cubed

1½ cups round buttery crackers, crushed

4 tablespoons butter, melted

Preheat oven to 350 degrees. In large mixing bowl, combine cream cheese, soup, poppy seeds, pepper, and cheese. Fold in chicken, mixing well to combine. Pour into prepared 9 x 13-inch baking dish. In small bowl, combine crackers and butter. Sprinkle on top of chicken. Bake, uncovered, 30 minutes.

Serves 4-6

James Wallace "Wally" Butts Jr. coached the University of Georgia football team from 1939 to 1960, leading the Bulldogs to four SEC titles, one undefeated season, and eight bowl games. His intense desire to win, knowledge of the game, and innovative techniques—including a devastating passing game—made him a coaching legend even before he retired.

Despite all good intentions, how much soup can a person under the weather realistically consume? The mild goodness of this dish makes it perfect to take over!

Crunchy Chicken Casserole

Great dish to take to a housewarming or to a "new mom."

½ cup sour cream

½ cup mayonnaise

1 (10¾-ounce) can cream of chicken soup

3 cups cooked chicken, chopped

1 cup shredded Monterey Jack or Cheddar cheese

½ cup slivered almonds

2 cups celery, finely chopped

1 (8-ounce) can water chestnuts, drained and chopped

1½ cups cooked rice

1½ cups French fried onion rings

Preheat oven to 350 degrees. In large mixing bowl, whisk together sour cream, mayonnaise, and soup. Fold in chicken, cheese, almonds, celery, water chestnuts, and rice. Pour into prepared 11 x 7-inch baking dish. Bake 40 minutes. Remove from oven and sprinkle with onion rings. Return to oven and bake 5 more minutes.

Serves 6

If you, like many people, dislike the texture of cooked celery, substitute one teaspoon each of celery salt and onion powder for an equally flavorful version of this hearty casserole.

Chicken Tetrazzini

1 small onion, chopped

½ pound mushrooms

2 tablespoons butter or margarine

2 (10¾-ounce) cans cream of mushroom soup

1½ cups shredded Cheddar cheese, divided

1 tablespoon sour cream

3 cups cooked chicken, shredded

4 ounces sliced pimentos, drained

1 (16-ounce) package spaghetti, broken and cooked al dente

1 cup chicken stock

Salt and pepper to taste

Preheat oven to 350 degrees. In large saucepan over medium high heat, sauté onion and mushrooms in butter. Stir in soup and reduce heat to low. Add 1 cup cheese, stirring until cheese melts. Stir in sour cream. Fold in chicken, pimento, and spaghetti. Add chicken stock, stirring well to combine. Season with salt and pepper to taste. Pour into prepared 9 x 13-inch baking dish. Sprinkle with remaining ½ cup cheese. Bake 25 to 35 minutes or until bubbly.

Serves 6-8

For those whose palates are sensitive to bolder flavors, an equal portion of marinated roasted peppers may be substituted for the pimentos without sacrificing anything that this dish derives from its Italian inspiration. Similarly, shredded mozzarella works as well here as the Cheddar does.

Chicken Boudini à la Bloomfield

1 large Vidalia onion, peeled and
    cut into 4 wedges

3 large chicken breasts, rinsed

6 large chicken thighs, rinsed

1 (10.5-ounce) can chicken stock

½ carrot, peeled and sliced

½ celery stalk, trimmed and
    sliced

1 garlic clove, minced

¼ teaspoon thyme

1 bay leaf

Water

Salt and pepper to taste

1 stick butter, divided

2 cups fresh mushrooms, sliced

1 cup slivered almonds

6 tablespoons all-purpose flour

4 cups whole milk

1 cup shredded sharp Cheddar
    cheese

½ cup dry sherry, or to taste

Dash of nutmeg

2 egg yolks, beaten

Cooked rice, egg noodles, or
    pastry cup

Paprika

Set aside 3 onion wedges and coarsely chop 1 wedge. Place chopped onion in large stockpot. Add chicken, stock, carrot, celery, garlic, thyme, and bay leaf to stockpot. Add enough water to cover chicken. Bring to a boil and cook until chicken is done. Remove chicken from stockpot and set aside to cool. Strain the chicken stock and return liquid to stockpot. Remove and discard bay leaf. Purée vegetables in food processor with small amount of stock. Set aside.

When the chicken is cool, remove skin. Debone chicken and cut into bite-sized pieces. Lightly season with salt and pepper and set aside.

In skillet over medium high heat, melt 1 tablespoon butter. Add mushrooms and sauté 5 minutes. Remove from heat, transfer mushrooms to bowl, and set aside. Melt 1 tablespoon butter in skillet and sauté almonds 5 minutes, or until lightly browned. Remove from heat, transfer almonds to bowl, and set aside.

Finely chop remaining onion wedges. Melt 5 tablespoons butter in same stockpot. Add onions and sauté 5 minutes over medium heat. Stir in flour, stirring 5 minutes. Stir in milk and 1 cup chicken stock. Increase heat to high, stirring constantly 2 minutes. Reduce heat to medium and stir until mixture starts to thicken. Reduce heat to low.

Add puréed vegetables, chicken, and sautéed mushrooms and almonds. Stir in Cheddar cheese. Add sherry and nutmeg.

In small mixing bowl, combine small amount of cooled soup mixture to egg yolks, making sure yolks do not curdle. Add yolk mixture to stockpot, stirring constantly until well combined. Serve over rice or egg noodles or in pastry cup. Sprinkle with paprika.

Boudinis have always been a traditional favorite for entertaining in Athens, dating back to before the Civil War. Boudinis are a form of creamed chicken enriched with egg yolks. Sometimes this dish is served over noodles or rice or in a pie shell.

There was a famous local caterer known for her Boudini, but no matter what your social status, every woman worth her salt in Athens had a Boudini in her cookbook.

If a southern cookbook seems long on chicken dishes, it's because we eat a lot of it. Athens is a mere hour's drive from Gainesville, Georgia, the "Poultry Capital of the World." Amusingly, some native Italian chefs view our beloved bird as "peasant food," fighting words in Gainesville: The Queen City of the Northeast Georgia Mountains.

Bruschetta Chicken Bake

1 (14½-ounce) can diced tomatoes, undrained

1 package herb-seasoned stuffing mix

½ cup water

2 garlic cloves, minced

Olive oil

1½ pounds boneless skinless chicken breasts, cut into bite-sized pieces

1 teaspoon basil

Pinch of salt

Dash of pepper

1 cup shredded mozzarella cheese

Preheat oven to 400 degrees. In mixing bowl, combine tomatoes, stuffing mix, water, and garlic. Drizzle with small amount of oil; set aside. Place chicken in prepared 9 x 13-inch baking dish and sprinkle with basil, salt, pepper, and cheese. Top with stuffing mixture. Bake 30 minutes, or until chicken is no longer pink.

Serves 4

Chicken and Spinach Enchiladas

1 to 1½ pounds cooked chicken breasts, shredded

1 (10-ounce) package frozen chopped spinach, thawed and drained

1 large can enchilada sauce, divided

1 (16-ounce) container reduced-fat sour cream, divided

1 (8-ounce) package shredded Monterey Jack cheese, divided

8 to 10 (8-inch) flour tortillas

Preheat oven to 350 degrees. In large mixing bowl, combine chicken, spinach, half of enchilada sauce, half of sour cream, and half of cheese. Spoon mixture down center of each tortilla and arrange in single layer seam side down in prepared 9 x 13-inch baking dish. Cover with remaining enchilada sauce and top with remaining cheese. Bake 30 minutes. Remove from heat and let stand 5 minutes before serving. Top with remaining sour cream and serve.

Serves 4-6

Creamy Chicken Enchiladas

1 tablespoon butter

1 medium onion, chopped

1 (4½-ounce) can chopped green chilies, drained

1 (8-ounce) package cream cheese, softened and cubed

3½ cups chopped, cooked chicken breasts

8 (8-inch) flour tortillas

2 (8-ounce) packages Monterey Jack cheese, shredded

2 cups whipping cream

Preheat oven to 350 degrees. In large skillet over medium heat, melt butter. Add onion and sauté 5 minutes. Add chilies and sauté 1 minute. Stir in cream cheese and chicken. Cook, stirring constantly until cheese melts. Spoon 2 to 3 tablespoons chicken mixture down center of each tortilla. Roll up tortillas and place seam side down in lightly prepared 13 x 9-inch baking dish. Sprinkle with cheese and drizzle with whipping cream. Bake 45 minutes or until cheese is lightly browned.

Serves 4-5

Sizzlin' Chicken Enchilada Casserole

2 (10¾-ounce) cans cream of chicken soup

1½ cups low-sodium chicken stock

2 (4½-ounce) cans chopped green chilies, drained

1 cup chopped onion

1 cup sour cream

1 teaspoon salt

¾ teaspoon cumin

¾ teaspoon freshly ground black pepper

1 garlic clove, minced

24 (6-inch) corn tortillas

4 cups shredded, cooked chicken breast (about 1 pound)

2 cups finely shredded sharp Cheddar cheese

Preheat oven to 350 degrees. In large saucepan over medium high heat, whisk together soup, chicken stock, chilies, onion, sour cream, salt, cumin, pepper, and garlic. Bring to a boil, stirring constantly. Remove from heat. Spread 1 cup sour cream mixture into prepared 9 x 13-inch baking dish. Dip 6 tortillas in mixture with tongs to moisten each side. Arrange tortillas over mixture and top with 1 cup chicken and ½ cup cheese. Repeat layers 3 times, ending with cheese. Spread remaining mixture over cheese and bake 30 minutes or until bubbly.

Serves 12

MARGARITA FRUIT SALAD

1 cantaloupe, cut into small pieces

1 honeydew melon, cut into small pieces

4 small oranges, peeled and sectioned

3 cups strawberries, hulled and halved

½ cup sugar

½ cup orange juice

¼ cup tequila

¼ cup Grand Marnier™

3 tablespoons lime juice

1 cup unsweetened coconut, toasted

In mixing bowl, combine cantaloupe, melon, oranges, and strawberries and set aside. In small saucepan over medium heat, heat sugar and orange juice over medium heat. Stir 3 minutes, or until sugar dissolves. Stir in tequila, Grand Marnier™, and lime juice. Let cool. Gently toss with fruit. Chill at least 4 hours. Just before serving, sprinkle with coconut.

Serves 8 to 12

Spicy Chicken and Rice

½ cup chicken stock

1 (10¾-ounce) can cream of mushroom soup

1 cup sour cream

2 (4-ounce) cans green chilies, drained

2 cups shredded sharp Cheddar cheese

3 cups cooked chicken, chopped

1 package chicken-flavored instant rice mix, prepared according to package directions

1 (6-ounce) can French fried onion rings

Preheat oven to 350 degrees. In large mixing bowl, combine stock, soup, sour cream, chilies, and cheese. Fold in chicken and rice. Pour into prepared 11 x 7-inch baking dish and bake 30 to 40 minutes. Remove from oven and sprinkle with onion rings. Return to oven and bake 3 more minutes.

Southern Chicken Divan

3 tablespoons butter, divided

3 tablespoons all-purpose flour

2 teaspoons chicken bouillon

2 cups milk

½ cup mayonnaise

2 tablespoons spicy brown mustard

1 (16-ounce) package frozen broccoli florets

3 cups cooked chicken, shredded

½ cup shredded Cheddar cheese

½ cup plain bread crumbs

Preheat oven to 350 degrees. In medium saucepan over medium-high heat, melt 2 tablespoons butter. Add flour and bouillon; stir in milk. Cook until mixture boils and thickens, stirring constantly. Add mayonnaise and mustard, stirring until blended. Remove from heat. Spread broccoli in ungreased 2-quart baking dish. Top with chicken. Spoon sauce over chicken and sprinkle with cheese. In small mixing bowl, combine bread crumbs and remaining 1 tablespoon melted butter. Sprinkle on top of cheese. Bake 30 to 35 minutes.

Serves 6

Company Chicken

Great with white rice, using sauce as gravy.

6 boneless, skinless chicken
  breasts

1 (10¾-ounce) can cream of
  mushroom soup

1 packet dry onion soup mix

1 (8-ounce) carton heavy
  whipping cream

1 to 2 tablespoons paprika

Preheat oven to 350 degrees. Place chicken in 9 x 13-inch baking dish. In small bowl, combine soup and dry soup mix. Whisk in whipping. Pour over chicken. Bake 1 hour.

Serves 4-6

Chicken Gorgonzola

2 cups penne pasta, uncooked

2 teaspoons olive oil

½ cup chopped onions

1 teaspoon sugar

1 (14.5-ounce) can diced
  tomatoes

½ pound cooked chicken,
  chopped

1½ cups chicken stock

¼ cup whipping cream

2 garlic cloves, minced

1 teaspoon salt

1 (5-ounce) package Gorgonzola
  cheese

½ cup freshly chopped basil

In large saucepan over medium high heat, cook pasta 15 minutes. While pasta cooks, heat oil in small skillet over medium heat. Add onions and sugar, cooking and stirring 2 to 3 minutes, or until onions are tender. Remove from heat and set aside. Drain and rinse pasta; transfer to large skillet. Add tomatoes and cook over medium heat 1 minute. Add chicken, stock, cream, and garlic; tossing gently to combine. Cook and stir 5 minutes, or until sauce slightly thickens. Add onion, salt, Gorgonzola, and basil. Cook 2 minutes, stirring occasionally.

Serves 6-8

Poppy Seed Chicken

3 pounds boneless, skinless
    chicken breasts, cooked and
    coarsely chopped

1 (10¾-ounce) can cream of
    mushroom soup

1 (8-ounce) container sour cream

1 tablespoon poppy seeds

1 garlic clove, minced

Salt and pepper to taste

1½ cups round buttery crackers,
    crushed

1 stick butter, melted

Preheat oven to 350 degrees. Arrange chicken in 9 x 13-inch glass casserole. In large mixing bowl, combine soup, sour cream, poppy seeds, garlic, salt, and pepper. Pour over chicken. Sprinkle with crushed crackers. Drizzle with melted butter. Bake 30 minutes.

Serves 6-8

> *This casserole may also be frozen. If frozen, let stand
> 1 hour at room temperature before baking.*

Herb-Encrusted Chicken

2 tablespoons lemon juice

1 teaspoon paprika

1 cup reduced-fat sour cream

2 teaspoons Worcestershire sauce

1 teaspoon celery salt

8 boneless, skinless chicken
    breasts

Italian-seasoned bread crumbs

8 tablespoons butter, melted

Preheat oven to 350 degrees. In large mixing bowl, combine lemon juice, paprika, sour cream, Worcestershire sauce, and celery salt. Dip chicken into sour cream mixture. Dredge chicken in bread crumbs. Roll up chicken and secure with toothpick. Arrange chicken in a 9 x 13-inch baking pan. Chill 30 minutes. Pour melted butter over chicken. Bake 45 minutes to 1 hour. Remove toothpicks before serving.

Serves 8

Southern Fried Chicken

2 to 3 pound chicken fryer, cut up

Milk and flour (enough to batter the chicken)

Salt and pepper

Oil for frying

Prepare chicken, separate, and lay out for frying. Salt well. Drain off excess water. Sprinkle with pepper. Dip each piece of chicken into milk, then into flour. Cook in hot oil (enough to cover chicken) until golden brown. Turn chicken so that each piece browns evenly. When cooked thoroughly, remove from frying pan to a hot platter. Drain most of the fat, leaving about ¼ cup to make gravy.

GRAVY

¼ cup reserved fat from fried chicken

2 tablespoons butter

6 tablespoons self-rising flour

2 cups cream

Mix fat, butter, and flour in the same skillet where the chicken was fried. Brown slightly, stirring constantly. Add milk and season with salt and pepper. Simmer 8 to 10 minutes.

Garrard's Homecoming Chicken

1 cup brown sugar

⅔ cup olive oil

½ cup cider vinegar

6 garlic cloves, minced

4 tablespoons stone ground mustard

3 tablespoons lemon juice

3 tablespoons lime juice

6 boneless, skinless chicken breasts, cut into large strips

In large mixing bowl, combine sugar, oil, vinegar, garlic, mustard, and juices. Pour over chicken strips and marinate overnight. Preheat grill and cook 6 to 8 minutes per each side, or until chicken is no longer pink in center.

Serves 6

FRIED GREEN TOMATOES

3 or 4 medium-sized green tomatoes, washed, cored, and sliced (do not peel)

Cooking oil

Cornmeal or flour, seasoned to taste with salt and pepper

1 egg

1 cup milk

Grease skillet with cooking oil and heat over medium heat. Spread thin layer of cornmeal on foil. In mixing bowl, beat together egg and milk. Dip each tomato slice in egg mixture. Dredge slice in cornmeal, creating a thin layer of batter. Place tomato slices in skillet and brown on both sides. Serve hot.

Saucy Soba Noodles with Broccoli and Chicken

1 (8.2-ounce) package soba noodles with soy ginger sauce

1 tablespoon cooking oil, divided

¾ pound chicken breast, cut into bite-sized pieces

1½ teaspoons dark sesame oil

3 cups quartered mushrooms

3 cups broccoli florets

1 red bell pepper, seeded and cut into 1-inch strips

1 tablespoon bottled ground fresh ginger

2 garlic cloves, minced

Cook noodles according to package directions. In large nonstick skillet over medium high heat, heat 2 teaspoons cooking oil. Add chicken and cook 4 minutes, or until chicken is no longer pink. Transfer chicken to plate and set aside. Heat sesame oil and 1 teaspoon cooking oil in same skillet over medium high heat. Add mushrooms, broccoli, bell pepper, ginger and garlic; cook 4 minutes, or until broccoli is slightly tender. Return chicken to skillet. Stir in half of soy ginger sauce from meal kit. Cook 1 minute, or until thoroughly heated. In large serving bowl, toss chicken and broccoli mixture with noodles. Stir in remaining soy ginger sauce and mix well.

Serves 4

PARMESAN PERKS

Parmesan cheese contains less fat than many cheeses – that's what makes it a hard cheese. Hard cheeses are higher in calcium. One ounce of freshly-grated Parmesan cheese contains a bone-strengthening 226 milligrams of calcium. Parmesan also packs a lot of flavor. That's what makes it a favorite pasta topper.

Chicken Marsala

6 boneless, skinless chicken breasts

Salt and pepper to taste

½ cup all-purpose flour

1½ sticks margarine, divided

¾ cup Marsala wine

1 cup chicken stock

1 cup shredded mozzarella cheese

½ cup shredded Parmesan

½ cup sliced mushrooms

Preheat oven to 350 degrees. Flatten chicken breasts to ⅛-inch thickness. Season with salt and pepper to taste. Dredge in flour. In skillet over medium high heat, sauté chicken in 1 stick margarine 3 to 4 minutes per side. Remove from heat and transfer chicken to prepared 13 x 9-inch baking dish. Stir wine and chicken stock into skillet drippings. Simmer 10 minutes. In small sauté pan over medium heat, sauté mushrooms in remaining 4 tablespoons margarine. Spoon mushrooms over chicken. Combine cheeses and sprinkle over mushrooms and chicken. Cover with sauce and bake 10 to 12 minutes. Remove from heat and place under broiler 1 to 2 minutes.

Easy Weeknight Chicken Pot Pie

4 boneless, skinless chicken breasts, chopped

1 (15-ounce) can mixed vegetables, drained

1 (15-ounce) can English peas, drained

1 (10¾-ounce) can cream of chicken soup

1 (10-ounce) can chicken stock

1 stick butter, softened

1 cup all-purpose flour

1 cup milk

Preheat oven to 375 degrees. In large mixing bowl, combine chicken, mixed vegetables, peas, soup, and stock. Pour into 3-quart baking dish. Combine butter, flour, and milk in blender and pulse until smooth. Pour over chicken and vegetables. Bake 30 to 45 minutes, or until crust is golden brown.

Mediterranean Chicken

Fast and easy!

1½ pounds boneless, skinless chicken breast, cut into bite-sized pieces

Salt and pepper to taste

3 teaspoons olive oil, divided

4 garlic cloves, minced

1 can chickpeas, drained and rinsed

1 cup water

4 Roma tomatoes, sliced ½-inch thick

2 tablespoons chopped, pitted kalamata olives

1 teaspoon white wine vinegar

Roasted garlic and olive oil flavored couscous, prepared according to package directions

Season chicken with salt and pepper. In large nonstick skillet over medium high heat, heat 2 teaspoons olive oil. Add chicken and cook until golden (3 to 4 minutes) and no longer pink. Transfer chicken to serving plate.

Reduce heat to medium low. Add remaining 1 teaspoon oil to skillet. Add garlic and sauté until fragrant. Add chickpeas and water. Bring to a boil and cook until liquid is reduced by half.

Add tomatoes and cook over medium heat about 3 to 4 minutes. Add olives, vinegar, and chicken, tossing until thoroughly heated. Serve over couscous. This dish may also be served over polenta, warm spinach, or grits.

Serves 4

Barbecued Chicken

2 whole chickens, cut into pieces
    or 8 boneless, skinless
    chicken breasts

3 tablespoons ketchup

2 tablespoons vinegar

1 tablespoon lemon juice

2 tablespoons Worcestershire
    sauce

4 tablespoons water

2 tablespoons butter, melted

3 tablespoons brown sugar

1 teaspoon dry mustard

1 teaspoon chili powder

1 teaspoon paprika

½ teaspoon black pepper

Preheat oven to 500 degrees. Wash chickens and pat dry. Place pieces, skin side up, in baking pan. In large mixing bowl, whisk together ketchup, vinegar, juice, Worcestershire, water, butter, brown sugar, mustard, chili powder, paprika, and pepper. Pour mixture over chicken and coat well. Cover pan with foil seal tightly. Bake 15 minutes. Reduce heat to 375 degrees and bake 1 hour, 20 minutes, or until done. Remove foil and baste chicken with sauce in bottom of pan. Place under broiler to brown.

Soft-Shell Crabs

These are heavenly in the morning with scrambled eggs, on a po'-boy at lunch, and especially for dinner. Fresh soft-shell crabs are of course best, and although they must be cleaned before cooking many places will do this for you. With frozen crabs, look for a nice size and proportion, both claws, and no freezer burn.

4 tablespoons butter

2 tablespoons lemon juice

4 soft-shell crabs, cleaned

1½ cups shrimp fry mix

Greek seasoning to taste

Paprika to taste

Cayenne to taste (optional)

In small skillet over medium heat, melt butter. Stir in lemon juice. Transfer to shallow bowl. Dip crabs in mixture, covering both sides. In separate bowl, combine Greek seasoning, paprika, and cayenne. Dredge crabs in seasoning, then transfer to skillet. Add remaining butter mixture. Sauté 4 to 5 minutes per side, or until golden brown. Remove from skillet and serve immediately.

Serves 2

Deviled Crab

1 stick butter

1 pound claw crabmeat, frozen or
    fresh

2 egg yolks, lightly beaten

1 medium onion, finely chopped

2 tablespoons flour

½ cup milk

Salt and pepper to taste

1 teaspoon Worcestershire sauce

Preheat oven to 350 degrees. Melt butter in a 2-quart boiler. Sauté onions in butter until yellow. Mix flour and milk together to make paste. Add slightly beaten egg yolks and milk paste to butter and onions. Cook over low heat 5 minutes, stirring constantly. Add crabmeat and Worcestershire sauce; stir and cook slowly for 20 minutes. Add salt and pepper to taste. Place in crab shells and brown 15 minutes.

Serves 4

Grouper Piccata

4 grouper fillets

Salt and pepper to taste

½ cup all-purpose flour

¼ cup extra virgin olive oil

1 garlic clove, minced

½ cup white wine

½ cup chicken stock

Juice of ½ lemon

1 tablespoon capers, rinsed and
    dried

3 tablespoons butter

2 tablespoons freshly chopped
    parsley

Lemon slices

Preheat oven to 250 degrees. Season both sides of grouper with salt and pepper. Dredge fish in flour. Heat oil in nonstick skillet over medium high heat. Add fish and sauté until lightly browned (about 2 minutes per side). Remove fish from skillet, place in oven-safe serving dish, and transfer to oven to keep warm. Add garlic to same skillet over medium high heat and sauté 15 seconds. Add wine and simmer until reduced by half. Stir in chicken stock and lemon juice. Simmer 3 to 4 minutes. Add capers and simmer 1 additional minute. Remove from heat and add butter, stirring until melted; stir in parsley. Remove fish from oven and pour sauce over fish. Garnish with lemon slices.

Serves 4

Coastal Shrimp & Grits

2 tablespoons minced garlic

2 to 3 tablespoons butter

1 small red onion, chopped

1 red bell pepper, seeded and diced

1 yellow pepper, seeded and diced

1 package real bacon bits

1½ pounds small shrimp, cooked, peeled, and deveined

1 package quick cooking grits

Milk

1 (8-ounce) package cream cheese, cubed

1 (8-ounce) package shredded sharp Cheddar cheese

1 tablespoon butter

Salt and pepper taste

In large skillet over medium heat, sauté garlic in butter, stirring until butter melts. Add onion and sauté 3 to 4 minutes. Add red and yellow peppers and sauté 6 to 8 minutes. Add bacon bits and shrimp and heat until shrimp is warm. Serve over grits below.

Prepare 4 to 6 servings of grits according to package directions. When grits start to thicken, stir in a splash of milk. Cover and simmer 1 to 2 minutes. Stir in cream cheese, cover, and simmer 2 minutes. Stir in Cheddar cheese and butter. Season with salt and pepper to taste. Cover and simmer 2 minutes before serving with shrimp.

Serves 4

Herbed Linguine with Shrimp

½ cup half-and-half

3 tablespoons freshly chopped basil

2 tablespoons freshly chopped parsley

2 tablespoons shredded Parmesan

¼ teaspoon salt

½ (8-ounce) package linguine, cooked al dente

½ pound, medium shrimp, cooked and peeled

¼ cup sour cream

In large nonstick skillet over medium heat, combine half-and-half, basil, parsley, Parmesan, and salt. Add linguine, tossing gently to coat. Cook 5 minutes; stir in shrimp. Cook 1 minute, or until thoroughly heated. Remove from heat and stir in sour cream.

2 servings

Crab Tortellini

1 tablespoon minced garlic

2 tablespoons extra virgin olive oil

4 tablespoons butter

1 bundle fresh asparagus, cut

1 jar roasted red peppers, drained and chopped

½ pound fresh lump crabmeat

½ cup herb-seasoned stuffing mix

2 packages fresh, stuffed tortellini, prepared according to package directions

In large skillet over medium heat, sauté garlic in olive oil and butter. Stir until butter melts. Add asparagus and roasted red peppers. Sauté 5 to 6 minutes. Add crabmeat and stuffing mix. Sauté until crab is golden brown (about 3 to 4 minutes). Add more butter if mixture begins to dry out. Toss tortellini with half of Roasted Red Pepper Cream Sauce. Top pasta with crab mixture and pour remaining sauce on top.

ROASTED RED PEPPER CREAM SAUCE

1 jar roasted red peppers, drained and chopped

1 package hollandaise sauce mix, prepared according to package directions

½ cup half-and-half

Purée roasted red peppers, hollandaise sauce, and half-and-half in blender.

Serves 4

Basil Shrimp with Feta and Orzo

½ cup orzo, uncooked

2 teaspoons olive oil, divided

1 cup chopped tomato

¾ cup sliced green onions

½ cup crumbled feta cheese

½ teaspoon lemon zest

1 tablespoon freshly squeezed lemon juice

¼ teaspoon salt

¼ teaspoon black pepper

¾ pound large shrimp, peeled and deveined

¼ cup freshly chopped basil

Preheat oven to 450 degrees. Coat inside of foil oven bag with cooking spray. Place bag in deep baking sheet. Cook pasta in boiling water, about 5 minutes, and drain. Place pasta in large bowl. Stir in 1 teaspoon oil, tomato, green onion, feta, zest, juice, salt, and pepper, tossing gently to combine. Place orzo mixture in oven bag. Toss shrimp with basil. Arrange shrimp over orzo. Fold over edge of bag to seal. Bake 25 minutes, or until shrimp turn pink. Remove from oven, cut open bag, and peel back foil. Drizzle with remaining 1 teaspoon olive oil. Serve immediately.

Serves 2

Salmon Au Poivre

4 (6-ounce) salmon fillets, skin removed

¼ teaspoon salt

2 teaspoons black pepper

2 tablespoons olive oil

1 can chicken stock

2 tablespoons honey

Sprinkle salmon with salt. Lightly coat both sides with pepper. In large skillet over medium high heat, heat olive oil. Cook salmon 1 minute; turn salmon over and gradually add chicken stock. Bring to a boil and reduce heat to simmer. Cover and simmer 5 minutes, or until cooked thoroughly. Transfer to serving plate and drizzle with honey.

Serves 4

Grilled Salmon with Balsamic Glaze

½ cup balsamic vinegar

½ cup dry white wine

2 tablespoons freshly squeezed
lemon juice

2 tablespoons dark brown sugar,
firmly packed

Salt and pepper to taste

6 (5 to 6-ounce) salmon fillets

In medium saucepan over medium high heat, whisk together vinegar, wine, juice, and brown sugar. Bring to a boil and simmer until mixture has reduced to ⅓ cup (about 17 minutes). Season with salt and pepper to taste. Pour glaze over fillets in shallow baking dish. Marinate in refrigerator 2 to 3 hours. Preheat grill to medium high heat. Remove fillets from dish and reserve glaze. Place salmon on grill and cook until half done. Brush with reserved glaze and cook to desired doneness.

Serves 6

Salmon Dijon

3 salmon steaks or 1 long side of
salmon, rinsed and patted
dry

Salt and pepper to taste

1 tablespoon melted butter,
divided

½ cup pecans

¼ cup chopped parsley

2 slices day-old French bread

4 tablespoons melted butter

¼ cup Dijon mustard

¼ cup brown sugar

Preheat oven to 375 degrees. Spray 1-inch deep baking pan with nonstick cooking spray. Place salmon, skin side down, in pan. Season with salt and pepper. Brush salmon with ½ tablespoon melted butter and set aside. In food processor, combine pecans, parsley, and bread. Pulse until finely chopped and set aside. In small mixing bowl, combine 4 tablespoons butter, mustard, and brown sugar. Brush top of salmon with butter mixture. Pat bread crumb mixture on top of salmon and drizzle with remaining ½ tablespoon butter. Bake 15 minutes, or until salmon flakes with fork.

Serves 2

Choose wild for flavor. Order wild salmon, as opposed to farm raised salmon, whenever possible.

Freshness above all else. The most important consideration when buying salmon is the freshness of the fish. A farm-raised salmon that is absolutely fresh might taste far superior to a wild Alaskan salmon that's been on ice for a while.

Carolyn's Shrimp and Pasta

This recipe is quick and easy to prepare.

3 garlic cloves, minced

5 green onions, sliced

2 tablespoons olive oil

1 can artichoke hearts, chopped

6 Roma tomatoes, chopped

1 cup sliced mushrooms

¼ cup dry white wine

¼ teaspoon rosemary

¼ teaspoon salt

¼ teaspoon pepper

1 pound medium fresh shrimp, peeled

1 (8-ounce) package linguine

Shredded Parmesan to taste

In large skillet over medium high heat, cook garlic and onion in olive oil until tender. Add artichokes, tomatoes, mushrooms, wine, rosemary, salt, and pepper. Bring to a boil, reduce heat, and simmer 5 minutes. Add shrimp, cooking 3 minutes, or until shrimp turn pink. Serve over linguine and sprinkle with Parmesan.

Serves 4

LIME SALSA PICANTE

4 ripe medium plum tomatoes, finely chopped

1 large onion, peeled and diced

⅓ cup freshly squeezed lime juice

2 jalapeño peppers, seeded and minced

1 tablespoon freshly chopped cilantro

1 tablespoon freshly chopped parsley

In mixing bowl, combine tomato, onion, lime juice, jalapeño peppers, cilantro, and parsley. Stir gently and chill until serving time. Serve with baked chips or as a garnish or accompaniment with grilled chicken or fish.

Mexican Stuffed Tilapia

6 large tilapia fillets

2 teaspoons cumin

2 cups shredded Monterey Jack cheese

1 cup salsa

1 cup crushed tortilla chips

½ cup finely chopped green onion

¼ cup freshly chopped cilantro

Preheat oven to 425 degrees. Sprinkle tilapia on one side with cumin; set aside. In large mixing bowl, combine cheese, salsa, chips, green onion, and cilantro. Spread mixture over fillets and roll up, securing each fillet with a toothpick. Place in 9 x 13-inch baking pan and bake 25 minutes. Remove toothpicks before serving.

Pistol Packin' Paella on the Porch

4 boneless, skinless chicken breast halves, cut into strips

1 tablespoon olive oil

¾ cup coarsely chopped onion

½ red bell pepper, cut into strips

½ cup sliced celery, cut into 1-inch pieces

2 garlic cloves, crushed

1 (26-ounce) jar Newman's Own Diavolo Spicy Simmer Sauce©

1 (14½-ounce) can salt-free stewed tomatoes

1 teaspoon cumin

½ pound large shrimp, peeled and deveined

12 to 24 asparagus tips, cut into 3-inch pieces

1 (10-ounce) box frozen sugar snap peas or shelled green peas

2 cups instant white rice, uncooked

In heavy 6-quart saucepan over medium heat, sauté chicken in oil. Add onion, bell pepper, celery, and garlic. Add spicy sauce, tomatoes, and cumin and bring to a boil. Cover and simmer 30 minutes, stirring occasionally. Increase heat to medium high and add shrimp, asparagus, peas, and rice. Bring to a boil, cover, and remove from heat. Let stand 5 to 7 minutes before serving.

For additional flavor, add 12 ounces andouille sausage.
Cut sausage into bite-sized chunks and sauté with chicken.

Serves 8-10

Spicy BBQ Shrimp

1½ sticks butter, melted

1 cup freshly squeezed lemon juice

1 cup Worcestershire sauce

1 tablespoon salt

1 tablespoon coarsely ground black pepper

1 tablespoon hot sauce

¼ teaspoon cayenne

3 garlic cloves, minced

3 pounds unpeeled jumbo shrimp

Preheat oven to 400 degrees. In large mixing bowl, whisk together butter, juice, Worcestershire, salt, pepper, hot sauce, cayenne, and garlic. Arrange shrimp in 3-quart baking dish and drizzle with butter mixture. Bake 30 minutes, stirring once.

Serves 6

An avid volunteer, Margie Kelly dedicates a good portion of her time to being a "Cuddler" to the children at Athens Regional Medical Center and St. Mary's Hospital in Athens, Georgia. A Cuddler steps in when young patients need to have a little extra company during their hospital stay. Margie's spirit of volunteerism inspired her to create Pistol Packin' Paella—an easy and elegant one-dish meal good enough to serve company.

Petite diced tomatoes with garlic may be used to add more flavor.

Shrimp Creole

1 medium white onion, finely chopped

1 green bell pepper, seeded and finely chopped

2 celery stalks, finely chopped

4 tablespoons butter

2 tablespoons all-purpose flour

½ teaspoon sage

½ teaspoon salt

¼ teaspoon black pepper

Dash of garlic salt

1 cup petite diced tomatoes

1 (15-ounce) can tomato sauce

1 teaspoon vinegar

1½ pounds cooked shrimp, peeled

Hot sauce (optional)

Cayenne (optional)

White rice, cooked

In skillet over medium high heat, sauté onion, bell pepper, and celery in butter. Gradually stir in flour, sage, salt, pepper, and garlic salt. Add tomatoes, tomato sauce, and vinegar. Cover and simmer 10 minutes. Add shrimp and bring to a boil. Cover and simmer for 5 minutes. Season with hot sauce and cayenne, if desired. Serve over white rice.

Serves 4

Serve this in a chafing dish at a brunch buffet along with rice or creamy grits served in a separate dish.

Low Country Shrimp

4 pounds uncooked shrimp, peeled and deveined

Salt to taste

Pepper to taste

Paprika

All-purpose flour

1 pound salt pork, finely chopped

1 cup sweet onion, chopped

1 cup green bell pepper, seeded and chopped

2 cups water

Cooked grits or white rice

½ bunch fresh parsley, chopped

Season shrimp with salt, pepper, and paprika. Dust with flour and set aside. In a large skillet over medium high heat, sauté salt pork until fat is rendered. Remove pork and set aside. Add dusted shrimp to hot drippings. Reduce heat and sauté 2 minutes. Add onion and bell pepper and sauté additional 2 minutes. Slowly add small amount of water to thin mixture; stir constantly and add pork. Cover and simmer 5 minutes. Add more water to thin mixture, if necessary. Serve over grits or rice. Garnish with freshly chopped parsley.

Calli's Pizza Lasagna

1 package commercially prepared pizza crust

1 jar commercially prepared puttanesca sauce

1 package sliced pepperoni

2 cups shredded mozzarella cheese or Italian cheese blend

½ cup shredded Parmesan

Preheat oven to 350 degrees. Loosely place one-third of pizza crust in bottom of shallow 11 x 7-inch baking dish. Top with 4 to 5 tablespoons puttanesca sauce. Arrange one-third of pepperoni on sauce. Repeat layers twice. Top with mozzarella. Sprinkle with Parmesan and bake 25 minutes, or until hot and bubbly.

Serves 4-6

This is quick, easy, and fun to eat. Serve it with a tossed green salad and fresh fruit.

Spinach Lasagna

1 (1½-ounce) spaghetti sauce seasoning packet

1 (15-ounce) can tomato sauce

1 (6-ounce) can tomato paste

2½ cups water

3 eggs, beaten

2 (10-ounce) package frozen spinach, thawed and drained

1 (16-ounce) container cottage cheese

1 cup grated Parmesan cheese

Lasagna noodles, uncooked

2 (8-ounce) packages mozzarella slices

Preheat oven to 350 degrees. In large saucepan over medium high heat, combine spaghetti sauce seasoning packet, tomato sauce, tomato paste, and water. Bring to a boil, remove from heat, and set aside. In large mixing bowl, combine eggs, spinach, cottage cheese, and Parmesan. Spoon 1½ cups tomato sauce mixture into 9 x 13-inch baking dish. Layer noodles, spinach mixture, and mozzarella cheese slices. Spoon tomato sauce over cheese. Repeat layers, ending with tomato mixture. Cover with foil and bake 1 hour.

Serves 8

An equal amount of ricotta cheese can be used instead of the cottage cheese. For an even greater depth of flavor tuck a chiffonade or fresh basil or oregano leaves into the tomato sauce.

In general thinner noodles are better for simple tomato sauces. The chunkier your sauce, the wider your noodle should be. The thinnest noodle is the capelli d'angelo (angel hair). Shaped pastas include: ziti (hollow tubes), rigatoni (ribbed hollow tubes), rotelle (wagon wheels), and farfalle (bow ties). Most shaped pastas are used for salads or baked dishes.

Black Bean Lasagna

1 (15-ounce) can black beans, drained

1 (28-ounce) can crushed tomatoes

1 cup chopped onion

½ cup salsa

½ cup chopped green bell pepper

½ teaspoon cumin

1½ teaspoons chili powder

1 cup ricotta cheese

¼ teaspoon garlic powder

1 egg

Lasagna noodles, uncooked

2 cups shredded mozzarella cheese

1 cup shredded Cheddar cheese

Preheat oven to 350 degrees. In large mixing bowl, lightly mash beans. Add tomatoes, onions, salsa, bell pepper, cumin, and chili powder; mix well to combine. In separate mixing bowl, combine ricotta, garlic powder, and egg; mix well to combine. Spread 1 cup black bean mixture onto bottom of prepared 9 x 13-inch baking pan. Layer with lasagna noodles. Top noodles with half of remaining black bean mixture. Spread ricotta mixture over beans. Sprinkle with half of cheese. Repeat layers: noodles, black bean mixture, and remaining cheese. Cover with foil and bake 1 hour, or until noodles are tender. Remove from oven, uncover, and let stand 20 minutes before serving.

Serves 8

Some pasta dishes are better made with dried pasta rather than fresh. By and large, most fresh pasta is softer and much more fragile, while dried pasta is heartier and a better complement to thicker sauces.

Spinach Fettuccini

1 (16-ounce) package fettuccini, prepared according to package directions

1½ tablespoons butter

1½ teaspoons minced garlic

2 ounces cream cheese, softened

1½ cups chicken stock, divided

3 tablespoons all-purpose flour

3 ounces grated Parmesan cheese

¾ cup half-and-half

1 teaspoon salt

1 teaspoon pepper

1 (10-ounce) package frozen spinach, thawed

10 bacon slices, cooked and crumbled

In large skillet over medium heat, melt butter. Add garlic and sauté 30 seconds. Add ½ cup chicken stock and cream cheese, whisking until cheese melts and mixture is smooth. Add remaining chicken stock and flour. Bring to a boil, stirring constantly. Cook 2 minutes. Remove from heat and add Parmesan cheese, stirring until smooth. Add half-and-half, salt, pepper, and spinach, stirring until thoroughly combined. Place pasta in large bowl. Pour spinach mixture over pasta, tossing well to coat. Serve in individual pasta bowls and garnish with bacon.

Serves 8

Cheesy Mostacolli

1 (8-ounce) package mostacolli noodles, prepared according to package directions

1 jar marinara sauce

1 (8-ounce) container ricotta cheese

¾ pound ground beef or sausage, cooked and drained

1 to 1½ cups shredded mozzarella cheese, divided

A tasty and quick alternative to lasagna or stuffed shells, and it tastes great with ground turkey substituted for ground beef or sausage.

Preheat oven to 375 degrees. In 3-quart casserole dish, combine pasta, sauce, ricotta, meat, and half of mozzarella, stirring gently to combine. Sprinkle with remaining mozzarella. Bake 35 to 40 minutes, or until cheese is bubbly.

Serves 6-8

Manicotti Spiñaci

1 box manicotti shells

1 pound ground chuck

¼ cup chopped onion

1 teaspoon garlic powder

1 (15-ounce) can chopped spinach, drained

1 cup ricotta cheese

1 cup shredded mozzarella cheese

½ cup shredded Parmesan cheese

2 eggs, lightly beaten

Salt and pepper to taste

1 (32-ounce) jar spaghetti sauce

Parmesan cheese

Preheat oven to 350 degrees. Cook shells according to package directions. Drain and cool on foil, keeping shells separate so they will not stick together, and set aside. In skillet over medium high heat, brown ground chuck. Add onion and garlic powder. Sauté 3 to 4 minutes, or until onion is tender, drain. Remove from heat and set aside. In mixing bowl, combine spinach, cheeses, eggs, salt, and pepper, stirring well to combine. Stir into meat mixture. Carefully spoon meat and spinach mixture into each shell. Transfer filled shells to prepared 9 x 13-inch baking pan. Pour spaghetti sauce evenly over stuffed shells. Sprinkle with Parmesan, if desired. Cover with foil and bake 20 minutes. Remove from heat and remove foil. Return to oven and bake additional 20 minutes.

Chicken Spaghetti

1 stick butter

1 green bell pepper, seeded and chopped

1 small onion, chopped

1 (8-ounce) package spaghetti, cooked al dente

4 boneless skinless chicken breasts, cooked and shredded

1 (10¾-ounce) can cream of mushroom soup

1 (10-ounce) can diced tomatoes with green chilies

1 (16-ounce) package processed cheese loaf, cubed

Crushed or diced tomatoes lend themselves better to this dish than whole tomatoes, but if you find yourself with the latter in the pantry, you can use a pair of kitchen shears to snip those pomodoros into bits—right in the can.

Preheat oven to 350 degrees. In large saucepan over medium heat, melt butter. Sauté bell pepper and onion until tender. Add spaghetti and chicken. Stir in soup and tomatoes. Add processed cheese loaf, stirring until cheese melts. Transfer to prepared 9 x 13-inch baking dish. Bake 30 to 45 minutes.

Serves 8

Cheese Ravioli with Tomatoes and Artichokes

1 tablespoon olive oil

1 pound Roma tomatoes, peeled, seeded, and chopped

1 (6½-ounce) jar marinated artichoke hearts

½ cup chopped green chilies

3 garlic cloves, crushed

½ teaspoon salt

¼ teaspoon black pepper

2 (9-ounce) packages fresh cheese ravioli, cooked according to package directions

1 teaspoon olive oil

2 tablespoons grated Parmesan

Extra virgin olive oil was not created to use for sautés— most of its flavor is lost cooking it in this manner. It was made to be used in salads or to be drizzled over roasted or steamed vegetables. Buy a cold-pressed olive oil for sautéing, and save the good stuff for when it really counts!

In large skillet over medium heat, heat 1 tablespoon oil. Add tomatoes, artichokes, green chilies, garlic, salt, and pepper. Cook 2 to 3 minutes, stirring occasionally until warm throughout. Remove from heat. Place pasta in large bowl and toss with 1 teaspoon of olive oil. Add half of tomato sauce and gently toss. Pour remaining sauce on top of ravioli and garnish with Parmesan.

Serves 6

Pasta Bolognese

1 pound lean ground beef

1 cup finely chopped red onion

2 medium green bell peppers, seeded and cut into strips

2 medium red bell peppers, seeded and cut into strips

2 garlic cloves, minced

⅔ cup finely chopped fresh basil

½ cup freshly chopped parsley

2 (14-ounce) cans whole, peeled tomatoes, cut into chunks

2 (8-ounce) cans tomato sauce

½ teaspoon salt

¼ teaspoon black pepper

1 (16-ounce) package spaghetti, prepared according to package directions

In large skillet over medium high heat, partially brown ground beef. Add onion and sauté until tender. Add peppers and sauté 3 minutes. Add garlic and sauté 30 seconds. Add basil, parsley, tomatoes, tomato sauce, salt, and pepper. Bring to a boil, reduce heat, and simmer 20 to 25 minutes. Serve over spaghetti.

Serves 8 to 12

Tuscan Pasta

1 head of escarole, cut into 1-inch strips

1 (12-ounce) package Italian sausage, casings removed

1 tablespoon olive oil

2 tablespoons minced garlic

1 (16-ounce) can white beans, drained

½ cup chicken stock

¼ cup shredded Romano cheese

1 (16-ounce) package rigatoni pasta, cooked al dente

Cayenne pepper

Soak escarole in bowl of water 5 minutes; drain and set aside. In large skillet over medium high heat, cook sausage in oil. Stir after 3 minutes. Add garlic; cook 1 minute. Add escarole and cook until wilted (about 3 minutes), stirring occasionally. Add beans and chicken stock. Reduce heat to medium and cook 6 minutes. Remove from heat. Add cheese and pasta. Gently toss to combine. Season with cayenne pepper.

PREPARING THE PERFECT PLATE OF PASTA

Boil 4 to 6 quarts of water for every pound of dry pasta. (You can divide this recipe depending on how much pasta you are cooking.) Add the pasta with a stir and return the water to a boil. Stir the pasta occasionally during cooking. Follow the package directions for cooking times. If the pasta is to be used as part of a dish that requires further cooking, undercook the pasta by one-third of the cooking time specified on the package. Taste the pasta to determine if it is done. Perfectly cooked pasta should be "al dente," or firm to the bite, yet cooked through. Drain pasta immediately, add sauce, and enjoy.

Serve with a crispy salad and crusty bread for a meal that is sure to please. Leftovers only get better and it also freezes well!

Bonnie's Lasagna

2 pounds ground beef, cooked and drained

1 pound ground sausage, cooked and drained

2 (26-ounce) jars tomato-basil spaghetti sauce

1 (12-ounce) can tomato paste

1 package dry spaghetti mix

3 cups water

1 (24-ounce) and 1 (8-ounce) container small curd cottage cheese

3 eggs, beaten

3 cups shredded mozzarella cheese, divided

1½ cups shredded Parmesan, divided

1 package no-boil lasagna noodles

Preheat oven to 350 degrees.

In large saucepan over medium heat, combine beef, sausage, spaghetti sauce, tomato paste, dry spaghetti mix, and water. Bring to a slow boil. Cover and simmer 1 hour, stirring occasionally.

In large mixing bowl, combine cottage cheese, eggs, half of mozzarella, and half of Parmesan; set aside.

In lasagna pan, spread 1 to 2 cups sauce on bottom. Layer half of noodles over sauce. Spoon one-third of remaining sauce over noodles. Spread half of cheese mixture over sauce. Repeat layers, ending with remaining one-third sauce. Cover with foil and bake 40 minutes. Remove from oven and remove foil. Top with remaining cheeses. Return to oven and bake 10 additional minutes. Remove from oven and let stand 8 to 10 minutes before serving.

Serves 10-12

Chan's Pork Loin

⅓ cup soy sauce

⅓ cup orange juice

3 tablespoons Worcestershire
    sauce

3 tablespoons lemon juice

2 tablespoons brown sugar

1 teaspoon dry mustard

1 garlic clove, minced

Rosemary

Black pepper

Pork tenderloin

In large mixing bowl or gallon-sized plastic zip top bag, combine soy sauce, orange juice, Worcestershire, lemon juice, brown sugar, dry mustard, garlic, rosemary, and pepper. Add pork tenderloin and marinate in refrigerator 4 to 8 hours.

Preheat oven to 350 degrees. Place tenderloin in roasting pan and bake until meat thermometer registers 160 degrees when inserted in center.

Both apple cider or red wine vinegar can provide the requisite acidity instead of the citrus juice. A shot of vodka also works beautifully as a tenderizer.

Grilled Pork Tenderloin

Perfect with cranberry salsa

½ cup peanut oil

⅓ cup soy sauce

¼ cup red wine vinegar

3 tablespoons lemon juice

2 tablespoons Worcestershire
    sauce

1 garlic clove, crushed

1 tablespoon freshly chopped
    parsley

1 tablespoon dry mustard

1½ teaspoons black pepper

2 (¾ to 1-pound) pork tenderloins

In large bowl, whisk together oil, soy sauce, vinegar, juice, Worcestershire, garlic, parsley, mustard, and pepper. Pour into gallon-sized zip top plastic bag. Place tenderloins in bag and marinate overnight, turning often.

Preheat grill. Remove tenderloins from bag; discard marinade and bag. Grill 6 inches from medium coals at 300 to 400 degrees 12 to 14 minutes on each side, or until meat thermometer inserted in center registers 145 to 160 degrees. Tenderloins may also be cook in oven at 350 degrees 30 to 45 minutes.

CRANBERRY SALSA

2 cups fresh cranberries,
    chopped

1 cup dried apricots,
    chopped

2 tablespoons cilantro,
    chopped

2 jalapeño peppers, seeded
    and finely chopped

2 tablespoons honey

2 tablespoons freshly
    squeezed lime juice

In mixing bowl, combine cranberries, apricots, cilantro, jalapeño, honey, and lime juice. Chill 1 to 2 hours before serving.

Makes 3 cups

Tenderize your tenderloin with enthusiastic jabs from a sharp fork, allowing the pork to soak up even more of this superlative marinade.

Ginger Honey Pork Tenderloin

½ cup soy sauce

1 tablespoon minced garlic

1 large pork tenderloin
(about 1½ pounds)

⅓ cup honey

¼ cup brown sugar, packed

2 teaspoons ginger

2 tablespoons ginger preserves

2 tablespoons sesame seeds,
toasted

Combine soy sauce and garlic in zip top plastic bag. Add pork and seal bag. Chill and marinate 2 hours, turning every 30 minutes to coat. Preheat oven to 400. Remove pork from bag and reserve marinade; set aside.

Preheat oven to 400 degrees. In small mixing bowl, whisk together honey, brown sugar, ginger, and ginger preserves. Stir in 2 tablespoons reserved marinade; set aside.

Line shallow roasting pan with foil, allowing 5 inches to hang from both sides. Place pork in pan and brush with half of honey mixture. Roast 10 minutes. Remove from oven, turn pork, and brush with remaining honey mixture. Sprinkle with sesame seeds. Return to oven and roast 15 minutes, or until meat thermometer inserted in center of pork registers 155 degrees. Remove from oven. Transfer pork in foil to cutting board. Tent foil around pork and seal tightly. Let stand 5 minutes, or until meat thermometer inserted in center of pork registers 160 degrees. Cut into ¼-inch slices. In small saucepan over medium high heat, bring remaining marinade to a boil and serve with pork.

Serves 6

Pork Loin with Herb Mustard Crust

1 tablespoon finely chopped thyme, plus 6 sprigs

1 tablespoon finely chopped parsley

1½ teaspoons finely chopped rosemary, plus 3 sprigs

1½ teaspoons finely chopped sage, plus 3 sprigs

½ cup Dijon mustard

6 tablespoons olive oil, divided

½ teaspoon kosher salt

⅛ teaspoon freshly ground black pepper

1 (3-pound) boneless center-cut pork loin, tied with kitchen twine at even intervals

Salt and pepper to taste

6 tablespoons unsalted butter, cut into ½-inch pieces, divided

2 pounds fingerling potatoes, halved lengthwise

8 large shallots, peeled and halved through the root

½ pound seedless red grapes, snipped into small bunches

½ cup red wine or port

½ cup chicken stock

In small mixing bowl, whisk together chopped thyme, parsley, rosemary, sage, mustard, 2 tablespoons olive oil, salt, and pepper. Place pork loin in shallow dish and coat evenly with mixture. Cover and chill at least 4 hours.

One hour before cooking, bring pork to room temperature. Reserve marinade from dish and set aside. Season pork with salt and pepper.

Place roasting pan in oven and preheat to 325 degrees. In large sauté pan over high heat, heat 2 tablespoons olive oil until smoking. Add pork and sear about 3 to 4 minutes per side, or until well browned, reducing heat to medium if necessary to prevent burning. Remove roasting pan from oven. Transfer pork, fat side down, to roasting pan. (Set sauté pan aside.) Rub reserved marinade over pork and top with 3 tablespoons butter and herb sprigs. Return pan to oven and cook 55 minutes to 1 hour, 5 minutes, or until meat thermometer inserted in center reaches 135 degrees.

In large mixing bowl, toss potatoes, shallots and grapes with remaining 2 tablespoons olive oil. Season with salt and pepper. After pork has cooked 15 minutes, place potatoes, cut side down, around pork. Arrange shallots and grapes over potatoes.

Drain sauté pan of fat and return to medium high heat. When hot, add wine or port and bring to a boil, scraping bottom of pan. When nearly evaporated, add chicken stock and return to a boil. Whisk in remaining 2 tablespoons butter. Season with salt and pepper and strain through a fine-meshed sieve. Cover and keep warm.

When pork is done (center of roast should register 145 to 150 degrees), transfer to cutting board. Tent lightly with foil and let rest 15 minutes before slicing. Serve with potatoes, shallots, and grapes accompanied with wine sauce.

Serves 6

Good with cornbread. Better with cornbread and bourbon. (Bourbon before meal, please!)

Oven Baby Back Ribs

1 cup ketchup

¼ cup cider vinegar

¼ cup water

1 tablespoon sugar

Hot sauce

1 slab baby back ribs

In small saucepan over medium heat, combine ketchup, vinegar, water, sugar, and hot sauce. Simmer 10 minutes.

Preheat oven to 350 degrees. Wash ribs and cut in 8 to 10 pieces. Place on baking sheet and cook 40 minutes. Remove from oven. Spoon sauce over ribs and continue cooking 30 additional minutes, spooning sauce once every 10 minutes.

Spareribs and Cabbage

3 pounds lean spareribs

1 large cabbage

4 small onions

1 cup water

3 tablespoons drippings from ribs

Soy sauce

Crack spareribs and bake in a 350 degree oven until brown and well done (about 40 minutes). Quarter cabbage and onions and place in large boiler along with water, ribs, and drippings. Cover and steam until cabbage is crisp but tender, stirring occasionally. Do not overcook cabbage! Sprinkle generously with soy sauce after serving.

Serves 4

Swiss Stuffed Pork Chops

4 (1-inch) pork chops

4 slices Swiss cheese, cut into pieces

¼ cup freshly chopped parsley

½ cup chopped mushrooms

½ teaspoon salt

1 egg, lightly beaten

½ cup bread crumbs

3 tablespoons cooking oil

1 cup white wine

Cut a pocket halfway through each pork chop. In mixing bowl, combine cheese, parsley, mushrooms, and salt. Stuff pockets with cheese mixture. Dip chops in egg and dredge in bread crumbs. In an electric skillet over medium high heat, brown chops on both sides in hot oil; add wine. Cover and simmer 1 hour, or until tender. Add more wine if skillet becomes dry.

Although they require a little more time than boneless chops, bone-in pork chops offer more flavor because the bone helps to flavor the meat. Look for either rib chops or loin chops.

Rosemary Pork Tenderloin

¼ cup red wine vinegar

½ cup olive oil

1 tablespoon whole grain Dijon mustard

1 tablespoon fresh rosemary leaves

½ teaspoon black pepper

2 (1-pound) pork tenderloins

Rosemary sprigs

In small mixing bowl, whisk together vinegar, oil, mustard, rosemary, and pepper. Pour into gallon-sized zip top plastic bag. Place tenderloins in bag and marinate 1 to 24 hours, turning often. Preheat grill. Remove tenderloins from bag; discard marinade and bag. Cook tenderloins over medium heat grill until meat thermometer inserted in center registers 145 to 160 degrees. Remove from grill and let meat stand 5 to 10 minutes, loosely covered. To serve, slice thinly across the grain and garnish with sprigs of rosemary.

Beef Tenderloin with Salt-Herb Crust

Serve this would-be Wellington with accompanying ramekins of hot beef juice and chilled horseradish sour cream.

2 cups, plus 3 tablespoons coarse salt

¼ cup, plus 3 tablespoons freshly chopped thyme

¼ cup, plus 3 tablespoons fresh rosemary

2 large eggs, separated

⅔ cup water

2½ cups all-purpose flour

All-purpose flour, for rolling out dough

1 (2 to 3-pound) beef tenderloin, tied and at room temperature

1 tablespoon unsalted butter

1 tablespoon extra virgin olive oil

10 to 12 fresh sage leaves

2 bay leaves

1 cup fresh flat-leaf parsley

7 garlic cloves, peeled and thinly sliced

2 tablespoons water

Freshly ground black pepper

In bowl of electric stand mixer fitted with paddle attachments and set on low, combine 2 cups salt, 3 tablespoons thyme, and 3 tablespoons rosemary. Add 2 egg whites and water, mixing thoroughly until combined. Gradually add up to 2½ cups flour, beating on medium speed, until mixture forms a firm dough (about 2 to 3 minutes). Dough should be firm, but not too moist or sticky. If necessary, knead in additional flour or water. Form dough into square shape and wrap in plastic wrap. Let rest at room temperature at least 2 hours or up to 24 hours.

Preheat oven to 350 degrees. Rinse tenderloin and pat dry. In large skillet over medium high heat, combine butter and oil. When skillet is hot, add tenderloin. Sear on all sides (about 1½ minutes per side). Transfer tenderloin to wire rack set over a baking pan and cool 5 minutes.

On lightly floured surface, roll out dough to an approximately 10 x 15-inch rectangle (rectangle should be large enough to completely encase tenderloin.) Sprinkle remaining ¼ cup thyme, ¼ cup rosemary, sage, bay leaves, parsley, and garlic over dough. Remove twine from tenderloin and place in center of dough. Completely wrap dough around beef. Press edges together to seal. Carefully transfer wrapped beef to roasting pan. In small bowl, mix egg yolks with 2 tablespoons water; brush entire dough surface with egg wash. Sprinkle top with remaining 3 tablespoons salt.

Place baking pan in center of oven. Roast until crust is lightly golden and an instant-read thermometer inserted into center registers 125 to 130 degrees (for medium rare); cook 10 to 12 minutes per pound. Remove pan from oven. Let rest at room temperature 1 hour.

When ready to serve, slice off crust at one end, remove beef to serving platter, and discard crust. Season with black pepper, slice, and serve.

Serves 6-8

Country Style Meatloaf

1½ pounds ground beef

1 (8-ounce) can tomato sauce

1 cup quick cooking oats, uncooked

2 eggs, beaten

½ cup chopped onion

½ cup chopped bell pepper

1 teaspoon salt

½ teaspoon pepper

¾ cup ketchup

Preheat oven to 350 degrees. In large mixing bowl, combine beef, tomato sauce, oats, eggs, onion, bell pepper, salt, and pepper. Mix well and transfer to loaf pan. Bake 45 minutes. Remove from oven and brush top with ketchup. Return to oven and bake 15 additional minutes.

Serves 6-8

Two cups of crustless, diced white bread will work as a binder instead of oats. Serve with mashed potatoes livened up with ground white pepper or grated Parmesan.

Mitchell's Good Beef

1 to 1½ pounds stew beef or chuck roast, trimmed of fat

Garlic powder to taste

Salt to taste

Pepper to taste

Worcestershire sauce to taste

1 can golden mushroom soup

1 cup red wine, beef stock, or water

½ cup Allegro® Original Marinade

Preheat oven to 325 degrees. Place beef in baking dish. Season beef with garlic powder, salt, pepper, and Worcestershire sauce to taste. In mixing bowl, combine soup, wine (or stock or water), and marinade. Pour over beef and cover with foil. Bake 3 hours.

Serves 4-6

This is great company fare and can be easily doubled. Serve over rice, egg noodles, or mashed potatoes along with garden peas and crusty bread for a great meal. It's sure to be a family favorite.

Barbequed Chuck Roast

1 (2 to 2½-pound) boneless chuck roast, trimmed

1 medium onion, chopped

¾ cup cola-flavored soda

¼ cup Worcestershire sauce

1 tablespoon apple cider vinegar

2 garlic cloves, minced

½ teaspoon dry mustard

½ teaspoon chili powder

¼ teaspoon cayenne

½ cup ketchup

2 teaspoons butter

Place roast and onion in slow cooker. In small mixing bowl, combine cola, Worcestershire, vinegar, garlic, mustard, chili powder, and cayenne. Reserve ½ cup mixture and chill. Pour remaining mixture over roast. Cook 6 hours on high temperature or 8 to 9 hours on low temperature. Remove roast from slow cooker and shred; set aside. In small saucepan over medium heat, combine reserved liquid, ketchup, and butter, stirring until thoroughly heated. Pour over shredded beef and stir. Serve with hamburger buns.

Classic Beef Stroganoff

5 tablespoons butter, divided

1 pound lean beef or top sirloin, cut into pieces

½ onion, thinly sliced

1 can mushrooms, drained

1 tablespoon all-purpose flour

½ cup beef stock

½ cup red wine

1 tablespoon Dijon mustard

¼ cup sour cream

1 (16-ounce) package egg noodles, cooked according to package directions

In large skillet over medium high heat, melt 2 tablespoons butter. Season beef with salt and pepper. Add to skillet and brown. Add onion and mushrooms and sauté 4 minutes. Remove from heat and set aside. In saucepan over low heat, melt 2 tablespoons butter; stir in flour to make a roux. When mixture begins to bubble, gradually stir in stock and wine. Increase heat and bring to a boil, stirring until mixture is smooth. Stir in mustard and sour cream. Add beef mixture and keep warm. Toss cooked noodles with remaining 1 tablespoon butter. Place noodles on serving plate and top with beef mixture.

Serves 3-4

King's Corned Beef

Wonderful on St. Patrick's Day with cabbage and potatoes.

1 (7½-pound) package corned
  beef with pickling spice
  packet

⅔ cup prepared mustard

½ cup brown sugar, firmly packed

½ teaspoon nutmeg

Black pepper to taste

In Dutch oven over medium-high heat cover corned beef with water. Bring to a boil, reduce heat to low, and simmer. Add spice packet and cook 1 ½ hours, per pound of meat. (The meat will shrink to about half its size during the boiling process.) Using a fork, scrape the fat from the corned beef. Add water as necessary as the liquid cooks off.

In mixing bowl, whisk together mustard, brown sugar, nutmeg, and pepper. Set aside half of mixture. Coat corned beef with mustard mixture. Preheat grill and cook until crusty on the outside. Serve with reserved sauce.

Serves 10

Corning is a form of curing; it has nothing to do with corn. The name comes from Anglo-Saxon times before refrigeration. In those days, the meat was dry-cured in coarse "corns" of salt. Pellets of salt, some the size of kernels of corn, were rubbed into the beef to keep it from spoiling and to preserve it.

Today brining—the use of salt water—has replaced the dry salt cure, but the name "corned beef" is still used, rather than "brined" or "pickled" beef.

Mexican Bake

1 pound ground beef

¼ cup chopped onion

1 (16-ounce) can kidney beans,
  drained

1 (15-ounce) can tomato sauce

1 (¼-ounce) packet taco
  seasoning mix

1 cup shredded Cheddar cheese,
  divided

3½ cups corn chips, divided

1¼ cups sour cream

In large Dutch oven, cook beef and onion until meat is browned and onion is tender. Drain and return to Dutch oven. Stir in beans, tomato sauce, taco seasoning mix, and ¾ cup Cheddar. Sprinkle 2½ cups corn chips in bottom of an 8 x 8 x 2-inch baking dish. Cover with beef mixture. Bake at 350 degrees 20 to 25 minutes. Spread sour cream over beef. Top with remaining corn chips and cheese. Bake additional 3 to 4 minutes, or until cheese melts.

Serves 6

As more and more Mexican groceries open in and around Athens, we are delighted to be able to find wonderful cheeses such as asadero and cotija, authentic alternatives to the trusty Cheddar used here.

Simple Stroganoff

A quick and easy weeknight meal.

¾ pound ground beef

1½ tablespoons chopped green
    bell pepper

¼ cup chopped onion

2 tablespoons cooking oil

½ cup cream of mushroom soup

½ cup sour cream

1 tablespoon chopped pimento

1 (10-count) container regular
    sized canned biscuits

In large skillet over medium high heat, cook beef, onion, and bell pepper in oil. Brown lightly and salt to taste. Add soup, reduce heat, and simmer 10 minutes. Stir in sour cream and pimento; remove from heat. Preheat oven to 350 degrees. Transfer mixture to 9 x 13-inch baking dish and top with uncooked biscuits. Bake 25 minutes, or until biscuits are cooked and browned.

Homemade Hamburger Helper

Great for kids!

1 pound ground beef

1 small onion, chopped

1 (10¾-ounce) can cream of
    mushroom soup

1 (15-ounce) can tomato sauce

1 (10-ounce) can diced tomatoes
    with green chilies

Salt and pepper to taste

2 cups macaroni noodles, cooked
    al dente

½ cup shredded Parmesan cheese

In large skillet over medium high heat, brown ground beef with onion and drain. Remove from heat and set aside. In large mixing bowl, combine beef mixture, soup, tomato sauce, and tomatoes. Season with salt and pepper to taste. Add macaroni, tossing gently to combine. Preheat oven to 350 degrees. Transfer to a 2-quart baking dish and sprinkle with Parmesan. Bake until bubbly and cheese melts.

Serves 4-6

Mom's Chalupas

1 (5 to 6-pound) boneless pork
    roast

1 to 2 packages dried pinto beans,
    soaked overnight, drained,
    and rinsed

2 to 3 onions, chopped

3 to 4 tablespoons minced garlic

4 (4-ounce) cans chopped green
    chilies, drained

1½ tablespoons chili powder

1 tablespoon oregano

1½ tablespoons cumin

Salt and pepper to taste

Corn chips

Lettuce, shredded

Cherry or grape tomatoes, halved
    or quartered

Avocado, pitted, peeled, and
    chopped

Onion, finely chopped

Sharp Cheddar cheese, shredded

Salsa

In large stockpot over medium-high heat, combine roast, beans, onion, garlic, chilies, chili powder, oregano, and cumin. Cover with water. Bring to a boil, reduce heat to low, and simmer. Cook covered for 3 hours, 30 minutes, to 4 hours, stirring frequently. Add water as needed. Uncover, continuing to stir as needed. Cook until mixture thickens, usually another 1 hour, 30 minutes. Season to taste with both salt and pepper.

Place corn chips on individual plate and top with pork mixture. Garnish with lettuce, tomato, avocado, onion, cheese, and salsa.

Spinach and Cheese Pizza

1 (9-ounce) package frozen,
    creamed spinach, cooked
    according to package
    directions

¼ cup freshly shredded Parmesan

½ teaspoon oregano

1 large prepared pizza crust

1 (4-ounce) package shredded
    mozzarella cheese

4 Roma tomatoes, thinly sliced

1 small jar artichoke hearts,
    sliced

1 (4-ounce) package feta cheese

Preheat oven to 400 degrees. In mixing bowl, combine spinach, Parmesan, and oregano. Place pizza crust on baking sheet and cover with spinach mixture. Sprinkle with mozzarella. Arrange tomatoes and artichoke hearts over cheese and sprinkle with feta. Bake 10 to 15 minutes, or until cheese melts and pizza is thoroughly heated. Remove from oven and let cool 5 minutes before slicing.

Make 4 servings

If one or more of your children (or perhaps your spouse) is averse to feta cheese, divide into two smaller prepared pizza crusts and leave the feta off of one out of consideration for the finicky. Then treat yourself to a glass of wine (not a chorus of whines) and enjoy!

When choosing eggplant, look for heavy, firm fruit with unblemished skin. Male eggplants have fewer seeds (which are often bitter) than the female; they have a rounder, smoother blossom end or base. The blossom end of a female eggplant is generally indented. Store an eggplant in a perforated plastic bag in the refrigerator where it should keep for several days. It may be steamed then frozen for up to six months.

Eggplant Parmesan with Tomato Basil Sauce

1 large eggplant, peeled and
    thinly sliced
Self-rising flour
Parmesan cheese, finely shredded
Salt and pepper to taste

¼ cup olive oil
¼ cup canola oil
1 (16-ounce) package shredded
    mozzarella cheese, divided
½ cup shredded Parmesan,
    divided

Preheat oven to 375 degrees. Soak eggplant slices at least 10 minutes in salted water. (Leave slices in water until ready to coat and cook.) In large shallow bowl, combine flour and Parmesan. Season with salt and pepper to taste. In large skillet over medium high heat, combine olive and canola oils. Dredge eggplant in flour mixture. Carefully place slices into hot oil. Cook on both sides until lightly brown. Remove from skillet and drain on paper towels. Spoon a thin layer of Tomato Basil Sauce into 9 x 13-inch baking dish. Arrange half of eggplant slices in baking pan. Sprinkle half of mozzarella then Parmesan over eggplant. Spoon half of remaining sauce over cheeses and repeat layers. Bake 15 to 20 minutes or until lightly browned. Allow to cool 5 minutes before slicing.

TOMATO BASIL SAUCE

Fresh basil leaves
2 (14½-ounce) cans petite diced
    tomatoes

2 garlic cloves
3 tablespoons olive oil

Bruise basil by sandwiching the leaves between two sheets of plastic wrap. Crush with rolling pin or meat mallet. In saucepan over medium heat, combine tomatoes, garlic, and oil; add basil. Simmer 20 minutes.

When basil leaves are mostly dark, they are sufficiently bruised. Use your time wisely—let the sauce simmer while you are cooking the eggplant!

Party Turkey Breast

Easy, healthy recipe that always gets rave reviews!

1 (5 to 7-pound) fresh turkey
    breast
1 cup cider vinegar
¼ cup olive oil

¼ teaspoon salt
¼ teaspoon black pepper
2 teaspoons freshly chopped
    parsley

Preheat oven to 300 degrees. Place turkey in oven bag. In small mixing bowl, combine vinegar, oil, salt, pepper, and parsley. Pour over turkey breast. Seal bag and place in baking dish. Pierce bag several times. Place turkey thermometer in turkey and bake until thermometer pops up.

One-Dish Dirty Rice

6½ ounces turkey kielbasa,
    thinly sliced
⅔ cup chopped onion
½ cup chopped celery

3 cups water
1 (8-ounce) package dirty rice
    mix
1 (10-ounce) package frozen,
    chopped spinach

Spray large nonstick skillet with cooking spray. Sauté onion, celery, and kielbasa over medium high heat 5 minutes. Add water, rice mix, and spinach, stirring well. Bring to a boil. Reduce heat, cover, and simmer 25 minutes, or until rice is cooked and liquid is nearly absorbed.

Serves 4

HOW TO CARVE A TURKEY

Grasp the end of a drumstick. Place a knife between the drumstick/thigh and the body of the turkey and cut through skin to joint. Remove the entire leg by pulling out and back, using the point of the knife to disjoin it. Separate the thigh and drumstick at the joint.

Insert a fork in upper wing to hold the turkey steady. Make one long horizontal cut above the wing, through to the body.

Slice straight down beginning halfway up the breast. When knife reaches the cut above the wing joint, a slice will fall free.

Continue to slice breast meat, starting the cut at a higher point each time.

Baked Lamb Chops

3 eggs

1½ tablespoons Worcestershire
    sauce

Dash of salt and pepper

12 (5½-ounce) lamb chops

2 cups Italian bread crumbs

Preheat oven to 375 degrees. In small mixing bowl, whisk together eggs, Worcestershire, salt, and pepper. Dip each lamb chop in egg mixture. Lightly dredge in bread crumbs. Arrange chops in 9 x 13-inch baking dish. Bake 20 minutes, remove from oven, and turn over. Bake additional 20 minutes.

Serves 6

These are so easy and delicious! Goes well with mashed potatoes and something green.

Queen Mother Mariella's Leg of Lamb

1 leg of lamb, have butcher
    remove BOTH gland and
    bone

Mrs. Dash

Minced garlic

Freshly ground black pepper

Preheat oven to 425 degrees. Coat entire piece of lamb with Mrs. Dash, garlic, and pepper. Cook, uncovered, 45 minutes. While the lamb is cooking, prepare sauce for basting. Reduce oven temperature to 350 degrees and baste with sauce. Continue basting lamb every 30 minutes for 4 hours. Pour remaining sauce over lamb. Cover and bake 1 additional hour. Remove from oven and allow to cool before serving.

SAUCE

3 to 4 cups beef stock

2 chopped onions

½ cup minced garlic

½ cup ketchup

½ cup vinegar

½ cup red wine

4 to 5 tablespoons Worcestershire
    sauce

2 tablespoons Mrs. Dash

1 to 2 tablespoons thyme

1 to 2 tablespoons rosemary

In large saucepan over medium high heat, combine beef stock, onion, garlic, ketchup, vinegar, wine, Worcestershire, Mrs. Dash, thyme, and rosemary. Bring to a boil, stirring frequently to avoid sticking. Reduce heat and simmer until first basting.

Sauce and drippings make fabulous gravy for both the lamb and a side dish such as wild rice or garlic smashed potatoes.

Ernie's Smoked Pheasant

1 tablespoon garlic powder

1 tablespoon salt

1 tablespoon pepper

2 pheasants, dressed

4 slices bacon, uncooked and
   divided

In small mixing bowl, combine garlic powder, salt, and pepper. Coat pheasants with spice mixture. Place 2 bacon slices over each pheasant breast. With cooking twine, tie legs up around the breasts. Cook on grill away from fire 1 hour to 1 hour, 30 minutes.

Serves 4

Serve this with wild rice, fruit salad, and your favorite glass of something white and light.

Quail in Mushroom Gravy

1 tablespoon garlic powder

1 tablespoon salt

1 tablespoon pepper

6 quail, dressed

1 stick butter, melted

1 (10¾-ounce) can cream of
   mushroom soup

1 cup water

Preheat oven to 300 degrees. In small mixing bowl, combine garlic powder, salt, and pepper. Coat quail with spice mixture. In heavy skillet over medium-high heat, brown quail in butter on all sides 5 to 7 minutes. Remove quail from pan and combine soup and water with pan drippings from browning. Place quail in baking dish and cover with soup mixture. Cover and bake 35 minutes.

Serves 6

Stuffed Venison Tenderloin

Pork tenderloin can be substituted for venison.

1 venison tenderloin

4 ounces cream cheese, softened

1 cup thawed, frozen chopped
    spinach

¼ cup teriyaki sauce

1 tablespoon salt

1 tablespoon pepper

1 tablespoon garlic powder

4 bacon slices, uncooked

Cut slit into tenderloin, creating a pocket. In mixing bowl, combine cream cheese, spinach, and teriyaki sauce. Stuff mixture into pocket of tenderloin and secure slit using toothpicks or twine. Season tenderloin with salt, pepper, and garlic powder and wrap with bacon. Secure bacon to tenderloin with toothpicks. Cook on hot grill about 30 minutes, or until thoroughly cooked.

Serves 4-6

Red Wine Garlic Sauce

1 (75-milliliter) bottle Burgundy
    or other dry red wine

1 head garlic, crushed
    (approximately 12 cloves)

In large saucepan over medium high heat, combine wine and garlic. Simmer 45 minutes, or until mixture is reduced to approximately 1 cup. Pour through wire mesh strainer into small container and discard garlic. Serve over steak or other meat. Store unused sauce in refrigerator up to 1 week. Sauce will keep in freezer for up to 3 months.

Fat-Free Alfredo Sauce

2 cups non-fat cottage cheese

3 tablespoons shredded Parmesan

2 tablespoons butter flavored
    granules

½ cup evaporated skim milk

½ teaspoon chicken bouillon

½ teaspoon dried basil

¼ teaspoon black pepper

Dash of cayenne

In large saucepan over medium high heat, combine cottage cheese, Parmesan, butter flavored granules, milk, bouillon, basil, black pepper, and cayenne. Stir constantly until smooth. Watch closely, being careful not to overcook because sauce will separate.

Makes 2¾ cups

Authentic Italian Sauce

1 (16-ounce) package Italian
    sausage

4 to 6 country style, bone-in pork
    ribs

Salt and freshly ground black
    pepper to taste

Olive oil

1 large onion, chopped

2 garlic cloves, minced

2 cans plum tomatoes

1 (6-ounce) can tomato paste

Dry oregano, fresh thyme, or
    other Italian spice to taste

Freshly chopped flat leaf parsley

Preheat oven to 375 degrees. In large skillet, cook sausage until lightly browned, but not all the way through. Remove from heat and set aside. Season ribs with salt and pepper to taste and drizzle with olive oil. Roast ribs in oven until lightly browned.

In large saucepan over medium high heat, sauté onion and garlic in olive oil. Add tomatoes, tomato paste, oregano, thyme, salt, and pepper. Bring to a simmer. Add sausage and ribs. Simmer over low heat 1 hour, 30 minutes to 2 hours. Gently stir in parsley. Serve over favorite pasta and sprinkle with Parmesan, if desired. Serve sausage and ribs on the side.

Serves 8

Brown and drain ground veal or pork and add close to the end of the cooking time for something a bit more Bolognese. A thin disc of fresh buffalo mozzarella atop each portion makes a great garnish, especially with a sprinkle of red pepper flakes.

Supreme Marinara Sauce

1 stick butter

¼ cup extra virgin olive oil

1 cup fresh basil, chopped

7 garlic cloves, minced

2 tablespoons sugar

1 large onion, chopped

2 red bell peppers, seeded and
 chopped

1 cup chopped fresh mushrooms
 (optional)

4 ounces tomato paste

¼ cup balsamic vinegar

1 cup red wine

2 (28-ounce) cans plum tomatoes,
 puréed

In large skillet over medium heat, melt butter with olive oil. Add basil, garlic, sugar, onion, and peppers, cooking until slightly browned. Add mushrooms and cook 3 to 4 minutes. Add tomato paste and stir until combined. Add balsamic vinegar and wine and cook additional 8 to 10 minutes. Add puréed tomatoes and stir until heated through.

This sauce is great on pasta, in lasagna, or as a sauce for homemade pizza. Serve with a robust red wine.

Simple Blue Cheese Pasta Sauce

4 to 6 ounces crumbled blue
 cheese

1 stick butter

1 garlic clove, minced

1 (16-ounce) package pasta,
 cooked al dente

1 pound cooked shrimp, chicken,
 or scallops, chopped
 (optional)

In skillet over medium low heat, combine blue cheese, butter, and garlic, stirring until smooth. Gently toss pasta with blue cheese sauce. Add cooked shrimp, chicken, or scallops, if desired.

Serves 4-6

Bay scallops are small enough to eliminate any need for chopping, and combine well with small to medium shrimp. A tablespoon of jarred minced garlic means none of your knives need to leave the block—the only thing cut will be prep time.

Vegetables
& Sides

Wilson's Soul Food Eggplant Casserole

1 eggplant, peeled	1 cup shredded cheese
2 eggs, beaten	½ (10¾-ounce) can cream of chicken soup
½ teaspoon pepper	
1 teaspoon salt	1 tablespoon minced green bell pepper
1 small onion, diced	
	Bread crumbs

Preheat oven to 300 to 325 degrees. In large saucepan over medium heat, bring enough water to cover eggplant to a boil. Boil eggplant until tender and drain well. Remove eggplant from heat, pat dry, and mash in large mixing bowl. Add eggs, pepper, salt, onion, cheese, soup, and bell pepper, mixing well to combine. Pour into 9 x 13-inch casserole dish. Top with bread crumbs. Cook 25 minutes, or until firm.

Serves 8

Wilson's Soul Food in downtown Athens opened in 1981. Mrs. Wilson is quoted as saying, "Anybody can cook. You've got to give it time to let things simmer. That's where the love comes in. Cooking is just getting it done. Simmering is where the real taste comes from. Don't get in a hurry."

Slow Cooker Macaroni and Cheese

Cooking oil	1 (10-ounce) package sharp Cheddar cheese, shredded
1 (12-ounce) can evaporated milk	
2 cups milk	2 (10-ounce) packages medium Cheddar cheese, shredded
1½ teaspoons salt	
4 tablespoons margarine, melted	1 (16-ounce) package macaroni, cooked and drained
2 eggs, lightly beaten	
	Paprika

Coat crock pot with cooking oil. In large mixing bowl, combine milks, salt, margarine, and eggs. Fold in cheeses and macaroni, gently stirring to combine. Transfer mixture to crock pot and sprinkle with paprika. Set to low heat and cook 3 hours, 30 minutes.

If this pasta is to be served alongside an Italian main dish, consider using olive oil to coat the inside of the crock pot and substitute Parmesan Reggiano for a portion of the sharp Cheddar.

Tillamook white Cheddar and a dash of white pepper can be used here for palates that crave highly spicy flavors.

Gayle's Macaroni and Cheese

1 pound shredded Cheddar cheese

¼ cup finely chopped onion

¼ green pepper, finely chopped

¼ cup diced pimentos

1 (10¾-ounce) can cream of mushroom soup

1 cup mayonnaise

1 (8-ounce) package macaroni, cooked

1 tube round buttery crackers, crushed

1 stick butter, melted

Preheat oven to 300 degrees. In large mixing bowl, combine cheese, onion, green pepper, pimientos, soup, and mayonnaise. Gently fold in macaroni. Transfer mixture to greased baking dish. In small bowl, combine crackers and butter; sprinkle on top of macaroni. Bake until cheese melts and topping has browned.

Serves 8-10

Cheese Soufflé

1½ cups milk

3 eggs, beaten

¼ teaspoon salt

Dash of pepper

1 stick butter (optional)

1 (8-ounce) package shredded sharp Cheddar cheese

½ cup small macaroni, cooked and drained

Paprika

Preheat oven to 350 degrees. In large mixing bowl, combine milk, eggs, salt, pepper, butter, and cheese. Gently fold in macaroni, mixing well. Pour into prepared 9 x 13-inch baking dish. Sprinkle with paprika and bake 30 minutes. Center will be soft when done. Let stand 10 minutes before serving.

Arroz à la Mexicana

1 (5-ounce) package yellow rice

1 (10¾-ounce) can cream of
chicken soup

1 (8-ounce) container sour cream

4 tablespoons melted butter

1 (8-ounce) can green peas,
drained

1 (12-ounce) can Mexican corn,
drained

1 (2-ounce) jar diced pimientos,
drained

1½ cups shredded Cheddar
cheese, divided

1 can French fried onions

Preheat oven to 350 degrees. Cook rice according to package directions and set aside. In large mixing bowl, combine soup, sour cream, and butter. Add rice, peas, corn, pimientos, and ¾ cup cheese. Pour into 7 x 11-inch baking dish. Top with remaining cheese and bake 30 minutes. Remove from oven and sprinkle with French fried onions. Return to oven and bake 5 minutes.

Serves 8-10

Yellow rice is sometimes confused with saffron rice, saffron being collected from the crocus flower and one of the more expensive spices. Luckily, yellow rice is sold at reasonable prices and can be enjoyed as often as you choose.

Chile Rice Casserole

2 cups rice

2 cups sour cream

1 teaspoon salt

2 cups shredded Monterey Jack
cheese

1 (4½-ounce) can green chilies

½ stick butter, sliced

¼ cup Parmesan

Preheat oven to 350 degrees. Cook rice according to package directions. In large mixing bowl, combine rice, sour cream, and salt. Transfer half of rice mixture to 11 x 7-inch casserole; sprinkle with Monterey Jack and chilies. Top with remaining rice. Sprinkle with butter and Parmesan. Bake, uncovered, 30 minutes.

Serves 8

Should there be any leftovers, this casserole can be spooned into soft flour tortillas with diced chicken and tomatoes for a piquant Mexican-style wrap.

Artichoke Rice

This recipe is good slightly warm with quail.

1 package chicken-flavored rice (Uncle Ben's)

4 green onions, sliced

½ green pepper, chopped

12 stuffed olives, sliced

2 (6-ounce) jars marinated artichoke hearts

¾ teaspoon curry powder

⅓ cup mayonnaise

Cook rice as directed. Cool completely. Add onions, pepper, and olives. Drain artichokes (reserve marinade) and cut them in half. Add to the onion mixture. Mix mayonnaise, curry, and marinade. Add to rice mixture and mix well. Serve room temperature, cold, or heated.

Add shrimp, almonds, mushrooms, or water chestnuts for variation.

Consommé Rice

1 stick butter

2 cups Uncle Ben's regular white rice

1 can beef consommé soup

1 can French onion soup

Preheat oven to 350 degrees. Melt 1 stick of butter. Then combine butter, rice, beef consommé, and French onion soup in a 2-quart casserole dish. Stir well and cover with foil. Bake for 45 minutes.

Hoppin' John can be served for New Year's Day lunch or dinner with pork and collard greens, atop tortilla chips for an appetizer, or even over fish.

Hoppin' John

2 slices bacon

1 medium onion, chopped

1 (15-ounce) can black-eyed peas, drained

1 (14.5-ounce) can stewed tomatoes, undrained

1 cup cooked rice

¼ teaspoon salt

¼ teaspoon pepper

Preheat oven to 350 degrees. Cook bacon in a large skillet until lightly browned. Remove bacon from skillet, crumble, and set aside. Sauté onion in bacon drippings until tender, about 5 minutes. Add peas, tomatoes, rice, salt, and pepper; gently stir to combine. Transfer mixture to 1½-quart casserole. Bake 30 minutes. Remove from oven and sprinkle with bacon.

Party Potatoes

This is an easy dish to make ahead of time.

8 to 10 medium-sized potatoes, peeled

1 (8-ounce) package cream cheese

1 (16-ounce) container sour cream

1 tablespoon butter

2 tablespoons Parmesan cheese

Salt to taste

Pepper to taste

Paprika to taste

Chives, chopped (optional)

Preheat oven to 350 degrees. In large saucepan, cover potatoes with water and bring to a boil. Drain, cut into chunks, and set aside. In mixing bowl, beat together cream cheese and sour cream with electric mixer on medium speed until blended. Gradually add hot potatoes, beating constantly until light and fluffy. Add Parmesan, butter, salt, and pepper, stirring until thoroughly combined. Transfer potato mixture to 2-quart casserole. Sprinkle with paprika and chives. Bake 25 to 30 minutes.

Serves 8-10

These are delicious with steak au poivre, and can be made ahead for a superb company dish.

Fancy Scalloped Potatoes

3 tablespoons butter

2 pounds Russet potatoes, peeled and sliced

1 large onion, thinly sliced

2 tablespoons parsley, chopped

2 slices bacon, cooked and chopped

2½ cups Gruyère cheese, grated

1 cup Parmesan cheese, grated

2½ to 3 cups half-and-half

Salt and pepper to taste

Preheat oven to 350 degrees. Grease a 2-quart casserole dish with butter. Layer the bottom of the dish with one-third of the potatoes. Sprinkle with salt and pepper. Layer half the onions and ½ cup Gruyère cheese. Layer half the bacon and half the parsley. Sprinkle with ⅓ cup of Parmesan cheese.

Repeat the layers, (half of the onions, ½ cup Gruyère, bacon, parsley, and ⅓ cup Parmesan) ending with a layer of potatoes. Pour the half-and-half over the entire dish and dot with butter.

Cover with aluminum foil and bake for 1 hour. After 1 hour, remove from the oven and remove the foil. Sprinkle with the remaining 1½ cups Gruyère and ⅓ cup Parmesan. Return to the oven for 35 minutes or until most of the liquid is absorbed.

Serves 6

This casserole can be finished under the broiler for a few minutes if a lightly brown crust is desired. Be sure to watch it carefully when doing this, as it will brown quickly.

Potato Casserole

1 stick butter

1 medium onion, chopped

1 can cream of chicken soup

1 pint sour cream

Salt and pepper, to taste

2 pounds frozen hash browns

10 ounces grated Cheddar cheese

Preheat oven to 375 degrees. Place the hash browns in a 2-quart, buttered casserole dish. Sauté onions in butter. Mix together soup, sour cream, salt, and pepper and pour over the hash browns. Let set for about 35-40 minutes. Sprinkle Cheddar cheese and bake for 50 minutes.

Serves 8-10

These toppings enhance the sweetness and add flavor without resorting to the old standby of marshmallows. Try making the soufflé in individual ramekins for single servings, reducing the cooking time accordingly.

Sweet Potato Soufflé

2 eggs, beaten

3 tablespoons butter, melted

½ cup milk

1 teaspoon vanilla extract

3 cups cooked, mashed sweet potatoes

1 cup sugar

½ teaspoon salt

Preheat oven to 350 degrees. In large mixing bowl, combine eggs, butter, milk, and vanilla. Add sugar and salt. Fold in sweet potatoes, stirring well to combine. Pour into greased 2-quart baking dish. Sprinkle with topping of choice and bake 35 minutes.

BROWN SUGAR TOPPING

1 cup brown sugar

⅓ cup all-purpose flour

1 cup chopped pecans

3 tablespoons butter, melted

In small mixing bowl, combine ingredients. Sprinkle over soufflé.

COCONUT TOPPING

1 (3.5-ounce) can flaked coconut

1 cup chopped pecans

1 cup brown sugar

3 tablespoons butter, melted

½ cup all-purpose flour

In small mixing bowl, combine ingredients. Sprinkle over soufflé.

Sweet Potato Pecan Casserole

4 medium sweet potatoes (about 2 pounds), peeled and quartered

2 large egg whites

2 tablespoons honey

1 tablespoon butter

¼ teaspoon salt

⅛ teaspoon ground nutmeg

2 tablespoons finely chopped pecans

Preheat oven to 350 degrees. In large saucepan, cover potatoes with water. Bring to a boil over high heat. Reduce heat and simmer, covered, 20 to 25 minutes; drain. In large mixing bowl, beat potatoes until almost smooth with electric mixer on low speed. Add egg whites, honey, butter, salt, and nutmeg; beat until fluffy. Spoon mixture into a 2-quart round baking dish. Sprinkle with pecans. Bake 25 minutes.

While we tend to associate this dish with Thanksgiving, it's delicious in any cold-weather month and goes well with loin of pork or even game hens.

Baked Pineapple Casserole

2 cups sugar

16 tablespoons butter, softened

1 (20-ounce) can crushed pineapple, drained

3 eggs, beaten

9 slices white bread, torn

2 tablespoons milk

Preheat oven to 350 degrees. In mixing bowl, combine sugar and butter with electric mixer. Fold in pineapple and eggs. Mix in bread and pour into greased 2-quart casserole dish. Sprinkle with milk. Bake 1 hour.

Pineapples were an integral symbol of welcome in colonial times, and de rigeur on polite tables. According to some accounts, confectioners would rent pineapples to less affluent hostesses and then later sell the prickly delights to richer people who could afford to actually consume them.

Cranberry Apple Casserole

1 cup sugar

4 tablespoons water

3 to 4 tart apples, peeled, cored, and sliced

2 cups fresh cranberries, rinsed

¾ cup uncooked oatmeal

¼ cup all-purpose flour

½ cup brown sugar

½ cup pecans, chopped

1 stick butter, melted

Preheat oven to 350 degrees. In large mixing bowl, combine sugar and water. Add fruit, tossing well to coat. Pour mixture into 2-quart greased casserole and set aside. Combine oatmeal, flour, brown sugar, pecans, and butter. Spread over fruit or mix with fruit. Bake 1 hour.

This recipe is easily doubled and is great during the holidays. Not only does skipping peeling save time, should you choose to do so, it adds color for a different twist on presentation.

Aunt Jane's Squash Casserole

6 to 8 yellow squash, sliced

1 medium onion, chopped

2 eggs, beaten

4 tablespoons butter or margarine

½ cup milk

½ teaspoon salt

Pepper to taste

1 cup shredded sharp Cheddar
   cheese

8 to 12 crackers, crushed

Preheat oven to 350 degrees. In large saucepan, cover squash and onion in water. Bring to a boil and cook until tender. Drain, mash, and allow to cool. Transfer to mixing bowl; add eggs, butter, milk, salt, and pepper. Fold in cheese and half of cracker crumbs. Pour mixture into 2-quart casserole and top with remaining cracker crumbs. Bake until edges brown.

Serves 6

Garden Pea Casserole

1 (10¾-ounce) can cream of
   chicken soup

1 (10¾-ounce) can cream of
   mushroom soup

2 tablespoons evaporated milk

1 (15-ounce) can English peas,
   drained

1½ cups shredded sharp Cheddar
   cheese

Salt and pepper to taste

1 stick margarine, melted

1 tube round buttery crackers,
   crushed

Preheat oven to 350 degrees. In mixing bowl, combine soups. Add evaporated milk and mix well. Gently fold in peas and pour mixture into 2-quart casserole. Season with salt and pepper, sprinkle with cheese, and set aside. In small bowl, combine butter and crackers and sprinkle on casserole. Bake 30 minutes or until bubbly.

Serves 8

The common garden, or English, pea served as the basis for Gregor Mendel's pioneering experiments in genetics. We're sure that everyone is born with the appetite for this culinary take on an old favorite!

Cauliflower with Cheese Sauce

1 head cauliflower

1 tablespoon water

½ cup mayonnaise

1 tablespoon minced onion

1 teaspoon prepared mustard

¼ teaspoon salt

½ cup shredded Cheddar cheese

In mixing bowl, combine mayonnaise, onion, mustard, and salt. Fold in cheese, mixing well to combine; set aside. Place cauliflower in microwaveable dish with water. Cook 9 to 11 minutes. Cover cauliflower with cheese mixture and microwave on medium-high heat (70%) 1 to 2 minutes.

Corn Soufflé

1 stick butter, melted

½ pint whipping cream

1 egg

1 (15¼-ounce) can whole kernel sweet corn, drained

1 (14¾-ounce) can cream style corn

Salt to taste

1 (8½-ounce) box corn muffin mix

In season, this soufflé is especially wonderful using fresh corn cut from the cob, but if you're busy year 'round then a premium brand of canned corn will do beautifully.

Preheat oven to 350 degrees. In 9 x 13-inch baking dish, combine butter, whipping cream, and egg; mix well. Add whole kernel corn, creamed corn, and salt to taste, stirring to combine. Cover corn mixture completely with corn muffin mix, being careful not to mix the corn muffin mix with the corn. Bake for 1 hour or until lightly browned and bubbling on top.

Corn Pudding

2 cups corn (corn scraped from 6 full fresh ears or a 16-ounce can of cream-style golden corn)

¼ cup sugar

2 tablespoons flour

1 teaspoon salt

5 beaten eggs

2 cups milk

4 tablespoons butter

Preheat oven to 350 degrees. Mix corn, sugar, salt, and flour. Add beaten eggs and mix well; add milk and mix well. Pour into an ungreased 2-quart casserole dish and dot butter on top. Bake for 50 minutes.

Herbed Corn Soufflé

6 ears fresh corn, kernels
removed or 2 (15¼-ounce)
cans whole kernel corn

2 tablespoons all-purpose flour

2 eggs

1½ cups evaporated skim milk

2 tablespoons sugar

¼ teaspoon nutmeg

1 tablespoon freshly chopped
basil

1 teaspoon freshly chopped
chives

1 tablespoon freshly chopped
parsley

Dash of salt

Dash of pepper

Paprika

Preheat oven to 325 degrees. Remove kernels from cobs, scraping cobs
with flat knife to include corn milk, or drain canned corn, leaving small
amount of liquid. In mixing bowl, sprinkle flour over kernels and set aside.
In large mixing bowl with electric mixer, beat eggs until slightly frothy;
add evaporated milk, sugar, nutmeg, basil, chives, and parsley, mixing
well to combine. Add corn mixture to egg mixture and combine. Season
with salt and pepper. Pour into 2½-quart casserole coated with non-stick
cooking spray. Sprinkle with paprika. Bake 45 to 50 minutes or until set.

Serves 6-8

This is especially good if
made using "Silver Queen"
corn, but it can be difficult
to find unless you're growing
your own. We're fortunate
to have roadside stands in
the countryside surrounding
Athens, and the proprietors
are usually more than happy
to discuss which of their
offerings has a similar (or
even better) flavor.

Vidalia Corn Bake

1 cup sour cream

½ cup milk

¼ teaspoon salt

2 cups shredded Cheddar cheese,
divided

2 large Vidalia onions (or other
sweet onion), thinly sliced

1 stick butter or margarine

1 egg

1 (14¾-ounce) can cream style
corn

1 (8½-ounce) box corn muffin
mix

Preheat oven to 350 degrees. In mixing bowl, combine sour cream,
milk, and salt. Fold in 1 cup cheese and set aside. In large skillet over
medium-high heat, sauté onions in butter until tender. Add sour cream
mixture; remove from heat and set aside.

In mixing bowl, combine egg, corn, and corn muffin mix. Pour into
greased 13 x 9-inch baking pan. Spoon onion mixture over mix. Sprinkle
with remaining cheese. Bake, uncovered, 45 to 50 minutes or until set and
lightly browned. Let stand 10 minutes before cutting.

Try this in individual tartlets
for a scrumptious finger
food, heeding the baking
instructions found on the
package of frozen miniature
pie shells.

Vidalia Onion Pie

3 medium Vidalia onions, thinly
    sliced and quartered

1 stick butter

3 eggs, lightly beaten

1 cup sour cream

¼ teaspoon salt

½ teaspoon pepper

¼ teaspoon cayenne pepper

1 (9-inch) pie shell, unbaked

½ cup grated Parmesan cheese

Preheat oven to 450 degrees. In skillet over medium heat, sauté onions in butter until tender and transparent. Remove from heat and set aside. In large mixing bowl, combine eggs, sour cream, salt, pepper, and cayenne pepper until thoroughly mixed. Transfer onions to pie shell. Pour egg mixture over onions and sprinkle with cheese. Bake 15 minutes, then lower temperature to 325 degrees and bake additional 15 to 20 minutes or until lightly browned and set. Serve warm.

Vidalia, Georgia, hosts its Onion Festival usually on or around the last weekend in April. Remember, if they're not grown in this region, they're not Vidalias.

Green Beans Sorrento

2 (14½-ounce) cans green beans,
    drained

1 (4-ounce) can sliced black
    olives, drained

2 tablespoons red wine vinegar

2 tablespoons olive oil

1 teaspoon dried basil

1 teaspoon dried oregano

1 teaspoon garlic salt

In large mixing bowl, combine ingredients, tossing well to coat. Cover, chill, and marinate overnight.

If using fresh green beans, be sure to snap them into pieces of relatively the same size to ensure even distribution of seasonings, and consider substituting one pound of wax beans for added variation of color.

Spicy French Beans

4 slices bacon

1 tablespoon sugar

2 tablespoons water

½ teaspoon seasoned salt flavor
    enhancer

1 onion, sliced in rings

2 tablespoons vinegar

½ teaspoon salt

1 package frozen French green
    beans, thawed

Fry bacon until crisp and set aside. Measure out 2 tablespoons of the bacon drippings. Add remaining ingredients and simmer about 1 hour. When ready to serve, sprinkle with chopped bacon. When using unthawed beans, omit the water.

Serves 4

This bean dish gives you all the flavor of fresh beans without all of the trouble. They go great with just about anything and are always a great side for your buffet meal.

Asparagus Bundles with Prosciutto

A delicate and dainty complement to grilled meats.

1 bundle fresh asparagus

Olive oil

Salt and pepper to taste

¼ pound sliced prosciutto

2 to 3 ounces shredded Parmesan cheese

Preheat oven to 350 degrees. Wash asparagus; trim and discard ends. Arrange asparagus on baking sheet. Drizzle with olive oil and season with salt and pepper. Bake 10 minutes and remove from oven. Arrange asparagus into bundles of 4 to 5 stalks and wrap with prosciutto. Sprinkle with Parmesan. Return to oven and bake 7 minutes or until cheese melts.

Serves 4-6

Prosciutto is thinly sliced from ham that has been salt-cured and air-dried but not smoked, and although it traditionally accompanies melon or figs, as part of these asparagus bundles, it also complements grilled meats.

 # Asparagus for a Buffet Meal

1 tall can green asparagus spears

1 cup slivered (naked) almonds

1 can large whole button mushrooms

¼ pound New York sharp Cheddar cheese

Drain liquid off asparagus and place a layer in a casserole dish. Add a layer of almonds combined with mushrooms. Repeat layers. Pour white sauce over asparagus, mushrooms, and almonds. Grate cheese on top and heat.

Serves 6

WHITE SAUCE

3 tablespoons butter or margarine

3 tablespoons flour

1 cup milk

Blend flour into melted butter; add milk and cook until medium thick.

There's no reason to reach for a packet when there's a white sauce as simple and delectable as this one, and best of all, this recipe can easily be doubled!

Roasted Asparagus

1 pound fresh asparagus, trimmed

¼ cup olive oil

3 tablespoons lemon juice

½ teaspoon salt

¼ teaspoon pepper

⅓ cup freshly grated Parmesan cheese

Preheat oven to 400 degrees. Place asparagus on baking sheet and drizzle with olive oil, lemon juice, salt, and pepper. Sprinkle with Parmesan cheese and bake for 15 to 18 minutes, until asparagus is crisp tender.

Asparagus Italiano

2 pounds asparagus, trimmed

4 garlic cloves, chopped

3 tablespoons olive oil

8 vine-ripe tomatoes, peeled, or canned whole tomatoes

Salt

2 tablespoons basil, finely chopped

¼ cup bread crumbs

¼ cup freshly grated Parmesan cheese

Preheat oven to 450 degrees. Blanch asparagus and drain, then arrange in a single layer in a shallow dish.

Sauté the garlic in a pan with 2 tablespoons of olive oil. When it starts to brown, add the tomatoes and salt. Cook over medium-high heat until it thickens, about 6 minutes. Pour over the asparagus and top with the chopped basil. Combine the bread crumbs and Parmesan and sprinkle over the top. Drizzle with the remaining olive oil.

Bake for about 7 to 10 minutes, or until the top is golden brown. Serve immediately.

Dijon Green Beans Amandine

2 tablespoons Dijon mustard

¼ teaspoon salt

¼ teaspoon black pepper

¼ cup slivered almonds

1½ pounds green beans

2 teaspoons butter

¾ cup thinly sliced shallots

1 tablespoon sour cream

In small mixing bowl, combine mustard, salt, and pepper; set aside. Toast almonds in skillet over low heat until golden; set aside. Steam green beans until tender; set aside. In skillet, melt butter over low-medium heat. Add shallots and sauté over medium heat. Add green beans and mustard mixture, gently stirring to combine. Cook 2 minutes or until thoroughly heated. Stir in sour cream and almonds and remove from heat. Serve immediately.

Serves 10

This recipe is eminently adaptable. You might substitute garlic for the shallots, or add sliced mushrooms that have been simmered in a bit of red wine.

Ranch Style Beans

½ cup cold water

1 cup ketchup

2 tablespoons prepared mustard

2 tablespoons cider vinegar

1 (1¼-ounce) package onion soup mix

1 pound ground chuck, cooked and drained

2 (15-ounce) cans pork and beans

1 (15-ounce) can dark red kidney beans, drained

Preheat oven to 400 degrees. In large mixing bowl, combine water, ketchup, mustard, and vinegar. Add soup mix, stirring to combine. In 9 x 13-inch casserole, combine meat and beans. Add ketchup mixture, gently stirring to combine. Bake uncovered 45 to 55 minutes.

Tangy Baked Beans

⅓ cup dark brown sugar, firmly
    packed

1 tablespoon vinegar

1 teaspoon dry mustard

½ teaspoon salt

½ cup strong coffee

2 (16-ounce) cans oven baked
    beans

1 large onion, thinly sliced

6 slices bacon, cut up

Preheat oven to 350 degrees. In a saucepan, mix brown sugar, vinegar, dry mustard, salt, and coffee; simmer for 5 minutes. In a 2-quart casserole, layer beans, sliced onion, and half of the brown sugar mixture. Repeat layers. Top with bacon pieces and bake 45 minutes or until bacon is cooked.

Serves 8

Good with a green salad and any meat cooked on the grill for a patio meal. Beans will keep moist and warm for several hours after cooking if covered with foil and left in a 200 degree oven.

Copper Carrots

2 pounds small carrots

2 chopped onions

1 (10¾-ounce) can tomato soup

½ cup red wine vinegar

½ cup oil

1 cup sugar

1 teaspoon Worcestershire sauce

1 teaspoon salt

1 teaspoon pepper

In large saucepan over medium-high heat, cover carrots with water. Cook 30 minutes and drain. Add remaining ingredients to saucepan and cook 10 minutes over medium-high heat, stirring constantly. Remove from heat and chill. Reheat to serve.

Carrots were once grown for medicinal purposes and have the highest beta-carotene content of any vegetable.

Broccoli Puff

1 (16-ounce) container cottage cheese

3 eggs, lightly beaten

½ teaspoon salt

½ teaspoon onion powder

½ pound shredded Cheddar cheese

2 packages frozen broccoli, thawed

4 tablespoons butter, melted

1 cup bread crumbs

Preheat oven to 350 degrees. In large mixing bowl, combine cottage cheese, eggs, salt, and onion powder. Fold in Cheddar and broccoli. Pour into 9 x 13-inch casserole. In small mixing bowl, combine butter and bread crumbs. Sprinkle on top of broccoli. Bake 1 hour or until knife inserted in center comes out clean. Remove from oven and allow to set 10 minutes before serving.

Serves 8

If using fresh spinach, remember that it reduces in volume anywhere from two-thirds to three-quarters when cooked, so plan accordingly to maintain proper ratios of ingredients.

Spiñaci Risparmi

3 cloves garlic, minced

2 (10-ounce) packages frozen, chopped spinach, thawed and drained

2 tablespoons olive oil

Salt and pepper to taste

5 eggs, lightly beaten

½ cup grated Parmesan cheese

In large skillet over medium-high heat, sauté garlic and spinach in oil. Season with salt and pepper to taste. Reduce heat and add eggs, stirring frequently. When eggs have cooked, add cheese and cook additional 2 minutes.

Easy Spinach Bake

2 (10-ounce) packages frozen,
   chopped spinach, cooked
   and drained

1 (3-ounce) package cream
   cheese, softened

1 (10½-ounce) can cream of
   mushroom soup

1 large can French fried onion
   rings, divided

Preheat oven to 400 degrees. In medium bowl, combine spinach and cream cheese, stirring until cheese melts. Add soup and half of onion rings. Transfer mixture to 8 x 8-inch casserole dish and bake 10 minutes. Remove from oven and sprinkle with remaining onions. Bake additional 5 minutes or until bubbly.

Serves 6

This is a superb twist on the traditional green bean casserole and can also be made using chard for a similarly delicious result.

Burgundy Mushrooms

4 sticks butter

1 quart Burgundy wine

1½ tablespoons Worcestershire
   sauce

1 teaspoon dill weed

1 teaspoon black pepper

1 teaspoon minced garlic

2 cups boiling water

4 beef bouillon cubes

4 chicken bouillon cubes

4 pounds mushrooms, wiped
   clean

In stockpot, melt butter over medium heat. Add wine, Worcestershire, seasonings, water, and bouillon cubes, mixing well; fold in mushrooms. Bring to a slow boil on medium heat. Reduce heat, cover, and simmer 3 to 5 hours. Remove lid and cook additional 3 to 5 hours or until liquid just covers mushrooms. Allow to cool to room temperature. Do NOT stir! Transfer mushrooms to covered container and chill. Reheat to serve.

Serves 12

We are always mindful not to cook with anything we wouldn't drink, so consider the popularity of white burgundies if contemplating a personalization of this recipe. The repeated cooking times of three to five hours are not a mistake and well worth the wait.

Rutabagas are also sold under the name "yellow turnips." Prior to the widespread availability of pumpkins, these turnips were once used to make jack-o-lanterns.

Glazed Garden-Fresh Jubilee

A recipe made from vegetables in the garden!

1 large yellow rutabaga

4 large carrots

4 small zucchini

2 tablespoons butter or margarine

3 tablespoons honey

2 tablespoons lemon juice

⅓ cup water

1 tablespoon fresh, finely chopped ginger

1 tablespoon fresh, finely chopped rosemary

Rosemary sprigs for garnish

Chop vegetables into 1 x ¼-inch matchstick-sized pieces. Steam vegetables separately until tender crisp and drain. In large skillet or Dutch oven, melt butter over low heat and stir in honey, lemon juice, water, and ginger. Cook over low heat until sauce thickens. Remove from heat and stir in vegetables, tossing until lightly coated. Sprinkle with rosemary. Serve hot or at room temperature. Garnish with rosemary sprigs just before serving.

Serves 4-6

The broiled tomato is one component of a traditional full English breakfast, but goes equally well alongside lunchtime sandwiches or with salmon steaks at dinner.

Broiled Tomatoes

4 medium tomatoes

2 tablespoons Dijon mustard

¼ teaspoon salt

¼ teaspoon pepper

⅛ teaspoon cayenne pepper

1 cup Italian bread crumbs

1 cup freshly grated Parmesan cheese

8 tablespoons butter, melted

Cut tomatoes in half, pat dry, and set aside. In small mixing bowl, combine mustard, salt, pepper, and cayenne pepper. Sprinkle over cut sides of tomatoes. In mixing bowl, combine bread crumbs, Parmesan, and butter. Spread evenly over tomatoes. Place on rack in broiler pan. Broil 6 inches from heat 2 to 3 minutes or until lightly browned. Ovens vary greatly, so watch carefully. Serve immediately.

Serves 8

Italian Stuffed Tomatoes

8 large tomatoes

1 cup chopped onions

3 tablespoons olive oil

1 (10-ounce) package frozen, chopped spinach, thawed and drained

1 cup ricotta cheese

2 egg yolks, beaten

½ cup parsley, chopped

½ cup shredded mozzarella cheese

⅔ cup freshly grated Parmesan cheese

½ cup slivered almonds, toasted

Salt and pepper to taste

Parmesan cheese

Preheat oven to 350 degrees. Wash tomatoes; remove and discard tops and pulp. Salt tomato cavity and turn upside down; allow to drain 30 minutes.

In sauté pan over medium heat, cook onions in oil 20 minutes or until tender. Add spinach to onions, stirring until thoroughly heated. Remove from heat and set aside.

In mixing bowl, beat together ricotta cheese and egg yolks. Add parsley, mozzarella, Parmesan, and almonds. Season with salt and pepper. Stir in onion mixture and blend until well combined.

Fill tomato shells with onion mixture. Transfer stuffed tomatoes to shallow, greased 9 x 13-inch baking dish. Sprinkle with additional Parmesan and bake 20 minutes or until tops are brown.

Serves 8-10

Tomato Casserole

2 (28-ounce) cans diced tomatoes

6 strips bacon

1 large onion, chopped

2 pieces white bread, torn into bite-sized pieces

½ teaspoon salt

½ teaspoon sugar

½ teaspoon black pepper

Preheat oven to 350 degrees. Fry bacon until crisp, drain, and reserve grease. Sauté chopped onion in the grease. Add to tomato in 11 x 7-inch baking dish. Stir in remaining ingredients. Bake 45 minutes.

Serves 6

Tomatoes were initially eyed with suspicion when first introduced to Spain from Latin America, as they are a member of the poisonous nightshade family. Stuffed this way, they're certainly "to-die-for," but neither you nor those you serve them to need worry about any such thing.

Tomato Pie

1 deep-dish pie crust

4 large tomatoes

¼ teaspoon black pepper

1 bunch spring onions, chopped

6 leaves basil, chopped

1 cup shredded Mozzarella cheese

1 cup shredded sharp Cheddar cheese

1 cup mayonnaise

Salt to taste

Preheat oven to 350 degrees. Cook deep-dish pie crust according to directions on package. Peel and slice tomatoes, season with salt, and set aside for 1 hour. Drain tomatoes and pat dry; layer in precooked pie crust. Cover tomato layer with black pepper, spring onions, and basil. In a separate bowl, mix together 1 cup Mozzarella cheese, 1 cup sharp Cheddar cheese, and 1 cup mayonnaise. Spread mixture on top of tomatoes and other ingredients. Bake for 35 minutes.

Serves 6 to 8

In the 1918 version of Fanny Farmer's Boston Cooking-School Cookbook, she writes, "Never allow more than two layers of oysters for Scalloped Oysters; if three layers are used, the middle layer will be underdone, while others are properly cooked." No doubt your family will be pleased with both layers of this decadent oyster dish as well.

Erwin Family Scalloped Oysters

4 to 5 cups crackers, crushed

3 sticks butter, melted

1½ quarts oysters, divided

Salt and pepper to taste

1 pint whipping cream, divided

Dash of hot sauce (optional)

Dash of Worcestershire sauce (optional)

Preheat oven to 400 degrees. In small mixing bowl, combine crackers and butter. Layer half of cracker mixture on bottom of 3-quart casserole. Cover with half of oysters. Sprinkle with salt and pepper. Pour half of whipping cream over oysters. Repeat oyster and cream layers. Sprinkle with remaining crackers. Top with dashes of hot sauce and Worcestershire, if desired. Bake 30 minutes.

Serves 12

Desserts

Zim's Mounds Pie

CRUMB CRUST

2 cups chocolate wafer cookie
    crumbs

6 tablespoons unsalted butter,
    melted

6 tablespoons confectioners'
    sugar

In mixing bowl, combine crumbs, butter, and confectioners' sugar. Mix well and firmly press crumb mixture into bottom of 9-inch round springform pan coated with nonstick cooking spray.

FILLING

2 (14-ounce) cans sweetened
    condensed milk

21 ounces (1½ packages) flaked
    coconut

Preheat oven to 350 degrees. In mixing bowl, combine sweetened condensed milk and coconut. Mix well and spread evenly over crust. Bake 25 minutes and let cool.

TOPPING

8 ounces semisweet chocolate
    chips

¾ cup heavy whipping cream

2 tablespoons unsalted butter

Place chocolate chips in heatproof bowl and set aside. In heavy saucepan over medium-high heat, combine whipping cream and butter. Remove from heat just before reaching a boil. Pour over chocolate chips and let stand 5 minutes-do not stir. After 5 minutes, whisk until smooth. Pour over coconut filling, spreading evenly. Chill overnight. Use a sharp knife to cut around edges of pie before releasing from springform pan.

Use a knife warmed under hot tap water to cut pie into pieces.
This dessert is also great to freeze. Just remove from freezer and
defrost in the refrigerator a day before use.

Since 1993, Zim's has been serving the only made from scratch, authentic NewYork Style bagels in Athens. Originally offering 35 different sandwiches, Zim's has expanded their repertoire to include the Amazin' Grazin' Table! A one of a kind food bar featuring delicious salads, yummy hot food, and scrumptious homemade desserts! Everything is made from scratch daily. Believe us, you'll taste the difference!

Trumps Chocolate Chip Pecan Pie

1 (9-inch) unbaked pie shell	1¼ cups sugar
1 cup semisweet chocolate chips	⅝ cup corn syrup
¾ cup pecans, chopped	¼ teaspoon salt
2 tablespoons bourbon	¼ teaspoon vanilla
5 eggs, beaten	4 tablespoons butter, softened

Preheat oven to 375 degrees. Line baking sheet with parchment paper. Pierce bottom of pie crust with fork. Cover bottom of pie shell with chocolate chips. In mixing bowl, combine pecans and bourbon. In separate mixing bowl with electric mixer on medium speed, beat together eggs, sugar, corn syrup, salt, vanilla, and butter. Drain pecans and fold into sugar mixture. Pour mixture into one 9-inch deep-dish or 2 regular pie shells. Place pie on paper-lined baking sheet. Bake pie exactly 1 hour. Serve at room temperature or slightly warm with ice cream.

Serves 8

Really Rich Pecan Brownie Pie

1 cup sugar	⅔ cup evaporated milk
2 tablespoons all-purpose flour	2 tablespoons butter
½ teaspoon salt	1 (6-ounce) package semisweet chocolate chips
2 eggs, beaten	1 teaspoon vanilla
1 cup pecans, chopped	1 deep-dish pie shell, unbaked

Preheat oven to 375 degrees. In large mixing bowl, combine sugar, flour, and salt. Stir in eggs, mixing well to combine. Fold in pecans and set aside. Combine evaporated milk, butter, and chocolate chips in double boiler over medium-high heat. Beat with whisk until chocolate melts. Stir in flour mixture, then add vanilla. Pour into unbaked deep-dish pie shell. Bake 35 minutes. Serve with vanilla ice cream.

Serves 8

Nana's Old-Fashioned Toasted Coconut Pie

Even more delicious with a scoop of vanilla ice cream!

3 eggs, beaten

1½ cups sugar

½ cup margarine, melted

4 teaspoons lemon juice

1½ teaspoons vanilla

1 (3½-ounce) can flaked coconut

1 (9-inch) pie shell, unbaked

Preheat oven to 350 degrees. In large mixing bowl, combine eggs, sugar, margarine, lemon juice, and vanilla with electric mixer on medium speed. Stir in coconut. Pour into pie shell. Bake 45 minutes or until set. Cool completely before serving.

Serves 8

South Georgia Pecan Pie

½ cup sugar

4 tablespoons butter, softened

1 cup dark corn syrup

¼ teaspoon salt

1 teaspoon vanilla

3 eggs

1½ cups pecans

1 (9-inch) deep dish pie shell, unbaked

Preheat oven to 350 degrees. In medium mixing bowl, cream together sugar and butter with electric mixer on medium speed. Add corn syrup, salt, and vanilla, mixing well to combine. Add eggs one at a time, beating well after each addition. Stir in pecans. Pour into pie shell. Bake 45 minutes, or until pie is set. Cool and serve with whipped topping.

Peak months for fresh coconut are October through December, but due to its prolific nature, it can be found year-round in many markets. Most markets will display fresh coconuts already removed from the outer husk, stripped down to the hard dark-brown shell with the three distinctive circular indentations at the base end.

As much as we love a peach cobbler, if you want to serve a quintessential Georgia dessert, pecan pie is the way to go, as the 'Peach State' actually leads the nation in pecan production.

Old-Fashioned Chocolate Pie

2 cups milk	2 tablespoons cocoa
2 tablespoons butter	½ teaspoon vanilla
3 egg yolks, beaten (reserve egg whites)	1 baked pie shell
	3 egg whites
¾ cup sugar	½ teaspoon vanilla
⅓ cup all-purpose flour	6 tablespoons sugar

Preheat oven to 325 degrees. In mixing bowl, combine sugar, flour, and cocoa, mixing well; set aside. In large saucepan over low heat, combine milk, butter, and egg yolks, removing from heat as necessary to prevent egg yolks from curdling. Whisk sugar mixture into liquid, cooking until mixture boils and thickens. Stir in vanilla and pour into baked pie shell. In chilled metal bowl, beat egg whites with electric mixer on high speed. Gradually add sugar and vanilla, beating until soft peaks form. Spread meringue over pie to edges of shell. Bake 12 to 15 minutes.

You can use canned pumpkin pie filling or roast a sugar pumpkin and purée it. It just depends on how much time you want to spend on the pie.

Holiday Pumpkin Pie

1 (16-ounce) can pumpkin	½ teaspoon nutmeg
¾ cup sugar	3 eggs, beaten
1 teaspoon cinnamon	1 (5½-ounce) can evaporated milk
½ teaspoon salt	½ cup milk
½ teaspoon ginger	1 (9-inch) pie pastry

Preheat oven to 375 degrees. In large mixing bowl, combine pumpkin, sugar, cinnamon, salt, ginger, and nutmeg with electric mixer on medium speed. Gently whisk in eggs; add milks and mix well. Pour into pastry lined pie plate, covering pastry edges with foil. Bake 25 minutes. Remove from oven and discard foil. Bake additional 25 to 30 minutes, or until knife inserted near center comes out clean. Cool completely. Cover and chill to store.

Serves 8

Easy Pumpkin Crisp

1 (15-ounce) can pumpkin

1 cup evaporated milk

1 cup sugar

1½ teaspoons vanilla

¾ teaspoon cinnamon

1 package super moist yellow cake mix

1½ cups chopped pecans

1 stick butter, melted

Frozen whipped topping, thawed

Nutmeg

Preheat oven to 350 degrees. In large mixing bowl, combine pumpkin, evaporated milk, sugar, vanilla, and cinnamon; pour into prepared 9 x 13-inch baking pan. Sprinkle cake mix evenly over mixture. Sprinkle with pecans and drizzle with melted butter. Bake 1 hour, 5 minutes, or until golden brown. Remove from oven and allow to cool at least 10 minutes before serving. Serve warm or at room temperature with whipped topping. Sprinkle with nutmeg.

Serves 12-15

 # Aunt Georgia's Lemon Chiffon Pie

3 eggs, separated

½ cup, plus ¼ cup sugar

Juice of 1 lemon

Grated rind from 1 lemon

Pinch of salt

3 tablespoons hot water

1 (9-inch) baked pie crust

Preheat oven to 325 degrees. Beat egg yolks until lemon colored. Add ½ cup of the sugar and beat well. Add lemon juice, lemon rind, salt, and hot water. Cook in double boiler to a custard, stirring constantly. Set aside. Beat egg whites until stiff. Fold in remaining ¼ cup sugar gradually so that grains dissolve. Fold custard slowly into egg whites. Pour into baked pie crust. (Do not use graham cracker crust.).

Bake 30 to 35 minutes, increasing oven temperature to 350 degrees for the last 5 or 10 minutes, to brown top to a golden color. Open oven door to cool a bit before removing pie. Slow cooling minimizes settling.

With flavors that range from mildly sweet to tart and tangy, blueberries are nutritional, bursting with flavor while being very low in calories. Blueberries are at their best from May through October when they are in season.

Fresh Blueberry Crisp

⅔ cup sugar

2 tablespoons cornstarch

2 tablespoons lemon juice

5 cups blueberries
(fresh or frozen)

¾ cup rolled oats

½ cup all-purpose flour

¼ cup brown sugar

2 tablespoons chopped walnuts or pecans

6 tablespoons light margarine or butter

Preheat oven to 375 degrees. Coat a 1-quart baking dish with butter. In large mixing bowl, combine sugar, cornstarch, and lemon juice; mix well. Gently fold in blueberries, tossing well to coat. Spoon into baking dish. In same bowl, combine oats, flour, brown sugar, and nuts. With fork or pastry blender, cut in margarine until crumbly. Sprinkle blueberries with mixture. Bake 45 minutes to 1 hour, or until lightly browned and bubbling.

Serves 8

 # Georgia Peach Cobbler

2 cups fresh sliced peaches, peeled

2 cups sugar

½ cup butter

2 teaspoons baking powder

¾ cup plain flour

¾ cup milk

Pinch of salt

Whipped cream

Preheat oven to 350 degrees. Toss sliced peaches with 1 cup sugar. Melt butter in a 9 x 9-inch deep baking dish. Mix together 1 cup sugar, baking powder, flour, milk and salt; pour melted butter into baking dish. Top with fresh peaches. Do NOT stir. Bake in the oven for 1 hour. Serve with whipped cream or vanilla ice cream.

Serves 6

Grammy's Buttermilk Pie

2 tablespoons all-purpose flour

1¾ cups sugar

½ teaspoon salt

1 stick butter, softened

3 eggs

¾ cup buttermilk

½ teaspoon vanilla

1 (9-inch) unbaked deep dish pie
   shell

Preheat oven to 350 degrees. In mixing bowl, combine flour, sugar, and salt; set aside. In large mixing bowl, beat together butter and eggs with electric mixer on medium speed. Stir in buttermilk and vanilla. Gradually add flour mixture, mixing well to combine. Pour into pie shell. Place pie on baking sheet and bake 45 minutes.

Serves 6-8

Dot's Mandarin Orange Nut Pie

1 cup pecans or walnuts

2 teaspoons cooking oil

1 can Mandarin oranges, drained
   and crushed

1 can sweetened condensed milk

½ cup lemon juice concentrate

1 (8-ounce) container frozen
   whipped topping, thawed

1 graham cracker pie crust

On microwavable plate, drizzle nuts with oil and toast in microwave 1 minute, 30 seconds. Set aside. In mixing bowl, combine oranges, sweetened condensed milk, lemon juice concentrate, and frozen whipped topping. Spread toasted nuts in bottom of pie crust. Pour orange mixture over nuts. Freeze at least 3 to 4 hours until firm.

Triple Layer Carrot Cake with Pecan Cream Cheese Frosting

Very moist and delicious.

4 eggs

2 cups sugar

1½ cups cooking oil

3 cups grated carrot

2 cups all-purpose flour

1 teaspoon salt

2 teaspoons baking soda

2 teaspoons cinnamon

1 cup chopped pecans (optional)

Preheat oven to 350 degrees. In large mixing bowl, cream together eggs, sugar, and oil with electric mixer on medium speed. In separate bowl, sift together flour, salt, baking soda, and cinnamon. Gradually add flour mixture to sugar mixture, beating to combine. Stir in carrot, mixing well. Add pecans if desired. Pour into three greased and floured 8-inch round baking pans. Bake 25 to 30 minutes. Remove from oven and cool completely before turning out. Cake will be very moist. Spread Cream Cheese Frosting between layers, around sides, and on top of cake.

PECAN CREAM CHEESE FROSTING

1 (8-ounce) package, plus
    1 (3-ounce) package cream
    cheese, softened

1 stick butter, softened

1 (16-ounce) package
    confectioners' sugar

1 teaspoon vanilla

1 cup pecans, finely chopped

In mixing bowl, combine cream cheese, butter, confectioners' sugar, and vanilla, beating with electric mixer on medium speed. Fold in pecans.

Serves 16

202

Lemon "Cheese" Cake with Cream Cheese Icing

2 cups all-purpose flour

1 teaspoon baking soda

2 cups sugar

½ cup shortening, softened

1 stick butter, softened

1 tablespoon vanilla

5 eggs, separated

1 cup buttermilk

Preheat oven to 350 degrees. In small mixing bowl, sift together flour and baking soda. In large mixing bowl, cream together sugar, shortening, butter, and vanilla. Add egg yolks one at a time, beating well after each addition. Add flour mixture alternately with buttermilk. In chilled metal bowl, beat egg whites until stiff peaks form. Gently fold egg whites into batter. Pour into three greased and floured 8-inch round cake pans. Bake 25 minutes, or until toothpick inserted in center comes out clean. Cool cakes completely on wire racks. Spread ½ cup Lemon "Cheese" Filling between each layer and on top of cake. Spread Cream Cheese Icing on sides of cake.

LEMON "CHEESE" FILLING

1 stick butter

1 cup sugar

1 tablespoon all-purpose flour

3 egg yolks

½ cup freshly squeezed lemon juice

Melt butter in a saucepan over heat. Whisk in sugar and egg yolks. Add lemon juice and flour, whisking well to mix. Increase heat to medium and bring to a low boil. Boil 5 minutes, stirring constantly, until mixture thickens and coats the back of a spoon. Cool and chill until ready to use. (Makes 2 cups)

CREAM CHEESE ICING

1 (8-ounce) package cream cheese, softened

1 stick butter, softened

1 tablespoon vanilla

1 (16-ounce) package confectioners' sugar

In small mixing bowl, cream butter and sugar with electric mixer on low, until fluffy. Gradually add confectioners' sugar, mixing well. Stir in vanilla.

Serves 10-12

For a lighter cake, separate the eggs and add just the yolks to the butter mixture first. Then whip the egg whites separately using clean beaters until they form soft peaks. Then fold them into your cake batter.

Lemon Cheese Cake is an old Southern cake that does not actually contain cheese. We added the Cream Cheese Icing to balance the tartness of the lemon filling.

Mayonnaise is used in replacement of eggs and oil in this recipe, but you can't taste the difference.

The mayonnaise in this recipe supplies the eggs and oil otherwise necessary in this mouth-watering cake. You may find yourself using mayonnaise in all of your desserts after you see how moist this cake turns out!

Gramma V's Chocolate Cake

3 cups all-purpose flour, sifted

1½ cups sugar

⅓ cup cocoa

2¼ teaspoons baking powder

1½ teaspoons baking soda

1½ cups real mayonnaise

1½ cups water

1½ teaspoons vanilla

Preheat oven to 350 degrees. Grease two 9-inch cake pans and line bottoms with waxed paper. In large mixing bowl, combine flour, sugar, cocoa, baking powder, and baking soda. Stir in mayonnaise. Gradually stir in water and vanilla, mixing until smooth. Pour into cake pans. Bake 30 minutes, or until toothpick inserted near center comes out clean. Cool on wire racks before turning out. Remove and discard waxed paper. Frost between layers, around sides, and on top of cake with your favorite icing.

Folks from Mississippi will tell you that it is always called a Mississippi Mud Cake, but if you look through cookbooks for recipes for "mud cake," you can never find any agreement among them (they include anything from cherry pie filling, to coconut, to crushed pineapple).

So we feel comfortable defining a mud cake as a dessert from the American South that includes chocolate.

Georgia Mud Cake

1 box fudge brownie mix

2 cups miniature marshmallows

1 cup chopped pecans

1 cup sugar

⅓ cup butter or margarine

⅓ cup milk

1 cup semisweet chocolate chips

Prepare brownies according to package directions in 9 x 13-inch baking pan. Remove from oven and sprinkle warm brownies with marshmallows and pecans.

In small saucepan over medium-low heat, combine sugar, butter, and milk. Bring to a boil, stirring constantly, for 1 minute. Remove from heat and add chocolate chips, stirring until smooth. Pour over brownies and cool completely. Slice into squares and serve.

Serves 20

Old Fashioned Coca-Cola Cake

1 stick butter or margarine

3 tablespoons cocoa

1 cup Coca-Cola

2 cups sugar

2 cups all-purpose flour

1 teaspoon baking soda

½ cup buttermilk

2 eggs, beaten

1 teaspoon vanilla

Preheat oven to 350 degrees. In small saucepan over medium heat, melt margarine. Stir in cocoa and Coke and bring to a boil. In large mixing bowl, combine sugar and flour. Add hot cocoa mixture to sugar mixture, combining well with electric mixer set on medium speed. In separate mixing bowl, add baking soda to buttermilk; stir into batter. Add eggs, one at a time, beating well after each addition. Stir in vanilla. (Batter will be very thin.) Pour into greased and floured 9 x 13-inch baking pan or Bundt pan. Bake 30 minutes. Allow to cool 10 minutes before removing from pan. Drizzle warm cake with Chocolate Pecan Icing.

CHOCOLATE PECAN ICING

1 stick butter or margarine

3 tablespoons cocoa

6 tablespoons Coca-Cola

1 (16-ounce) package
confectioners' sugar

1 cup chopped pecans

1 teaspoon vanilla

In small saucepan over medium heat, melt margarine. Stir in cocoa and Coca Cola and bring to a boil. Remove from heat and stir in confectioners' sugar, stirring until smooth. Stir in vanilla and fold in pecans.

Jacob's Pharmacy, on Peachtree Street in Atlanta, was where Dr. John S. Pemberton sold the first Coca-Cola. The drink was marketed as being medicinal until 1905. It contained the extracts of cocoa leaves from South America and kola nuts from Africa, hence the name Coca-Cola.

This cake is inspired by another old southern favorite, Watergate Salad. Although it's a safe bet that, unlike a certain creation from the Waldorf-Astoria, Watergate salad has nothing to do with a hotel of the same name. However, the recipe did grace the back of pistachio pudding boxes for years on end, and well withstands the transformation into this unbelievably moist baked delight.

Watergate Cake with Pistachio Frosting

1 package white cake mix

1 (3-ounce) package pistachio instant pudding mix

¾ cup cooking oil

1 cup club soda

3 eggs

1 (3-ounce) package pistachio instant pudding mix

½ cup milk

1 (8-ounce) container frozen whipped topping, thawed

Preheat oven to 350 degrees. In large mixing bowl, combine cake mix and pudding mix together. Add oil, club soda, and eggs, beating with electric mixer on medium speed until smooth. Pour into greased and floured 9 x 13-inch baking pan. Bake 35 minutes. Remove from oven and cool. In small mixing bowl, whisk together pudding mix and milk until powder is just moist. Fold in whipped topping. Frost cooled cake before pudding sets.

Serves 12-16

Mama Mary's Fruit Cake Cookies

3 cups all-purpose flour

1 teaspoon baking soda

½ teaspoon salt

2 teaspoons cinnamon

½ teaspoon ground cloves

½ teaspoon allspice

1½ cup light brown sugar, well packed

3 eggs

2 sticks butter

½ cup buttermilk

6 cups pecans

1 pound candied cherries

6 slices candied pineapple

2 cups dates

Preheat oven to 300 degrees. In large mixing bowl, sift together flour, baking soda, salt, cinnamon, ground cloves, and allspice; set aside. In separate bowl, cream together sugar and butter with electric mixer on medium speed. Add eggs, one at a time, beating well after each addition. Add flour mixture, alternating with buttermilk, beating well to combine. Fold in pecans and fruit, mixing well. Drop by tablespoonfuls on prepared baking sheet. Bake 20 minutes. Batter can be kept in refrigerator and baked later.

Amande Gâteau

1¼ cups sugar

⅔ cup milk

1 egg

1½ teaspoons pure almond
  extract

1¼ cups all-purpose flour

½ teaspoon baking powder

1 stick margarine, melted

Confectioners' sugar

Preheat oven to 350 degrees. In large mixing bowl, beat together sugar, milk, egg, and almond extract with electric mixer on medium speed. Add flour, baking powder, and margarine, mixing well to combine. Mix all ingredients well. Pour into prepared baking pan (decorative pans work well for this recipe). Bake 40 to 50 minutes. Cool completely and sprinkle with confectioners' sugar.

It Will Cause a Riot Cake

A beautiful and delicious dessert sure to cause a riot anywhere it's served!

1 (20-ounce) can crushed
  pineapple in juice

2 large eggs, beaten

2 cups all-purpose flour

1¾ cups sugar

¼ teaspoon salt

2 teaspoons baking soda

Fruit of choice, for decoration
  (strawberries, blueberries,
  kiwi, banana, star fruit, etc.)

Preheat oven to 325 degrees. In large mixing bowl, combine pineapple (with juice) and eggs; set aside. In separate bowl, combine flour, sugar, salt, and baking soda. Gradually add to pineapple mixture, mixing well to combine. Pour into two prepared 9-inch round cake pans. Bake 30 minutes or until toothpick inserted in center comes out clean. Remove from oven and cool on wire racks before turning out. Spread Cream Cheese Frosting between layers, around sides, and on top of cake. Arrange fruit between layers. Decorate top and sides of cake with fruit and chill.

CREAM CHEESE FROSTING

1 stick butter or margarine,
  softened

2 cups confectioners' sugar

1 (8-ounce) package cream
  cheese, softened

In mixing bowl, beat together butter, confectioners' sugar, and cream cheese with electric mixer on medium speed.

My Grandmother's Tea Cakes

1 egg
1 cup sugar
½ cup shortening
4 tablespoons buttermilk

1 teaspoon baking soda
1 teaspoon vanilla
4 to 5 cups flour (enough to make dough manageable)

Preheat oven to 400 degrees. Mix all ingredients together. Roll out very thin and cut with cookie cutters. Place on ungreased cookie sheets and bake for about 9 minutes. Run spatula under cookies immediately after removing the pan from the oven to prevent sticking.

Makes about 50 cookies

3-Day Coconut Sour Cream Cake

1 (18½-ounce) package butter flavored cake mix (prepared in two 8-inch round cake pans according to package directions)

Divide both cooled layers in half so there are four layers. Spread Coconut Filling between cake layers (cut side up). Frost top and sides of cake with Coconut Frosting. Seal in plastic airtight container and chill 3 days before serving.

COCONUT FILLING

2 cups sugar
1 (16-ounce) container sour cream

1 (12-ounce) package frozen coconut, thawed

In mixing bowl, combine sugar, sour cream, and coconut; mix well to combine. Chill several hours. Reserve 1 cup for frosting.

COCONUT FROSTING

1 cup reserved Coconut Filling

1½ cups frozen whipped topping, thawed

In mixing bowl, combine reserved Coconut Filling with frozen whipped topping.

Italian Cream Cake

2 cups all-purpose flour

1 teaspoon baking soda

1 stick margarine, softened

½ cup shortening, softened

2 cups sugar

5 egg yolks, beaten

1 cup buttermilk

1 teaspoon vanilla

1 (3½-ounce) can coconut

1 cup chopped pecans, divided

5 egg whites, stiffly beaten

Chopped pecans

Preheat oven to 350 degrees. In mixing bowl, combine flour and baking soda; set aside. In large mixing bowl, cream margarine and shortening with electric mixer on medium speed. Add sugar and beat until smooth. Add egg yolks, one at a time, beating well after each addition. Add flour mixture alternately with buttermilk to creamed mixture, beating well to combine. Stir in vanilla. Add coconut and ¾ cup nuts. Fold in egg whites. Pour into three greased and floured 9-inch round cake pans. Bake 25 minutes. Remove from oven and cool on wire racks before turning out. Spread Cream Cheese Frosting between layers, around sides, and on top of cake. Sprinkle pecans between layers and on top of cake.

CREAM CHEESE FROSTING

1 (8-ounce) package cream
   cheese, softened

4 tablespoons margarine, softened

1 (16-ounce) package
   confectioners' sugar

1 teaspoon vanilla

Milk (optional)

In mixing bowl, beat cream cheese and margarine with electric mixer on medium speed until smooth. Add confectioners' sugar and vanilla, beating until smooth. Add small amount of milk, if necessary, to create desired consistency.

This cake is great warm from the oven and gets better with age! Keeps for at least 5 to 7 days.

Inner Banks Chardonnay Cake

¼ cup chopped pecans (optional)

1 package yellow cake mix

1 (3-ounce) package instant vanilla pudding mix

¾ cup water

¾ cup cooking oil

¼ cup Chardonnay wine

4 eggs

¼ cup sugar

¼ cup brown sugar

2 teaspoons cinnamon

Preheat oven to 325 degrees. Sprinkle pecans in bottom of prepared Bundt or tube pan, if desired. In large mixing bowl, combine cake mix and pudding mix. Add water, oil, wine, eggs, sugars, and cinnamon, beating with electric mixer on medium speed about 1 to 2 minutes. Pour into baking pan and bake 1 hour. Remove from oven. Pour half of Chardonnay Glaze over hot cake still in pan. Cool 10 minutes. Turn cake onto serving plate and drizzle with remaining glaze.

CHARDONNAY GLAZE

1 stick butter

1 cup sugar

¼ cup water

¼ cup Chardonnay

In saucepan over medium heat, combine butter, sugar, and water; bring to a boil. Boil 2 to 3 minutes, or until butter melts. Remove from heat and stir in wine.

Chocolate Fudge Mint Cake

2 cups all-purpose flour

1 cup sugar

½ cup unsweetened cocoa powder

2 teaspoons baking soda

¼ teaspoon salt

1 cup water

1 cup mayonnaise

1 teaspoon vanilla

1 (4½-ounce) package chocolate covered thin mints

Preheat oven to 350 degrees. In large mixing bowl, sift together flour, sugar, cocoa, baking soda, and salt; set aside. In separate mixing bowl, combine water, mayonnaise, and vanilla, beating with electric mixer on medium speed for 3 to 4 minutes. Gradually add flour mixture to mayonnaise mixture, mixing well to combine. Pour into two 9-inch greased and floured baking pans. Bake 25 minutes. Turn oven off. Remove from oven and cool 10 minutes in pans. Turn out one layer onto serving plate and other layer onto cooling rack. Completely cover plated layer with mints. Return to oven 3 to 5 minutes to slightly melt mints. Remove from oven and spread mints evenly with spatula. Top with second cake layer and cool completely. Spread Fudge Frosting over top of cake.

FUDGE FROSTING

6 tablespoons unsweetened cocoa powder

2 cups sugar

⅔ cup milk

1 stick butter

Pinch of salt

1 teaspoon vanilla

In saucepan over medium high heat, combine cocoa, sugar milk, butter, and salt. Stir constantly and bring mixture to a boil. Reduce heat to low, boiling gently for 3 minutes without stirring. Remove from heat and pour into mixing bowl. Cool 3 minutes. Stir in vanilla. Beat with electric mixer on medium speed until just thick enough to spread without running off of cake.

Serves 24

WHAT IS A DESSERT WINE?

A dessert wine is one that is sweet and full of flavor. Dessert wines are thicker and sweeter than table wines. The grapes are picked late in the harvest to preserve residual sugars. Examples include fortified wines like port and sherry and late harvest wines, which originated from grapes that have shriveled a bit, concentrating their sweetness. As a rule of thumb, a dessert wine should always be sweeter than the dessert it accompanies. Some of the most popular fortified wines include Madeira, Vermouth, Marsala, Sherry, Cream Sherry, and Port.

Red Velvet Cake

2½ cups self-rising flour

1 teaspoon baking soda

1½ cups sugar

1½ cups cooking oil

2 large eggs, lightly beaten

1 teaspoon white vinegar

1 teaspoon pure vanilla extract

1 cup whole buttermilk

2½ tablespoons red food coloring

Preheat oven to 350 degrees. Grease three (9-inch) round cake pans and line with wax paper. Set aside.

In medium mixing bowl, combine flour and baking soda. Set aside. In separate mixing bowl, combine sugar, oil, eggs, vinegar, and vanilla. With electric mixer on medium speed, beat until light and fluffy, about 2 minutes. Gradually add flour mixture, and mix on low speed just until flour has just been incorporated. Slowly add buttermilk. Add food coloring and beat well to combine.

Pour batter equally into pans. Bake about 30 minutes. Remove pans to wire rack to cool 5 minutes. Invert pans onto wire racks until cake is completely cool.

To assemble, place one layer, top side down, on a cake plate, and spread with frosting. Repeat with remaining layers. Frost top and sides. Store in an airtight container for up to one week.

Serves 12

CREAM CHEESE FROSTING

2 sticks butter, softened

2 (8-ounce) cream cheese, softened

2 cup confectioners' sugar, sifted

2 teaspoons vanilla

¼ cup finely chopped pecans

Place butter in bowl of electric stand mixer and beat on medium-high speed until light and fluffy, about 2 minutes. Add cream cheese and beat until combined and fluffy, about 2 minutes. Add confectioner's sugar and vanilla and beat until well blended. Gently fold in pecans. Makes enough to generously frost a 3-layer cake.

A Southern specialty, the Red Velvet Cake owes its red color to history. Originally, its deep red color was thought to be due to a reaction between early varieties of cocoa and baking soda. But this reaction also gave the cake a soapy taste. Thereafter, cooks and bakers decided to use food coloring or an edible red dye to get the same effect.

Black Russian Cake

It is rich, moist, and delicious!

1 cup cooking oil	4 eggs
½ cup sugar	1 yellow cake mix (no pudding)
¾ cup water	1 (6-ounce) package chocolate instant pudding mix
¼ cup vodka	½ cup confectioners' sugar
¼ cup Kahlúa	¼ cup Kahlúa

Preheat oven to 350 degrees. In large mixing bowl, combine oil, sugar, water, vodka, and Kahlúa. Add eggs one at a time, beating well with electric mixer on medium speed after each addition. Add cake mix and pudding mix and beat 4 minutes. Pour into greased and floured Bundt pan. Bake 45 to 50 minutes. Cool 10 minutes before turning out onto serving platter. In small mixing bowl, combine confectioners' sugar and Kahlúa. Mix well to combine. With the end of a wooden spoon, make holes in cake and drizzle with Kahlúa Glaze. Cool completely and cover with plastic wrap and chill. Serve with ice cream or frozen whipped topping. Cake will keep up to one month.

Serves 16

Thanksgiving Pumpkin Pie Cake

3 eggs, beaten	1 teaspoon clove
3 cups canned pumpkin	1 teaspoon cinnamon
2 cups evaporated milk	1 box yellow cake mix
1½ cups sugar	1 stick butter, melted
1 teaspoon ginger	Crushed pecans (optional)

Preheat oven to 350 degrees. In large mixing bowl, combine eggs, pumpkin, evaporated milk, sugar, ginger, clove, and cinnamon, beating on low speed; set aside. In separate bowl, combine cake mix, melted butter, and pecans, gently stirring until mixture is crumbly. Pour pumpkin mixture into prepared bundt pan. Pour half of cake mixture over pumpkin. Bake 1 hour, 30 minutes. Halfway through baking (about 45 minutes), pour remaining cake mixture over cake and finish baking. Enjoy warm or cold.

Serves 12

According to one tradition, the Black Russian cocktail was created in 1949 to honor legendary hostess and then US ambassador to Luxembourg Perle Mesta. Even though southern hostesses were still probably passing Mint Juleps at the time, we're delighted that the cocktail caught on stateside every time we indulge in a slice of this decadent favorite.

This cake is a wonderful ending to a Thanksgiving dinner and the only dessert that promises no leftovers on the plate!

Chocolate Cream Cheese Pound Cake

3 sticks butter, softened
1 (8-ounce) package cream
    cheese, softened
3 cups sugar

3 cups cake flour
½ cup cocoa
6 eggs
1 tablespoon vanilla

In large mixing bowl, combine flour and cocoa; set aside. In separate mixing bowl, cream together butter and cream cheese with electric mixer on medium speed until fluffy. Add sugar in intervals, beating well after each addition. Add flour mixture alternately with eggs to creamed mixture, beginning and ending with flour mixture; beat well. Add vanilla flavoring, stirring until just mixed. Pour into greased and floured tube pan and transfer to COLD oven. Set temperature to 275 degrees and bake 1 hour, 30 minutes to 1 hour, 45 minutes.

Serves 10

Apricot Nectar Pound Cake

¼ cup apricot flavored dry gelatin
    mix
½ cup sugar
1 cup apricot nectar
⅔ cup cooking oil

4 eggs, beaten
1 box super moist lemon cake
    mix
Juice of 1 to 2 lemons

Preheat oven to 325 degrees. Reserve 1 teaspoon dry gelatin mix and set aside. In large mixing bowl, combine sugar, nectar, oil, and eggs, beating with electric mixer on medium speed. Gradually add cake mix and remaining dry gelatin mix. Pour into greased and floured tube pan or bundt pan. Bake 1 hour. Remove from oven and cool completely before turning out onto serving plate. In small bowl, whisk together lemon juice and reserved dry gelatin mix. Drizzle over cake.

Paw Paw's Pound Cake

3 cups sifted all-purpose flour
1 teaspoon baking powder
½ teaspoon salt
2½ cups sugar

1¼ cups shortening
6 eggs
1 cup evaporated milk
3 teaspoons vanilla

In large mixing bowl, sift together flour, baking powder, and salt; set aside. In separate mixing bowl, cream together sugar and shortening, beating with electric mixer on high speed until fluffy (about 10 minutes). Add eggs, one at a time, beating well after each addition. Add vanilla and mix well. Gradually add flour mixture alternately with milk and beat 1 minute (batter will become stiff). Pour into greased and floured tube pan and transfer to COLD oven. Set temperature to 325 degrees and bake 1 hour to 1 hour, 10 minutes. Remove from oven and cool cake in pan 20 minutes before turning out.

Almond, lemon, or orange extracts may be substituted for the vanilla.

Sour Cream Pound Cake

2 sticks butter, softened
3 cups sugar, divided
6 egg yolks
¼ teaspoon baking soda

1 cup sour cream
3 cups cake flour
6 egg whites

Preheat oven to 300 degrees. In large mixing bowl, cream together butter and 2 cups sugar with electric mixer on medium speed. Add egg yolks one at a time, beating well after each addition; set aside. In small mixing bowl, combine baking soda and sour cream. Add alternately with flour to creamed mixture and set aside. Wash and dry beaters. In chilled metal bowl, beat egg whites with electric mixer on high speed until stiff. Beat in remaining 1 cup sugar. Fold egg whites into batter. Pour into tube pan and bake 1 hour, 20 minutes.

Serves 12-16

EASY BERRY TOPPING

A creamy, flavorful topping that works well for pound cake, shortcake, or waffles.

1 cup berries, frozen or fresh
1 cup light or fat-free frozen whipped topping, thawed
½ teaspoon vanilla
Pinch of cinnamon

In mixing bowl, combine whipped topping, vanilla, and cinnamon. Gently fold in berries. Cover and chill until ready to serve (no longer than 6 hours).

Yields 2 cups

German Sweet Chocolate Cake

1 (4-ounce) package German sweet chocolate

½ cup boiling water

2 sticks butter or margarine, softened

2 cups sugar

4 egg yolks

1 teaspoon vanilla

2¼ cups all-purpose flour, sifted

1 teaspoon baking soda

½ teaspoon salt

1 cup buttermilk

4 egg whites, stiffly beaten

Preheat oven to 350 degrees. In large mixing bowl, sift together flour, baking soda, and salt; set aside. In saucepan over medium heat, melt chocolate in boiling water and cool. In separate mixing bowl, cream together butter and sugar with electric mixer on medium speed until fluffy. Add egg yolks, one at a time, beating well after each addition. Stir in vanilla and melted chocolate. Add flour mixture alternately with buttermilk to sugar mixture, beating after each addition until smooth. Fold in beaten egg whites. Pour batter into three prepared 9-inch round cake pans. Bake 30 to 35 minutes. Remove from oven and cool on wire racks before turning out. Spread Coconut-Pecan Frosting between layers, around sides, and on top of cake.

COCONUT-PECAN FROSTING

1 cup evaporated milk

1 cup sugar

3 egg yolks, lightly beaten

1 stick butter or margarine

1 teaspoon vanilla

1⅓ cups coconut flakes

1 cup pecans, chopped

In saucepan over medium heat, combine evaporated milk, sugar, egg yolks, butter, and vanilla, removing from heat as necessary to prevent egg yolks from curdling. Stir constantly, until thickened, about 12 minutes. Fold in coconut and pecans. Cook to desired spreading consistency. Makes 2½ cups.

Creamy Peanut Butter Bars

Great served warm!

1 stick butter or margarine

½ cup creamy peanut butter

2 eggs, whipped

1 cup self-rising flour

1½ cups sugar

1 tablespoon vanilla

Preheat oven to 350 degrees. Melt butter and peanut butter together in microwaveable bowl. Add whipped eggs, flour, sugar, and vanilla. Mix ingredients thoroughly. Pour mixture into prepared 9 x 13-inch dish. Bake 25 minutes. Cut into squares.

Serves 12

Although Georgians naturally think of peanut farming as the livelihood of presidents, it was Missouri native George Washington Carver who introduced peanut butter to the world – and when you taste these you'll agree it wasn't a minute too soon!

Special Dark Brownies

2 cups sugar

4 tablespoons special dark cocoa

1½ sticks butter, melted

3 eggs, beaten

1½ cups self-rising flour, sifted

1 tablespoon vanilla

Preheat oven to 350 degrees. In large mixing bowl, combine sugar and cocoa. Stir in melted butter. Add eggs one at a time, beating with electric mixer after each addition. Add flour and vanilla and mix well. Pour into prepared 9 x 13-inch baking dish. Bake 40 minutes.

FUDGE ICING

1 stick butter

4 tablespoons cocoa

⅓ cup milk

1 (16-ounce) package confectioners' sugar

1 tablespoon vanilla

In small saucepan over medium heat, combine butter, cocoa, and milk. Bring to a boil, stirring constantly. Remove from heat. Add confectioners' sugar and vanilla. Pour over hot brownies.

Mint Chocolate Brownies

1 box chewy fudge brownie mix

1 (8-ounce) package cream cheese, softened

1 box (28 pieces) chocolate covered mint square candies

1 (16-ounce) box confectioners' sugar

Green food coloring

Butter a 9 x 13-inch dish. Prepare the brownies dish using instructions for "cake-like" brownies. Remove from the oven and allow to cool completely.

In a separate bowl, mix softened cream cheese with confectioners' sugar. Add 2 to 3 drops of green food coloring. Frost the brownies.

With kitchen scissors cut up 18 of the mint candies and sprinkle on the top of the iced brownies. Take the remaining candies and melt in a microwavable bowl for about 20 seconds. With a spoon, drizzle the melted candies over the top of the brownies. Allow to set overnight before cutting into squares.

Studies in two prestigious scientific journals say dark chocolate—not white chocolate or milk chocolate—is good for you. It helps lower your blood pressure and is full of antioxidants.

Unbelievable Blondies

1 stick butter	¼ teaspoon salt
2 cups brown sugar, well packed	1 teaspoon vanilla
2 eggs, beaten	½ cup chopped pecans
1½ cups all-purpose flour	½ cup chocolate chips
2 teaspoons baking powder	Confectioners' sugar

Preheat oven to 350 degrees. In medium saucepan over medium heat, melt butter. Remove from heat; add brown sugar, stirring until smooth. When cool, stir in egg and set aside. In separate bowl, sift together flour, baking powder, and salt. Fold flour mixture into brown sugar mixture, stirring until well mixed. Stir in vanilla; fold in nuts and chocolate chips. Pour into prepared 9 x 13-inch baking pan and bake 30 minutes. Allow to cool; dust with confectioners' sugar.

Serves 24

Esther's Lemon Squares

2 sticks butter, softened	6 tablespoons lemon juice
2 cups all-purpose flour	1 tablespoon all-purpose flour
½ cup confectioners' sugar	½ teaspoon baking powder
4 eggs, lightly beaten	Confectioners' sugar
2 cups sugar	

Preheat oven to 325 degrees. In large mixing bowl, combine flour and confectioners' sugar. Cut in butter using pastry mixer or fork. Press into 10 x 14-inch baking pan. Bake 15 minutes.

In large mixing bowl, combine eggs, sugar, and lemon juice with electric mixer on medium speed. Add flour and baking powder, beating well to combine. Pour over baked pastry. Bake at 325 degrees for 40 to 50 minutes. Sprinkle with confectioners' sugar. Cool completely and cut into squares.

Serves 24

Better Butter Bars

1 package yellow cake mix

3 eggs, divided

1 stick butter, melted and divided

1 (8-ounce) package cream
cheese, softened

1¼ teaspoons vanilla

1 stick butter, melted

1 (16-ounce) package
confectioners' sugar

Preheat oven to 350 degrees. In large mixing bowl, combine cake mix, 1 egg, and 8 tablespoons melted butter. Spread mixture into 13 x 9 x 2-inch baking pan. In separate bowl, beat cream cheese until smooth. Add remaining eggs and vanilla, beating until mixed. Add remaining 8 tablespoons melted butter and confectioners' sugar and beat well. Spread over cake mixture and bake 40 to 45 minutes. The center should be "gooey," so be careful not to overbake!

Serves 15-20

Grown Up Magic Cookie Bars

4 cups chocolate cookie wafers,
crushed into crumbs

1 stick butter, melted

2 cups pecan pieces

1 cup macadamia nuts

1 cup semisweet chocolate chips

1½ cups white chocolate chips

3 cups sweetened shredded
coconut

1½ cans sweetened condensed
milk

Preheat oven to 325 degrees. Combine chocolate cookies crumbs and butter and press into bottom of prepared 9 x 13-inch baking pan.

In large mixing bowl, combine pecans, macadamias, chocolate chips, white chocolate chips, coconut, and condensed milk. Spread over prepared crust. Bake 25 minutes, or until lightly browned. Do not overcook. Cool and store, tightly covered, in refrigerator.

Raspberry Yum Yums

2 sticks butter, softened
2 egg yolks
½ cup sugar
2½ cups all-purpose flour

1 (10-ounce) jar raspberry
preserves
4 egg whites
1 cup sugar
1½ cups chopped pecans

Preheat oven to 350 degrees. In large mixing bowl, cream butter, yolks, and sugar; gradually add flour until dough forms. Press dough into 10 x 15-inch baking sheet and prick with fork. Bake 15 to 20 minutes or until golden brown.

Spread preserves over baked crust. In chilled metal bowl, beat egg whites until stiff; add sugar and beat. Fold in chopped pecans. Spread over preserves. Bake 25 minutes. Cut into squares while warm.

Serves 24

A wonderful addition to any fall festival bake sale!

Frosted Pumpkin Bars

1 can pumpkin
2 cups sugar
4 eggs

2 tablespoons cinnamon
2 cups biscuit baking mix

Preheat oven to 350 degrees. In large mixing bowl, combine pumpkin, sugar, eggs, and cinnamon with electric mixer on medium speed. Gradually add biscuit baking mix, beating well to combine. Pour into prepared 15 x 10 x 1-inch jellyroll pan. Bake 25 minutes. Cool completely before frosting generously with Cream Cheese Frosting. Cut into bars.

CREAM CHEESE FROSTING

2 cups confectioners' sugar
2 (8-ounce) packages cream
cheese, softened

½ teaspoon vanilla
Butter, softened

In mixing bowl, combine cream cheese, confectioners' sugar, and vanilla with electric mixer on medium speed. Add butter, ½ tablespoon at a time, until frosting is of desired consistency.

Serves 30

Buttery Sugar Cookies

2 sticks butter, softened
1½ cups sugar
3 eggs
1 teaspoon vanilla

3½ cups all-purpose flour
2 teaspoons cream of tartar
1 teaspoon baking soda
½ teaspoon salt

Preheat oven to 350 degrees. In large mixing bowl, cream butter and sugar together with electric mixer on medium speed. Add eggs one at a time, beating after each addition. Stir in vanilla and set aside. In separate bowl, sift together flour, cream of tartar, baking soda, and salt. Gradually add to creamed mixture, mixing well. Chill dough overnight.

Preheat oven to 375 degrees. Roll out dough on well-floured surface to ¼-inch thickness. Cut into shapes with cookie cutters. Transfer cookies to baking sheet. Bake 6 to 8 minutes.

VANILLA BUTTERCREAM ICING

1 (16-ounce) package
    confectioners' sugar
1 stick butter, softened
¼ cup milk

1 teaspoon vanilla
½ teaspoon salt
Food coloring

In small mixing bowl, combine sugar, butter, milk, vanilla, salt, and food coloring; beat with electric mixer on high for 2 to 3 minutes. Spread on cooled cookies.

Serves 36

WHY COOKIES SPREAD

Cookies spread for a variety of reasons. So before baking an entire batch, bake a test cookie. If it spreads more than desired, the dough may be too soft. Try refrigerating the dough until it is well chilled (1 to 2 hours). If the dough is still too soft, stir in 1 tablespoon of flour. Another reason that cookies spread is the use of low-fat or non-fat margarine. When there is less than a 60 percent fat content used, cookies may spread. Also, be sure too cool and then clean cookie sheets between batches.

White Chocolate Cranberry Oatmeal Cookies

1 stick butter or margarine,
    softened

1 cup brown sugar, firmly packed

½ cup granulated sugar

2 eggs

1 teaspoon vanilla

1½ cups all-purpose flour

1 teaspoon baking soda

½ teaspoon salt

3 cups old-fashioned oats

1 cup dried cranberries

1 cup white chocolate chips

Preheat oven to 350 degrees. In large mixing bowl, cream together margarine and sugars with electric mixer on medium speed. Add eggs and vanilla, beating well. In separate mixing bowl, sift together flour, baking soda, and salt. Add to sugar mixture, beating well. Fold in oats, cranberries, and white chocolate chips, mixing well by hand. Drop dough by heaping teaspoons onto ungreased baking sheet. Bake 10 to 12 minutes, or until lightly golden brown. Cool completely. Store in airtight container.

Makes 4 dozen

This cookie dough may be cut thick for lunch boxes or rolled paper thin for party cookies. They never lose their shape in cooking. An excellent basic dough for filled or for decorated cookies.

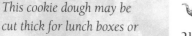

A Perfect Cookie

2½ cups flour

½ teaspoon baking powder

½ teaspoon baking soda

1 stick butter

¾ cup sugar

1 egg

1½ tablespoons buttermilk

1 teaspoon vanilla

Flour for rolling

Preheat oven to 325 degrees. Cream butter and sugar. Add whole egg, buttermilk, and vanilla and beat well. Work in the flour, in which baking powder and baking soda have been sifted. Roll to desired thickness on floured board, and cut in desired shapes. Bake until golden brown.

Makes 2 to 5 dozen, depending on size and thickness

Classic Chocolate Chip Cookies

½ cup shortening, softened

½ cup sugar

¼ cup firmly packed brown sugar

1 egg

1 teaspoon vanilla

1 cup unsifted all-purpose flour

½ teaspoon salt

¼ teaspoon baking soda

1 (6-ounce) package semisweet
    chocolate chips

½ cup chopped nuts (optional)

Preheat oven to 375 degrees. In large mixing bowl, beat together shortening, sugars, egg, and vanilla with electric mixer on medium speed until light and fluffy. In separate bowl, combine flour, salt, and baking soda. Gradually add to sugar mixture, mixing well to combine. Fold in chocolate chips and nuts. Drop by teaspoonfuls two inches apart onto ungreased baking sheet. Bake 8 to 10 minutes, or until lightly browned. Cool on wire racks.

Serves 48

Giant Chocolate and Peanut Butter Cup Cookies

2¼ cups all-purpose flour

⅓ cup cocoa

1 teaspoon baking powder

½ teaspoon salt

1 stick butter, softened

¾ cup creamy peanut butter

¾ cup firmly packed light brown
    sugar

¾ cup sugar

2 teaspoons vanilla

2 eggs

1 (10-ounce) package peanut
    butter cups, coarsely
    chopped

1 (6-ounce) package semisweet
    chocolate chips

Preheat oven to 350 degrees. In large mixing bowl, combine flour, cocoa, baking soda, and salt; set aside. In separate mixing bowl, beat together butter, peanut butter, brown sugar, sugar, and vanilla for 3 minutes with electric mixer on medium speed until light and fluffy. Add eggs one at a time, beating well after each addition. Reduce speed to low and gradually beat in flour mixture. Fold in peanut butter cups and chocolate chips. Drop dough (3 tablespoons per cookie) onto ungreased baking sheet, spacing each cookie about one inch apart. Bake 13 to 15 minutes. Cool on wire racks and store in airtight container.

Serves 24

COOKIE SWAPS

The holidays can be a very stressful time. It can be difficult to find time to get ready for the holidays and socialize at the same time. A fun way to help you cut-down on the amount of baking that you need to do and socialize at the same time is to have a cookie swap. The way a cookie swap works is that you coordinate with a group of friends and family and share cookies that you bake ahead of time. Everyone bakes four or five dozen of their favorite cookies; then you get together and swap the cookies. It's that easy, and you end up with a multitude of cookies to bring to your holiday events.

Heavenly Peanut Butter, Chocolate Chip, Oatmeal Cookies

3 cups old-fashioned oats

½ cup whole wheat flour

1 teaspoon baking soda

1 teaspoon baking powder

½ teaspoon salt

1 cup firmly packed light brown sugar

1 cup sugar

1 stick unsalted butter, softened

½ cup natural peanut butter

2 large eggs

1 teaspoon vanilla

2 cups salted peanuts

2 cups semisweet chocolate chips

Preheat oven to 350 degrees. In large mixing bowl, combine oats, flour, baking soda, baking powder, and salt; set aside. In separate bowl, beat together sugars, butter, and peanut butter with electric stand mixer on medium speed, using paddle attachment, about 5 minutes. Mixture should be light and fluffy. Add eggs and vanilla, scraping down sides of bowl as needed. Reduce mixer speed to low. Add oat mixture and mix until just combined. Gently stir in peanuts and chocolate chips. Using small ice cream scoop (½ tablespoon), scoop dough and place 2 inches apart on parchment paper lined baking sheet. Bake 13 to 15 minutes, or until cookies are golden. Remove from oven and cool on baking sheets 5 minutes. Transfer to wire racks and cool completely.

Serves 48

For cookies with more chocolate flavor, reduce the amount of peanuts to 1 cup and use 3 cups chocolate chips.

JoAnn's Famous Gingerbread Cookies

¾ cup light or dark molasses

¾ cup margarine

¾ cup firmly packed light brown sugar

3⅔ cups all-purpose flour

2½ teaspoons ground ginger

2 teaspoons cinnamon

1 teaspoon baking powder

½ teaspoon baking soda

½ teaspoon nutmeg

1 egg, beaten

Preheat oven to 350 degrees. In 3-quart saucepan over medium heat, bring molasses, margarine, and brown sugar to a boil, stirring occasionally. Remove from heat and cool completely. In large mixing bowl, sift together flour, ginger, cinnamon, baking powder, baking soda, and nutmeg. Stir egg into cooled molasses mixture. Stir molasses mixture into flour mixture until smooth. Wrap dough in plastic wrap; chill 1 hour. Divide dough in half. On floured surface, roll dough to ⅛ to ¼-inch thickness. Cut dough with floured 5 x 3-inch cookie cutter. Carefully lift cookies with metal spatula onto lightly greased baking sheet. Bake 10 to 14 minutes, or until indentation remains when touched. Remove from baking sheet and cool on wire rack. Decorate with icing and candies, as desired. Store in airtight container for up to two weeks.

Serves 24

Mighty Molasses Cookies

⅔ cup cooking oil

1 cup sugar

1 egg

4 tablespoons dark molasses

2⅛ cups all-purpose flour

1 tablespoon ground ginger

2 teaspoons baking soda

1 teaspoon cinnamon

½ teaspoon salt

¼ cup sugar

½ teaspoon cinnamon

Preheat oven to 350 degrees. In large mixing bowl, combine oil, sugar, egg, and molasses with electric mixer on medium speed. In separate bowl, sift together flour, ginger, baking soda, 1 teaspoon cinnamon, and salt. Add to sugar mixture, beating well to combine. Refrigerate dough until firm. In small mixing bowl, combine ¼ cup sugar and ½ teaspoon cinnamon. Form teaspoon-sized balls of dough and roll in sugar-cinnamon mixture. Place on parchment paper lined baking sheet and bake 8 to 10 minutes. Cookies will flatten during baking.

Serves 36

In food lore, ladies gave gingerbread cookies to knights before tournaments involving jousting and the like. In modern times, people are merely fighting over who gets the last one.

OUR FAVORITE CHRISTMAS MOVIES TO WATCH WHILE EATING CHRISTMAS COOKIES

* Rudolph, the Red-Nosed Reindeer

* Santa Claus is Comin' to Town

* How the Grinch Stole Christmas

* A Christmas Carol

* A Charlie Brown Christmas

* It's a Wonderful Life

* Miracle on 34th Street

* A Christmas Story

Dark molasses is the result of the second boiling of cane or beet sugar syrup (light molasses coming from the first). Dark molasses is the variety most often used in baking, and then there's black strap (from the third boiling) which is commonly incorporated into cattle food. Stick with dark, and there'll be a stampede into your kitchen lickety-split.

In double boiler over medium-low heat, whisk together chocolate chips and milk, stirring constantly until chocolate melts. Dip baked cookie (without preserves) halfway into chocolate or drizzle cookie (with preserves) with chocolate and dry on waxed paper.

Santa's Shortbread Cookies

4 sticks butter

1 cup firmly packed brown sugar

4½ cups all-purpose flour

1 teaspoon vanilla (optional)

½ teaspoon almond extract (optional)

¼ cup fruit preserves of choice (optional)

1 (6-ounce) semisweet chocolate chips

¼ cup milk (optional)

Preheat oven to 325 degrees. In large mixing bowl, cream butter and brown sugar with electric mixer on medium speed. Add vanilla or almond extract, if desired. Gradually add 3 to 3 ¾ cups flour, mixing well to combine. Sprinkle surface with remaining flour. Knead dough 5 minutes, adding only enough flour to form a soft dough. Cover in plastic wrap and chill 30 minutes or until firm. Drop teaspoon-sized balls of chilled dough on baking sheet. Make thumbprint indention on top of cookie and spoon small amount of preserves in indention, if desired. Chill again until firm. Bake 20 to 25 minutes.

Serves 48

Nutty Caramel Popcorn

3 quarts freshly popped popcorn

1 cup slivered almonds, blanched

1 cup pecan halves

1 cup cashews

1 stick butter

1 cup firmly packed brown sugar

¼ cup honey

1 teaspoon vanilla

Preheat oven to 250 degrees. Toss together popcorn, almonds, pecans, and cashews in lightly greased 14 x 11-inch roasting pan. In medium saucepan over low heat, melt butter. Stir in brown sugar and honey; bring to a boil. Boil 5 minutes without stirring. Gently stir in vanilla. Pour over popcorn mixture, stirring until evenly coated. Bake 1 hour, stirring every 15 minutes.

Makes 4 quarts

Dawg Chow

1 stick butter

1 cup semisweet chocolate chips

½ cup creamy peanut butter

8 cups assorted crispy octagonal
    or square-shaped cereal

3 cups confectioners' sugar

In medium mixing bowl, microwave butter, chocolate chips, and peanut butter until melted; stir until smooth. Place cereal in large mixing bowl; pour chocolate over cereal. Gently toss to coat, taking care not to crush the cereal. Place confectioners' sugar into 2-gallon plastic zip-top bag. Pour coated cereal into bag and gently toss to coat. Transfer bag to refrigerator until ready to serve.

Serves 10

Great for Georgia tailgates since it looks like real dog food kibbles! You can even serve it from new and clean dog bowls!

Double Decker Fudge

4 tablespoons melted butter

½ cup cocoa

1 teaspoon vanilla

2 cups peanut butter chips,
    divided

4½ cups sugar

4 tablespoons butter

1 (7-ounce) jar marshmallow
    creme

1½ cups evaporated milk

Line baking pan with foil and butter it well. In large mixing bowl, combine 4 tablespoons melted butter, cocoa, and vanilla, mixing until smooth. Stir in 1 cup peanut butter chips and set aside.

In 4-quart heavy bottom saucepan over medium heat, combine sugar, 4 tablespoons butter, marshmallow creme, and evaporated milk. Stirring constantly, bring mixture to a rolling boil and cook 5 minutes, adjusting heat as necessary to prevent scorching. Remove from heat and set aside.

Pour remaining 1 cup peanut butter chips into a large mixing bowl. Add half of marshmallow creme mixture to chips and beat until chips are melted and incorporated. Spread mixture evenly into prepared pan and cool 5 minutes. Pour remaining marshmallow creme mixture into reserved cocoa mixture, stirring until thickened and smooth. Spread over first layer and cool 5 minutes. Chill until firm and cut into 1-inch squares to serve.

Easy Peanut Butter Fudge

12 ounces semisweet chocolate chips

12 ounces peanut butter

14 ounces sweetened condensed milk

In a 1½-quart microwavable bowl, melt chocolate and peanut butter on high setting 3 minutes. Stir well. Add sweetened condensed milk and stir until well blended. Pour mixture into 8 x 8-inch dish lined with waxed paper. Chill until firm.

Makes 42 pieces

Peanut Orange Balls

1 cup peanuts, chopped

1 (14-ounce) package flaked coconut

1 (12-ounce) package orange slice candies, diced

1 (14-ounce) can sweetened condensed milk

⅔ cup confectioners' sugar

In large mixing bowl, combine peanuts, coconut, and orange slices. Add sweetened condensed milk, mixing well. Shape into 1-inch balls and roll in confectioners' sugar.

Makes 9 dozen

If the mixture begins to harden too fast to drop, you should stir in about 1 to 2 tablespoons of warm water to thin the mixture.

If you don't cook them long enough, they remain "sticky" and never become firm.

 # Southern Pralines

½ cup sugar

¾ cup light brown sugar, packed

½ cup, plus 2 tablespoons half-and-half

½ stick butter

1½ cups pecans

1 teaspoon vanilla

In heavy saucepan over medium heat, combine sugars, half-and-half, and butter. (Mixture will be thick.) Bring to a boil, stirring constantly. Reduce heat to low. Stir occasionally. Spoon mixture up on sides of pan to melt any sugar that hasn't melted. Cook until mixture registers 239 degrees with candy thermometer. If you don't have a candy thermometer, bring it to the soft ball stage.

Remove from heat. Stir in pecans and vanilla. Stir until mixture begins to thicken and becomes creamy and cloudy. Spoon onto waxed paper to harden. Wrap them individually and store them in an airtight container.

Cherry Coconut Bonbons

1½ (16-ounce) boxes
    confectioners' sugar

1 stick margarine

1 teaspoon vanilla

1 (8-ounce) jar maraschino
    cherries, drained and
    chopped

1 cup pecans, finely chopped

1 (3½-ounce) can coconut

2 packages chocolate bark, for
    dipping

In large mixing bowl, combine confectioners' sugar, margarine, and vanilla. Add cherries, pecans, and coconut. Dust hands in confectioners' sugar and shape mixture into 1-inch balls. Place on baking sheet lined with waxed paper and freeze 30 minutes. Melt chocolate bark according to package directions. Dip candy in chocolate, place on waxed paper, and chill. Store candy in refrigerator.

Maraschino cherries were historically marinated in their namesake Italian liqueur, although now the appellation merely denotes pitted fruits that have been soaked in sugar syrup.

Simple Divinity

2 cups sugar

½ cup white corn syrup

½ cup water

2 egg whites

Pinch of salt

1 tablespoon vanilla

½ cup chopped pecans

In saucepan over medium heat, combine sugar, corn syrup, and water. Heat, stirring constantly until sugar dissolves. Bring to a boil without stirring to the hard ball stage when tested in cold water, until mixture registers 265 degrees on a candy thermometer.

In cold metal bowl, beat egg whites with electric mixer until stiffened. Add salt and hot syrup, beating constantly, pouring slowly at first and then faster. Once mixture is stiff, beat with wooden spoon until creamy. Stir in pecans and vanilla and pour into buttered dish.

Makes 24 pieces

Strawberry Pizza

2 sticks butter, melted

2 tablespoons sugar

1 cup nuts, chopped

2 cups all-purpose flour

1 (8-ounce) package cream
    cheese, softened

1 (16-ounce) package
    confectioners' sugar

1 large container frozen whipped
    topping, thawed

3 cups strawberries, washed,
    stemmed, and sliced

2 cups sugar

6 tablespoons cornstarch

1 (3-ounce) package strawberry
    flavored gelatin mix

2 cups water

Preheat oven to 325 degrees. In large mixing bowl, combine butter, sugar, and nuts. Gradually add flour, mixing to dough consistency. Press into 13 x 9-inch baking pan. Bake 30 to 35 minutes. Remove from oven and cool completely.

In large mixing bowl, cream together cream cheese, confectioners' sugar, and frozen whipped topping with electric mixer on low speed. Spread over cooled crust. Top with sliced strawberries.

In saucepan over medium heat, combine sugar, cornstarch, gelatin, and water. Bring to a boil. Boil until thickened, stirring constantly. Remove from heat and cool. Pour over entire pizza and chill overnight.

Southerners do love banana pudding, and Athens has always turned out some memorable versions. One noteworthy batch was toted around at our Classic Center in the hands of one Harry Connick, Jr., who had enjoyed some backstage before his performance and pronounced it too good not to share with the audience!

Creamy Banana Pudding

2 (3-ounce) packages instant
    vanilla pudding

3 cups milk

1 can sweetened condensed milk

1 to 1½ teaspoons vanilla

1 extra-large carton frozen
    whipped topping

1½ to 2 packages vanilla wafers

8 to 10 large bananas, sliced

In large mixing bowl, beat together pudding and milk with electric mixer on medium speed. Slowly stir in sweetened condensed milk and vanilla. Stir in frozen whipped topping and mix well. In large bowl or serving dish, layer vanilla wafers, bananas, and pudding mixture. Best if chilled at least 8 hours before serving.

Serves 20

Chocolate Chip Cheese Ball

1 (8-ounce) package cream
  cheese, softened
1 stick butter, softened
¾ cup confectioners' sugar
2 tablespoons brown sugar
¼ teaspoon vanilla

½ teaspoon cinnamon
¾ cup miniature semisweet
  chocolate chips
¾ cup chopped pecans, finely
  chopped
Graham crackers

In medium mixing bowl, beat together cream cheese and butter with electric mixer on medium speed until smooth. Beat in confectioner's sugar, brown sugar, vanilla, and cinnamon. Stir in chocolate chips. Cover and chill at least 2 hours. Shape mixture into ball. Wrap with plastic wrap and chill at least 1 hour. Roll cheese ball in pecans and serve with graham crackers.

Serves 24

This recipe tastes a lot like Cookie Dough Cheesecake, but it's much easier to make! It keeps well overnight, so you can make it ahead of time.

Black Bottom Cupcakes

1⅔ cups all-purpose flour
1 cup sugar
¼ cup cocoa
1 teaspoon baking soda
1 teaspoon salt
1 cup water
1 tablespoon vinegar
½ cup cooking oil

1 teaspoon vanilla
1 (8-ounce) package cream
  cheese, softened
1 egg, beaten
⅓ cup, plus 2 tablespoons sugar
⅛ teaspoon salt
1 (8-ounce) package chocolate
  chips

Preheat oven to 350 degrees. In large mixing bowl, combine flour, sugar, cocoa, baking soda, and salt. Add water, vinegar, oil, and vanilla, beating with electric mixer until thoroughly combined; set aside. In separate mixing bowl, combine cream cheese, egg, sugar, and salt, beating well until mixed. Stir in chocolate chips. Pour ¼ cup cocoa mixture into prepared muffin pan. Top with 1 tablespoon cream cheese mixture.

Bake 18 to 20 minutes.

Serves 20-24

Ooey Gooey Chocolate Peanut Butter Delight

1 (21-ounce) package fudge
   brownie mix

1 (10-ounce) package peanut
   butter chips

24 regular-sized peanut butter
   cups, divided

1 (5-ounce) package vanilla
   instant pudding mix

3 cups milk

¾ cup creamy peanut butter

2 teaspoons vanilla

¼ cup sweetened condensed milk

1 extra-large carton frozen
   whipped topping, thawed
   and divided

½ cup chocolate syrup, divided

Line baking pan with foil, allowing two inches of foil to extend over sides. Prepare brownie mix according to package directions; fold in peanut butter chips. Bake as directed on brownie mix. Remove from oven and cool completely.

Lift foil out of pan and invert onto cutting board. Remove and discard foil. Cut brownies into bite-sized pieces and set aside. Coarsely chop 20 peanut butter cups and set aside.

In large mixing bowl, combine pudding mix and milk, beating on low speed two minutes until thickened. Add peanut butter, vanilla, and sweetened condensed milk. Gently fold in three-fourths container whipped topping.

Place half of brownies in bottom of trifle bowl; drizzle with ¼ cup chocolate syrup. Sprinkle with half of chopped candy and spread with half of pudding mixture. Repeat layers. Top with remaining whipped topping. Cut remaining peanut butter cups in half and use as garnish.

Serves 12-16

Chocolate Kahlúa Trifle

1 (21-ounce) package brownie
   mix (prepared according
   to package directions and
   cooled)

½ cup Kahlúa, divided

2 packages chocolate cooked
   pudding mix (prepared
   according to package
   directions and cooled)

1 container frozen whipped
   topping, thawed and divided

2 cups chopped chocolate-covered
   toffee candy bar, divided

Cut brownies into squares, making a hole in each brownie with the end of a wooden spoon. Place on bottom of trifle dish. Pour Kahlúa and half of chocolate pudding over brownies. Spread half of frozen whipped topping over pudding until covered. Sprinkle half of candy bars over frozen whipped topping. Pour remaining pudding over candy, then spread remaining frozen whipped topping over pudding. Sprinkle with remaining candy. Chill 2 hours before serving.

Serves 8

Extraordinarily Simple Chocolate Fondue

16 ounces dark, sweet or
   semisweet chocolate, broken
   into pieces

1½ cups whipping cream

1 teaspoon vanilla

Prepare fondue pot according to directions. Drop chocolate into fondue pot. Add whipping cream (which prevents the chocolate from being lumpy) and stir gently but constantly until chocolate melts and is smooth. Stir in vanilla. Enjoy!

POPULAR FONDUE DIPPERS

Whole strawberries

Apple slices

Kiwi

Banana slices

Pineapple chunks

Pear slices

Orange sections

Seedless grapes

Angel food cake

Butter cookies

Ladyfingers

Marshmallows

Appendices

Appendices

Special Menus

Three Course Dinner Party
Easy Sour Cream Biscuits
Green Bean and Fennel Salad with Champagne Vinaigrette
Rosemary Pork Tenderloin
Roasted Asparagus
Arroz à la Mexicana
Inner Banks Chardonnay Cake

Formal Five-Course Dinner
Pastry Wrapped Mushrooms
Creamy Broccoli Soup
Fig, Parmesan, and Pecan Salad
Grouper Piccata
Spicy French Beans
Triple Layer Carrot Cake with Cream Cheese Frosting

Summer Supper on the Porch
Summer Sipper
Sun-Dried Tomato Pâté
Simple Summer Spinach Salad
Pistol Packin' Paella on the Porch
Creamy Banana Pudding

Holiday Buffet Menu
Party Turkey Breast
Beef Tenderloin with Salt-Herb Crust
Party Potatoes
Spiced Peaches
Vidalia Corn Bake
Green Beans Sorrento
Copper Carrots
Tart Cherry Salad
Super Veggie Caesar Salad
It Will Cause a Riot Cake
Old Fashioned Chocolate Pie
South Georgia Pecan Pie

Easy Autumn Supper
A to Z Bread
Spinach Salad with Savory Dressing
Crunchy Chicken Casserole
Asparagus Rolls
Nana's Old Fashioned Toasted Coconut Pie
Tennessee Tea

Ladies Luncheon Menu
Cold Cucumber Soup
Mini Cream Cheese Muffins
Southern Chicken Divan
Broccoli Puff
Cranberry Apple Casserole
Buttermilk Pie

Tailgate Menu
Old Fashioned Bloody Mary
Sanford Slush
Bulldog Salsa
BLT Dip
Cajun Shrimp
Cream Cheese and Amaretto Spread
Easy Fall Salad
Garrard's Homecoming Chicken
Grilled Pork Tenderloin
Grown Up Magic Cookie Bars
Esther's Lemon Squares
Dawg Chow
Classic Chocolate Chip Cookies

Special Menus

Taylor Grady Tea Party

Russian Tea
Creamy Mocha Punch
Cheese Wafers
Game Day Party Pleasers
Caprese Tartlets
Classic City Chef Sweet Potato Biscuits
Banana Tea Bread
Krista's Favorite Chicken Salad
White Chocolate Cranberry Oatmeal Cookies

An Evening of Sweet Indulgence Dessert Party

Italian Cream Cake
Red Velvet Cake
Mama Mary's Fruitcake Cookies
Buttery Sugar Cookies
Cherry Chocolate Bonbons
Double Decker Fudge
Orange Peanut Balls
Elegant Strawberry Champagne Punch
Very Berry Eggnog Punch
Coffee

A special thanks to Cindy Haygood and Debra Lastinger of Perfectly Polished for their help in creating the Special Menus section

Recommended Safe Cooking Temperatures

Heating food to the right temperature destroys harmful microorganisms.

	FAHRENHEIT	CELSIUS
Beef/Lamb/Veal		
Rare	140^0	60^0
Medium	160^0	71^0
Well Done	170^0	77^0
Chicken/Duck/Goose	175^0 to 180^0	79^0 to 82^0
Eggs		
Fried, poached, coddled	cook until yolk and white are firm	
Casseroles, sauces, custards	160^0	71^0
Fish	120^0 to 137^0	49^0 to 58^0
Ground Meats		
Beef, lamb, pork	160^0	71^0
Chicken, turkey	165^0	74^0
Ostrich/Emu	160^0	71^0
Pâté	170^0	77^0
Pork		
Chops, roast	160^0 to 165^0	71^0 to 74^0
Cured	140^0	60^0
Rabbit	180^0	82^0
Sausage	160^0	71^0
Stuffing *(inside or outside poultry)*	180^0	82^0
Turkey		
Bone-In	180^0	82^0
Boneless roast	170^0	77^0

U.S. Measurements Equivalents

Pinch/dash	$\frac{1}{16}$ teaspoon
½ teaspoon	30 drops
1 teaspoon	$\frac{1}{3}$ teaspoon
3 teaspoons	1 tablespoon
½ tablespoon	1½ teaspoons
1 tablespoon	3 teaspoons; ½ fluid ounce
2 tablespoons	$\frac{1}{8}$ cup; 1 fluid ounce
3 tablespoons	1½ fluid ounces; 1 jigger
jigger	1½ fluid ounces; 3 tablespoons
4 tablespoons	¼ cup; 2 fluid ounces
5$\frac{1}{3}$ tablespoons	$\frac{1}{3}$ cup; 5 tablespoons plus 1 teaspoon
8 tablespoons	½ cup; 4 fluid ounces
10$\frac{2}{3}$ tablespoons	$\frac{2}{3}$ cup; 10 tablespoons plus 2 teaspoons
12 tablespoons	¾ cup; 6 fluid ounces
16 tablespoons	1 cup; 8 fluid ounces; ½ pint
$\frac{1}{8}$ cup	2 tablespoons; 1 fluid ounce
¼ cup	4 tablespoons; 2 fluid ounces
$\frac{1}{3}$ cup	5 tablespoons plus 1 teaspoon
$\frac{3}{8}$ cup	¼ cup plus 2 tablespoons
½ cup	8 tablespoons; 4 fluid ounces
$\frac{2}{3}$ cup	10 tablespoons plus 2 teaspoons
$\frac{5}{8}$ cup	½ cup plus 2 tablespoons
¾ cup	12 tablespoons; 6 fluid ounces
$\frac{7}{8}$ cup	¼ cup plus 2 tablespoons
1 cup	16 tablespoons; ½ pint; 8 fluid ounces
2 cups	1 pint; 16 fluid ounces
3 cups	1½ pints; 24 fluid ounces
4 cups	1 quart; 32 fluid ounces
8 cups	2 quarts; 64 fluid ounces
1 pint	2 cups; 16 fluid ounces
2 pints	1 quart; 32 fluid ounces
1 quart	2 pints; 4 cups; 32 fluid ounces
4 quarts	1 gallon; 8 pints
1 gallon	4 quarts; 8 pints; 16 cups; 128 fluid ounces
4 pecks	1 bushel

Ingredient Equivalents

FOOD	AMOUNT	APPROXIMATE EQUIVALENT
Almonds	1 lb in shell	1⅓ to 2 cups
	1 lb shelled	3 to 3½ cups whole; 4 cups slivered
	1 cup	4-oz
Anchovies	2-oz can	10 to 12 anchovies
	1 fillet	½ tsp anchovy paste
Anchovy Paste	2-oz tube	4 tbsp
Apples	1 lb fresh	3 medium; 2¾ cups chopped; 3 cups sliced, 1⅓ cups sauce
	1 lb dried	4⅓ cups; 8 cups cooked
Apricots	1 lb fresh	8 to 14; 2½ cups sliced or halved
	1 lb dried	2¾ cups; 5½ cups cooked
Asparagus	1 lb fresh	12 to 20 spears; 3½ cups chopped
	10-oz frozen	2 cups
Avocados	1 lb	2½ cups chopped; 1½ cups puréed
	1 medium	1 cup purée
Bacon	1 lb raw	18 to 22 regular slices; 20 thin; 10 to 14 thick
	1 lb cooked	1½ cups crumbled
	1 slice, cooked	1 tbsp crumbled
Bamboo shoots	8-oz can	1¼ cups sliced
Bananas	1 lb fresh	3 to 4 medium; 2 cups sliced; 1¾ cups mashed; 1 cup dried slices
	1 medium	½ cup puréed
	1 lb dried	4½ cups slices
Barley	1 cup medium	3½ to 4 cups cooked
	1 cup quick-cooking	3 cups cooked
Bean curd (see Tofu)		
Beans, black	1 lb dried	2⅓ cups; 4¾ cups cooked
	1 cup dried	2 cups cooked
	15½-oz can	2 cups
Beans, fava	1 lb dried	2 cups; 4½ cups cooked
	1 cup dried	2¼ cups cooked
Beans, fresh shell	1 lb	1 cup shelled
Beans, garbanzo	1 lb dried	2 cups; 5 cups cooked
	1 cup dried	2½ cups cooked
Beans, green	1 lb fresh	3½ cups whole
	9-oz frozen	1½ cups
	15 ½-oz can	1¾ cups

Ingredient Equivalents

FOOD	AMOUNT	APPROXIMATE EQUIVALENT
Beans, kidney	1 lb dried 1 cup dried	2½ cups; 5½ cups cooked 2½ cups cooked
Beans, lima	1 lb dried 1 cup dried	2⅔ cups; 6 cup cooked 2½ cups cooked
Beans, navy	1 lb dried 1 cup dried	2⅓ cups; 5½ cups cooled 2¼ cups cooked
Beans, pinto	1 lb dried 1 cup dried	2 cups; 5 cups cooked 2¼ cups cooked
Beans, refried	16-oz can	1¾ cups
Beans, soy	1 lb dried 1 cup dried	2 cups; 5 cups cooked 2½ cups cooked
Bean sprouts	1 lb	3 to 4 cups; 1½ to 2 cups cooked
Beets	1 lb, trimmed 15-oz can	2 cups, chopped or sliced and cooked 1¾ cups
Bell peppers (see Peppers, bell)		
Berries (see individual listings)		
Blackberries	1 pint fresh 10-oz frozen	2 cups 2 cups
Blueberries	1 pint fresh 10-oz frozen	2 cups 1½ cups
Brazil nuts	1 lb shelled 8-oz shelled	3 cups 1½ cups
Bread	1 lb loaf 1 slice	14 to 18 regular slices; 24 to 28 thin slices; 7 cups crumbs ½ cup fresh crumbs; ⅓ cup dried crumbs; 1 scant cup fresh cubes; ¾ cup toasted cubes
Breadcrumbs	8-oz package 7 cups fresh ½ cup fresh ⅓ cup dry	2⅓ cups 1 lb bread, crust removed 1 slice bread 1 slice toast
Broccoli	1 lb fresh 10-oz frozen	2 cups chopped 1½ cups chopped
Brussels sprouts	1 lb fresh 10-oz frozen	3 cups; 20 to 24 sprouts 18 to 24 sprouts
Bulgur	1 cup	3¾ cups cooked
Butter/margarine	1 lb regular ¼ lb regular 1 lbs whipped	2 cups; 4 sticks; 2 small tubs 1 stick; ½ cup; 8 tbsp; ⅓ cup clarified 3 cups regular

Ingredient Equivalents

FOOD	AMOUNT	APPROXIMATE EQUIVALENT
Butter-flavored granules	¾ tsp	1 tbsp butter
Cabbage	1 lb	3½ to 4½ cups shredded; 2 cups cooked
Cantaloupe	1 medium	2 lbs; 3 cups diced
Carrots	1 lb, trimmed	3 cups chopped; 2½ cups grated; 2 cups cooked
	1 to 2 medium	1 cup shredded
	14-oz frozen	2½ cups sliced
Cashew nuts	1 lb	3⅓ cups
Cauliflower	1 lb fresh	2½ to 3 cups florets; 1½ to 2 cups chopped
	10-oz frozen	2 cups chopped or sliced
Caviar	1-oz	1 heaping tbsp
Celery	2 medium ribs	½ cup chopped or sliced
Celery root (*celeriac*)	1½ lbs	4 cups grated; 1¾ cups cooked, puréed
Cheese (*blue*)	4-oz	1 cup crumbled
Cheese (*cheddar, Jack*)	1 lb	4 cups grated or shredded
Cheese (*cottage*)	16-oz	2 cups
Cheese (*cream*)	8-oz	1 cup
	3-oz	6 tbsp
Cheese (*Parmesan, Romano*)	¼ lb	1 cup grated
Cheese, ricotta	7½-oz	1 cup
Cherries	1 lb fresh	2½ to 3 cups pitted
	10-oz frozen	1 cup
	16-oz can	1½ cups drained
Chestnut purée	10-oz can	25 whole chestnuts; 1⅓ cups purée
Chestnuts	1½ lbs unpeeled	35 to 40 large; 1 lb peeled
	1 lb peeled	2½ cups; 2 cups purée
Chicken	3 to 3½ lbs	3 cups cooked meat
	1 large whole breast	1½ cups cooked, chopped meat
Chickpeas (*see Beans, garbanzo*)		
Chocolate	6-oz chips	1 cup
	8-oz squares	8 (1-oz) squares
Clams, medium	3 dozen in shell	4 cups shucked
Cocoa powder	8-oz package	2¾ cups

Ingredient Equivalents

FOOD	AMOUNT	APPROXIMATE EQUIVALENT
Coconut	1 medium	4 to 5 cups shredded
	7-oz bag, shredded or flaked	3 cups
	3½-oz can	1⅓ cups
Cookies		
Chocolate wafers	18 to 20 cookies	1 cup crumbs
Oreos or Hydrox (single cream)	22 cookies	1½ cups crumbs
Vanilla wafers	22 cookies	1 cup crumbs
Corn	2 medium ears	1 to 1¼ cups kernels
	10-oz frozen kernels	1¾ cups
	12-oz can	1½ cups
Cornmeal	1 lb	3 cups uncooked
	1 cup	4 cups cooked
Cornstarch	1 lb	3 cups
Corn syrup, light or dark	16-fluid oz	2 cups
Cottage cheese (see Cheese, cottage)		
Couscous	1 cup	2½ cups cooked
Crab	1 lb in shell	1 to 1½ cups meat
	1 lb meat	3 cups
	7½-oz can	1 cup
Crackers	15 graham squares	1 cup crumbs
	28 soda/saltine crackers	1 cup crumbs
Cranberries	12-oz fresh or frozen	3 cups; 4 cups sauce
Cranberry sauce	1 lb can	1⅔ cups
Cream	½ pint light	1 cup; 8-oz
	½ pint whipping	1 cup; 2 cups whipped
	½ pint sour	1 cup
Cream cheese (see Cheese, cream)		
Crenshaw melon	1 medium	3 lb; 4 to 5 cups cubed
Cucumber	1 medium	1½ cups chopped or sliced
Currants	10-oz package dried	2 cups
Dates	1 lb unpitted	2½ cups pitted and chopped
	8-oz package pitted	¼ cups chopped
Eggplant	1lb	3½ cups diced raw; 1¾ cup cooked

FOOD	AMOUNT	APPROXIMATE EQUIVALENT
Egg roll skins *(wrappers)*	1 lb	14 wrappers
Eggs, whole, large	1 dozen	2⅓ cups
	5 eggs	1 cup
	1 egg	3 tbsp
Egg whites, large	1 dozen	1½ cups
	7 to 8 whites	1 cup
	2 whites	2½ to 3 cups stiffly beaten
	1 white	2 tbsp
Egg yolks, large	1 dozen	⅞ cup
	11 to 12 yolks	1 cup
	1 yolk	1 to 1½ tbsp
Eggs, hard-cooked	1 egg	6 slices; ¼ to ⅓ cup chopped
Egg substitute	¼ cup liquid	1 large egg
	2 tbsp	1 large yolk
Figs	1 lb fresh	12 medium
	1 lb dried	3 cups chopped
Filberts *(see Hazelnuts)*		
Flour	1 lb all-purpose, bread, self-rising	3 cups sifted
	1 lb cake, pastry	4½ to 5 cups sifted
	1 lb gluten	3 cups sifted
	1 lb rice	3½ cups sifted
	1 lb rye	5 cups; 3½ cups sifted
	1 lb whole wheat	3½ cups unsifted
Fruit, most kinds	15-oz can	1⅓ cups, drained
	16-oz frozen	1¼ cups
Garlic	1 head	12 to 16 cloves
	1 medium clove	½ tsp minced; ¼ tsp garlic powder
Gelatin, unflavored	¼-oz package	1 tbsp granulated; 3½ (4″ x 9″) sheets
Ginger	2-inch piece	2 tbsp minced
Graham crackers *(see Crackers)*		
Grapefruit	1 lb fresh	1 medium; 1½ cups segments; ¾ to 1 cup juice
Grapes	1 lb	2½ to 3 cups
Green beans *(see Beans, green)*		
Green onions *(see Onion, green)*		
Greens *(beet, chard, kale, etc.)*	1 lb fresh	1⅓ to 2 cups cooked

Ingredient Equivalents

FOOD	AMOUNT	APPROXIMATE EQUIVALENT
Grits	1 lb	3 cups
	1 cup	3⅓ cups cooked
Half & Half (see Cream)		
Ham	½ lb boneless	1¼ to 1½ cups chopped
Hazelnuts	1 lb in shell	1½ cups
	1 lb shelled	3½ cups whole
Hearts of palm	14-oz can	6 to 7 pieces
Herbs	1 tbsp fresh, chopped	1 tsp dried, crumbled
Hominy	1 lb whole	2½ cups
	1 cup whole	6⅔ cups cooked
	1 cup grits	4½ cups cooked
Honey	1 lb	1⅓ cups
Horseradish	1 tbsp bottled	2 tsp freshly grated
Ice cream/ice milk/sherbet	1 qt	4 cups
Ice cubes, standard size	3 to 4 cubes	1 cup crushed ice
Kasha	1 cup	2½ to 3 cups cooked
Ketchup	16-oz bottle	1⅔ cups
Kiwifruit	2	¾ cup chopped or sliced
Lard	1 lb	2 cups
Leeks	1 lb	2 cups trimmed, chopped; 1 cup cooked
Lemons	1 lb	4 to 6 medium; 1 cup juice
	1 medium	3 tbsp juice; 2 to 3 tsp zest
Lentils	1 lb dried	2¼ cups; 5 cups cooked
Lettuce	1 lb	6 cups pieces
Limes	1 lb	6 to 8 medium; ¾ cup juice
	1 medium	1 to 2 tbsp; 1 tsp zest
Lobster	1 to 1½ lbs	2½ to 3 cups meat
Macaroni, elbow	8-oz	4 cups cooked
	1 cup	1¾ cups cooked
Mangoes	1 medium	12-oz; ¾ to 1 cup chopped
Maple syrup	16-fluid oz	2 cups
Margarine (see Butter)		
Marshmallow crème	7 to 7½-oz jar	2½ cups
	16-oz jar	5¼ cups
	1 tbsp	1 large marshmallow

Ingredient Equivalents

FOOD	AMOUNT	APPROXIMATE EQUIVALENT
Marshmallows	1 lb large	30; 4 cups
	1 cup large	6 to 7 marshmallows
	1 cup miniature	85 marshmallows
	10½-oz mini	400 pieces
Meat, ground	1 lb	2 cups uncooked
Melon (see Cantaloupe; Crenshaw; Watermelon)		
Milk, all types	1 qt fresh	4 cups
Milk, evaporated	5-oz can	⅔ cup
	12-oz can	1½ cups
Milk, powdered	1⅓ cups	1 quart reconstituted
	⅓ cup	1 cup reconstituted
Milk, sweet, condensed	14-oz can	1¾ cups
Molasses	12 fl-oz	1½ cups
Mushrooms, common	1 lb fresh	5 cups sliced; 6 cups chopped; 3-oz dried, reconstituted
	4-oz	⅔ cup sliced
	3-oz dried	1 lb fresh
Mussels	1 lb medium	9 to 12 mussels; ¾ to 1 cup meat
Mustard	1 tsp dry	1 tbsp prepared
Nectarines	1 lb	3 to 4 medium; 2 cups chopped; 2½ cups sliced; 1½ cups puréed
Noodles, 1-inch pieces	8-oz	4 cups cooked
Nuts (see individual listings)	1 cup	1¾ cups cooked
Oats, rolled	1 lb	5 cups uncooked
	1 cup	1¾ cups cooked
Oil, all types	1 quart	4 cups
	24-oz bottle	3 cups
Okra	1 lb fresh	2¼ cups chopped, cooked
	10-oz frozen	1¼ cups chopped
	15½-oz can	1¾ cups chopped
Onions, green	5, bulbs only	½ cup chopped
	5 with tops	1¾ cups chopped
Onions, white or yellow	1 lb fresh	4 medium onions; 3½ to 4 cups chopped or sliced
	1 medium	¾ to 1 cup chopped or sliced
	12-oz frozen	3 cups chopped

Ingredient Equivalents

FOOD	AMOUNT	APPROXIMATE EQUIVALENT
Oranges	1 lb	3 medium; 1 to ¼ cup juice
	1 medium	⅓ to ½ cup juice; 1½ tbsp zest
Oranges, Mandarin	11-oz can	1¼ cups segments, drain
Oysters	1 cup shucked	13 to 19 medium
	3.66-oz can smoked	14 to 16 oysters
Papaya	1 medium	10 to 12-oz; 1½ to 2 cups chopped or sliced
Parsnips	1 lb	4 medium; 2 cups chopped; 2½ cups sliced
Pasta (*see Macaroni; Noodles; Spaghetti*)		
Peaches	1 lb fresh	4 medium; 2½ cups chopped or sliced; 1½ cups purée
	1 medium	½ to ¾ cup chopped or sliced
	10-oz frozen	1½ cups sliced
	15-oz can	6 to 8 halves; 1¾ cups slices
	1 lb dried	2¾ cups; 6 cups cooked
Peanut butter	18-oz jar	1¾ cups
Peanuts	1 lb in shell	2 cups shelled
	1 lb shelled	3½ to 4 cups
	2 cups nuts	1 cup peanut butter
Pears	1 lb fresh	3 medium; 2 cups sliced
	1 medium	½ cup sliced
	1 lb dried	2¾ cups; 5½ cups cooked
Peas, black-eyed	1 lb fresh	2⅓ cups; 5½ cups cooked
	10-oz frozen	1½ cups
	15½-oz can	1¾ cups
Peas, green	1 lb fresh, in pod	1 cup shelled
	10-oz frozen	2 cups
	15-oz can	2 cups
Peas, split	1 lb dried	2¼ cups; 5 cups cooked
Pecans	1 lb in shell	2 cups shelled
	1 lb shelled	4 cups halves; 3¾ cups chopped
Peppers, bell	1 lb	2 large; 2½ cups chopped; 3 cups sliced
Phyllo	1 lb package	25 sheets
Pineapple	1 medium	5 cups cubed
Pine nuts	8-oz	1½ cups
Pistachios	1 lb in shell	2 cups shelled
	1 lb shelled	3½ to 4 cups

Ingredient Equivalents

FOOD	AMOUNT	APPROXIMATE EQUIVALENT
Plums	1 lb fresh 15½-oz can	2½ cups sliced; 2 cups cooked 3 cups sliced or chopped
Pomegranate	1 medium	½ cup seeds
Popcorn	3 tbsp	6 cups popped
Potatoes. sweet	1 lb fresh 15½-oz can	3 medium; 3½ to 4 cups chopped or sliced 1½ to 1¾ cups
Potatoes, white, red, russet	1 lb	3½ to 4 cups chopped or sliced; 2 cups mashed
Prunes	1 lb	2½ cups; 4 to 4½ cups cooked
Pumpkin	1 lb fresh 15-oz can 29-oz can	1 cup cooked and mashed 1¾ cups mashed 3½ cups mashed
Radishes	½ lb	1½ cups sliced; 10 to 14 radishes
Raisins	15-oz	2½ cups
Raspberries	½ pint fresh 10-oz frozen	1⅓ cups 1¾ cups
Rhubarb	1 lb fresh 12-oz frozen	2 cups chopped and cooked 1½ cups chopped and sliced
Rice	1 cup regular 1 cup converted 1 cup instant 1 cup brown 1 cup wild	3 cups cooked 3¾ cups cooked 2 cups cooked 3½ to 4 cups cooked 3½ to 4 cups cooked
Rutabaga	1 lb	2½ cups cubed
Saltines (see Crackers)		
Sauerkraut	1 lb	2 cups
Scallions (see Onions, green)		
Scallops	1 lb medium	2 cups
Shallots	4-oz	½ cup chopped
Shortening, vegetable	1 lb	2½ cups

Shrimp	1 lb in shell
	
	1 lb shelled
		11 to 15 jumbo; 16 to 20 extra large;
		    21 to 30 large; 31 to 35 medium;
		    36 to 45 small; 100+ miniature
		8-oz meat; 2 cups cooked

Soda crackers (see Crackers)		
Sour Cream (see Cream)		
Spaghetti (12 inches long)	1 lb	7 to 8 cups cooked

Ingredient Equivalents

FOOD	AMOUNT	APPROXIMATE EQUIVALENT
Spinach	1 lb fresh	10 cups; 1½ cups cooked
	10-oz frozen	1½ cups; 1 cup cooked and drained
Sprouts (see Bean sprouts)		
Squash	1 lb summer	3 medium; 3 cups sliced
	1 lb winter	1 cup cooked and mashed
Strawberries	1 pint fresh	1½ to 2 cups sliced
	10-oz frozen	1½ cups
Sugar	1 lb brown	2¼ cups packed
	1 lb confectioners'	3½ to 4 cups unsifted; 4½ cups sifted
	1 lb granulated	2 cups
	1 lb superfine	2⅓ cups
Sweet potatoes (see Potatoes, sweet)		
Tangerines	1 lb	4 medium; 2 cups sections
Tofu	1 lb	2¾ cups cubes; 2 cups crumbled; 1⅔ cups puréed
Tomatoes	1 lb	3 medium; 1½ cups chopped; 2 cups sliced
	14½-oz can	1¾ cups, including juice
Tomato paste	4½-oz tube	5 tbsp
	6-oz can	¾ cup
Tuna	6-oz can	⅔ to ¾ cup, drained
Turkey	6 lb	7 cups cooked meat
	12 l	16 cups cooked meat
Turnips	1 lb	3 to 4 medium; 2½ cups cooked, chopped
Walnuts	1 lb in shell	2 cups nuts
	1 lb shelled	3¾ cups halves; 3½ cups chopped
Watermelon	10 lb	20 cups cubed
Wheat germ	12-oz	3 cups
Wine	375 ml	half bottle; 12.7-oz; ample 1½ cups
	750 ml	regular bottle; 25.4-oz; scant 3¼ cups
	1 liter	33.8-oz; 4¼ cups
	magnum	1.5 liters; 50.7-oz; 6⅓ cups
Won ton skins	1 lb	60 wrappers
Yeast, active dry	¼-oz package	1 scant tbsp; 0.6-oz compressed fresh
Yogurt	8-oz	1 cup; ½ pint

Guide to Cooking Terms and Techniques

Al dente- Italian phrase used to describe pasta or other food that is cooked only until it offers a slight resistance when bitten into, but which is not soft or overdone.

Allspice- Dried berries of the pimiento tree that are dark brown and can be purchased whole or ground. The spice is so named because it tastes like a combination of cinnamon, nutmeg, and cloves.

Andouille sausage- A spicy, heavily smoked sausage made from pork chitterlings and tripe. It's the traditional sausage used in specialties like Jambalaya and Gumbo.

Aspic- A savory jelly, usually clear, made of clarified meat, fish, or vegetable stock and gelatin.

Au gratin- A French phrase referring to food that is topped with breadcrumbs mixed with bits of butter, or with grated cheese, and then broiled until brown and crisp.

Bake- To cook food, covered or uncovered, using the indirect, dry heat of an oven.

Baste- To moisten foods during cooking with pan drippings or a sauce in order to add flavor and prevent drying.

Beat- To make a mixture smooth by briskly whipping or stirring it with a spoon, fork, wire whisk, rotary beater, or electric mixer.

Blend- To combine two or more ingredients until smooth and uniform in texture, flavor, and color; may be done by hand or with an electric mixer.

Bouillon Cube- A compressed, flavor-concentrated cube of dehydrated beef, chicken, or vegetable stock.

Braise- To cook food slowly in a small amount of liquid in a tightly covered pan on the range or in the oven.

Broil- To cook food a measured distance below direct, dry heat.

Broth- The liquid resulting from cooking vegetables, meat, poultry, or fish in water

Brown- To cook food in a skillet, broiler, or oven in order to develop a rich, desirable color on the outside, add flavor and aroma, and help seal in natural juices.

Butterfly- To split foods such as shrimp or steak through the middle without completely separating the halves, then spreading the halves to resemble a butterfly.

Canapé- Small, decorative pieces of bread that are topped with a savory garnish such as anchovy, cheese or some type of spread.

Consommé- A clarified meat or fish broth, can be served hot or cold, and is variously used as a soup or sauce base.

Cornstarch- A dense, powdery substance used as a thickening agent for puddings, sauces, soups, etc.

Crab boil- Sold packaged in supermarkets and specialty markets, it is a mixture of herbs and spices added to water in which crab, shrimp, or lobster is cooked.

Cream- To beat a fat, such as margarine, butter, or shortening, either alone or with sugar to a light, fluffy consistency. This process incorporates air into the fat so baked products have a lighter texture.

Cream of Tartar- A fine white powder that is added to candy and frosting mixtures for a creamier consistency, and to egg whites before beating to improve stability and volume.

Cut in- To work a solid fat, such as shortening, margarine, or butter, into dry ingredients, usually with a pastry blender.

Guide to Cooking Terms and Techniques

Deglaze- Adding a liquid such as water, wine, or broth to a skillet that has been used to cook meat. The liquid is poured into the pan after the meat is removed and is used to help loosen the browned bits in the pan to make a flavorful sauce.

Dredge- To coat a food, either before or after cooking, with a dry ingredient, such as flour, cornmeal, or sugar.

Egg wash- Egg yolk or egg white mixed with a small amount of water or milk. It's brushed over breads, pastry, and other baked goods before baking to give them color and gloss.

Emulsion- A suspension of two liquid or semi liquid ingredients, such as oil and vinegar, that don't naturally dissolve in each other.

Fold- A method of gently mixing ingredients- usually delicate or whipped ingredients that cannot withstand stirring or beating.

Giblets- The edible internal organs o poultry, such as the liver, heart, and gizzard; also may include the neck and wing tips.

Gluten- An elastic protein present in flour, especially wheat flour, that provides most of the structure of baked products.

Jelly Roll- Dessert made by spreading a filling- usually jelly, pudding, ice cream, or flavored whipped cream- on a sponge cake and rolling it up into a log shape.

Julienne- To cut food into thin, matchlike sticks about 2 inches long. For easier cutting, cut food into slices about 2 inches long and ¼ inch thick; then cut food lengthwise into ¼ wide strips.

Knead- To work dough with the heals of hands in a pressing and folding motion until it becomes smooth and elastic.

Pare- To cut off the skin or outer covering of a fruit or vegetable, using a small knife or vegetable peeler.

Pipe- To force a semi soft food, such as whipped cream, frosting, or mashed potatoes, through a bag to decorate a food.

Proof- To allow yeast dough to rise before baking.

Purée- To change a solid food into a liquid or heavy paste, usually by using a blender, food processor, or food mill; also refers to the resulting mixture.

Roux- A French term that refers to a mixture of flour and a fat cooked to a golden or rich brown color and used for thickening in sauces, soups, and gumbos.

Sauté- To cook or brown a food in a small amount of hot fat.

Stock- The thin, clear liquid in which the bones of meat, poultry, or fish are simmered with vegetables and herbs; usually richer and more concentrated than broth; gels when cooled.

Zest- The colored outer portion of citrus fruit peel. It is rich in fruit oils and often used as a seasoning.

Contributors

Jonessa Alexander
Katherine Alexander
Peggy Allen
Lauren Alley
Sherry Anderson
Anna Smith
Jennie Armstrong
Becca Atchison
Marilyn Ayers
Tania Bachman
Kris Bakowski
Beth Barnett
Don Barnett
Jill Bateman
Alicia Battle
Ann Begnaud
Mary Beisswenger
Raven Bennett
Lori Bigham
Elizabeth Blount
Elaine Bolton
Robyn Bolton
Jessica Boozer
Becky Boyd
Ashlie Bradford
Karen Bray
Jenny Broadnax
Katy Brodrick
Susan Brodrick
Whitney England Byce
Katherine Bynum
Katie Campbell
Joanna Carabello
Meg Carey
Kim Carmack
Ashley Carter
Ryan Cesare
Laura Childers
Amy Chisholm
Rebecca Chisolm
Sheila Coffeen

Sabrina Collins
Jodi Conner
Laurie Cooney
Jill Courson
Julie Cox
Ila Crenshaw
Lynn Crosland
Kelly Cucuzza
Carol Cuff
Michelle Culp
Erin DeLoach
Mary DeLoach
Michelle Dickens
Theresa Dickenson
Kasey Dillard
Rachael Dillon
Elsie Dodson
Lauren Dodson
Melanie Dodson
Susan Dodson
Barbara Dooley
Laurie Douglas
Sheila Dunham
Jennifer Duvall
Aynsley Eastman
Marjorie Edenfield
Sharon Edenfield
Ellen Elder
Lindsay Elwood
Chad Erwin
Kat Farlowe
Leon Farmer, Jr.
Marilyn Farmer
Rebecca Farmer
Therese Farmer
Vickie Farmer
Shona Foster
Valerie Franklin
Whitney Freeman
Luci Furlow

Ali Gant
Carolyn Garrard
Meghan Garrard
Sharon Gillespie
Samantha Goldman
Suzanne Goodroe
Elizabeth Grant
Linda Grant
Susan Greer
Beth Greeson
Nancy Greeson
Suzanne Griffeth
Mary Griner
Jenny Grogan
Kerri Hammond
Caroline Hamrick
Erin Hantske
Betsy Harter
Barbara Hartman
Laura Hartman
Ruth Hartman
Blaine Healan
Megan Henning
Tracey Daniels Hickey
Melody Higginbotham
Tiffany Hines
Mary Anne Hodgson
Lauren Hodurski
Doris Holcomb
Bernice Hudspeth
Susan Huff
Leslie Hunsinger
Joni Farmer Ingram
Ashley Ivey
Alma Jackson
Howard Jackson
Diane Jacobs
Jill Jereb
Anisa Sullivan Jimenez
Cress Johnson

Contributors

Laura Johnson
Heather Kaplan
Margie Kelly
Jodi Kerr
Michelle Kimbler
Mariella King
Suzanne Hofman King
Genevieve Knox
Janet Krepps
Christina LaFontaine
Leigh Anne Landers
Valerie Langley
Jan Lanier
Leigh Laughlin
Kitty Lay
Kacy Lehn
Kate Lindsey
Kathryn Lookofsky
Tina Lord
Cindy Loveless
Peggy Lowe
Sydney Lowry
Laurie Lunsford
Jennifer Mangum
Allison Marlow
Teresa McClure
Alison McCormick
Mary McCormick
Alison McCullick
Charlene McCullick
Caron McDonald
Joanne Meadors
Brenda Magill
Amy Miller
Natalie Miller
Bonnie Mitchell
Ernie Mitchell, Jr.
Krista Mitchell
Laura Morang
Margaret Morgan

Phyllis Barrow Nelson
Alison Norris
Crysty Odom
Danna Ogletree
Sunny Ortiz
Cal Oxford
Cathy Padgett
Elizabeth Patrick
Kimberley Patterson
Nan Peterson
Claire Phillips
Mariah Pierce
Colleen Pruitt
Jill Reichert
Katharyn Richt
R.E.M.
Lucy West Rice
Anna Richardson
Tina Eckard Riecke
Natalie Rittle
Beth Rivenbark
Johnette Rodgers
Kathryn Rodrigue
Kimberly Rogers
Diana Ryan
Kelly Sanders
Mary Lou Scesney
Deidra Schad
Jackie Schad
Carrie Scruggs
Beth Segars
Mandy Seigler
Katie Grant Shalin
Stacy Sharpe
Jan Shuford
Jeanne Sixtos
Hollie Smith
Kim Smith
Missey Smyth
Sheila Snead

Carolyn Stewart Morgan
Jackie Stokes
Brooke Stortz
Cindy Sullivan
Whitney Swann
Chris Taylor
Jenny Taylor
Larry Taylor
Kelly Thomas
Jennifer Thompson
Reagan Thompson
Lee Thornton
Susan Thweatt
Robin Towns
Rachel Bianco Tribble
Katie Trowbridge
Larry Tucker
Laura Tucker
Martha Turner
Michele Turner
Kim Tweedell
Erin Vaughn
Becky Waltman
Jill Walton
Caroline Ward
Virginia Wells
Beth West
Heather Whitaker
Mary Elizabeth Williams
Angelish Wilson
W. Terrell "Terry" Wingfield
Tonya Woody
Jennifer Wootton
Jennifer Worley
Amy Yarbrough
Jo'elle Yarbrough
Lynn Yarbrough
Meredith York
Amanda Young
Ann Zimmermann

Contributors for Classic Recipes from
A Cook's Tour of Athens

Mrs. Robert E. Argo (Jeane)

Mrs. Upshaw Bentley (Frances)

Mr. John "Buck" Griffin

Mrs. John "Buck" Griffin (Gwen)

Ms. Vickey Butler

Mrs. Herschel Carithers (Karen)

Mrs. Tom Dover (Vee)

Mrs. Bolling DuBose, Jr (Mary Neil)

Mrs. E. J. "Doc" Eldridge, Sr. (Jane)

Mrs. George Erwin (Tee)

Mrs. A. Paul Keller, Jr. (Sadie)

Ms. Helen Major

Mrs. Charles McMullin (Jane)

Dr. J.B. Neighbors

Mrs. M. R. Redwine (Bonnie)

Mrs. Harry H. Robinson (Lou)

Mrs. Albert Sams (Nita)

Mrs. L. L. Scruggs, Sr. (Nancy)

Mrs. John Terrell, Jr. (Elinor)

Mrs. Henry H. West

Mrs. Phillip Warga

Mrs. John J. Wilkins III (Lovat)

Mrs. W.T. "Terry" Wingfield (Joy)

Proceeds from the sale of Beyond the Hedges: From Tailgating to Tea Parties *will be returned to the community through the League's support of these and other volunteer projects.*

JLA Volunteer Projects: Past and Present

Athens Area Homeless Shelter

Athens Regional Attention Home

Athens Regional Foundation Golf Tournament

Athens Regional Medical Center Guest House

Athens Regional Koffee Klinic

Boys and Girls Club

Clarke County After School program

Community Service Awards

DFACS Adopt A Family

DFACS Kid's Count Carnival

Don't Wait to Vaccinate

Done In A Day projects

Family Connection, Athens Holiday Lights

Food Bank of Northeast Georgia

Food 2 Kids

Georgia Museum of Art

Habitat for Humanity

Kids in the Kitchen

Kids on the Block Puppets

Leadership Academy

OneAthens

Open Hearts Center

Prevent Child Abuse Athens

Project Safe

Recording for the Blind and Dyslexic

Rutland Comprehensive Academy

Taylor Grady House

The Granny House

Youth Violence Prevention Forum

Beyond the HEDGES

FROM TAILGATING TO TEA PARTIES

634 Prince Ave.
Athens, Georgia 30601
Phone: 706-549-8688
www.juniorleagueofathens.org

Please send _____ copies of **Beyond the Hedges**   @ $27.95 each $ _____

Shipping and Handling   @ $ 5.00 each $ _____

TOTAL $ _____

_____Check, payable to *Junior League of Athens*, enclosed

_____Charge to ___ Visa or ___ MasterCard   Card Number #_____

Expiration Date _____Signature _____

Name_____

Address _____

City _____ State _____ Zip _____

Telephone _____ E-mail _____

Beyond the HEDGES

FROM TAILGATING TO TEA PARTIES

634 Prince Ave.
Athens, Georgia 30601
Phone: 706-549-8688
www.juniorleagueofathens.org

Please send _____ copies of **Beyond the Hedges**   @ $27.95 each $ _____

Shipping and Handling   @ $ 5.00 each $ _____

TOTAL $ _____

_____Check, payable to *Junior League of Athens*, enclosed

_____Charge to ___ Visa or ___ MasterCard   Card Number #_____

Expiration Date _____Signature _____

Name_____

Address _____

City _____ State _____ Zip _____

Telephone _____ E-mail _____